WITHDRAWN

WITHDRAWN

TOO YOUNG TO RUN?

TOO

YOUNG

TO

RUN

**A PROPOSAL FOR AN AGE AMENDMENT
TO THE U.S. CONSTITUTION**

JOHN SEERY

The Pennsylvania State University Press
University Park, Pennsylvania

Library of Congress Cataloging-in-Publication Data

Seery, John Evan.
    Too young to run? : a proposal for an age amendment to the U.S.
Constitution / John Seery.
        p.   cm.
Includes bibliographical references and index.
Summary: "Examines the history, theory, and politics behind the age
qualifications for elected federal office in the United States Constitution.
Argues that the right to run for office ought to be extended to all adult-age
citizens who are otherwise office-eligible"—Provided by publisher.
ISBN 978-0-271-04853-6 (cloth : alk. paper)
    1. Nominations for office—United States.
    2. United States. Constitution.
    I. Title.
JK2063.S44   2011
342.73'055—dc22
                                        2010046445

In memory of
Francis Thomas Seery

Contents

Acknowledgments

Pursuing this unwonted topic has not been as lonely as one might suppose. I've received a great deal of help and encouragement along the way, for which I am inordinately grateful. I want to thank publicly such friends and colleagues, while emphasizing that they bear absolutely no responsibility for any errors that remain. Shortcomings that follow are mine alone. First, Sanford Thatcher and Sanford Levinson quietly assisted me in this project even when it needed still more time and work. One desperately needs such background supporters, and I hope that I haven't betrayed their early trust. Many colleagues read drafts of various portions at various stages of this undertaking, and they provided crucial editorial feedback and criticism. I thank them all in one sweep here, which I regret doesn't do justice to the care, rigor, and attention to detail they extended so graciously to me: Derek Barker, Robert W. Bennett, Aaron Bruhl, Samuel Chambers, Justin Crowe, Patrick Deneen, Derek Galey, William Galston, Jennifer Hochschild, Dallas Holmes, Alexander Jakle, Bronwyn Leebaw, Andrew B. Lewis, Lee McDonald, Susan McWilliams, Paul Seaton, Simon Stow, Tracy Strong, and several anonymous reviewers (one especially to whom I owe an unspeakable debt). At timely junctures, a number of individuals offered me key insights or telling leads or wise counsel or bits of consolation, to the extent that I feel compelled to announce here that I well remember their specific contributions and want to express my abiding appreciation: Gordon Babst, Judith Baer, Terrell Carver, Daniel Conway, Jack DiStefano, Kelly Douglass, Elisabeth Ellis, Richard Flathman, Leo Flynn, Farah Godrej, Bonnie Honig, Bill Katovsky, Joseph Knippenberg, Henry Krips, Cary Nederman, Jake Oken-Berg, Michael Owen, Kim Peasley, Boris Ricks, Stephanie Simon, Sharon Snowiss, Jacqueline Stevens, James Sullivan, Greg Ver Steeg, and the late David Foster Wallace. I thank Arianna Huffington for providing me with a regular forum for several years in which I could try to extend some ideas outside the classroom. Last but not less, a number of my undergraduate students at Pomona College, and at some other colleges, influenced the direction of the manuscript in decided ways, and I am very pleased to acknowledge their thoughtful contributions here: Sara Aceves, Laura Aylward, Genna Beier, Galen Benshoof, Zachary Berne, Trevor Bisset, Diego Bustamante, Lauren Calton, Gregory Carter, Jemel Derbali, Allison Don, Keegen Dresow, Martie Finkelstein, Erin Fitts, Caroline Fleetwood, Kevin Frick, Daniel Garrett-Steinman, Jediah Grobstein, Brian Hardesty, Benjamin Heidlage, Sheri Irvin, Brandon Jacobsen, Yael Japha, Danielle Joseph, Matthew Kelberg, Sara Kendall, Jessie Lewis, Jordan Liew, Zachary Mandelblatt, Katie McDonald, Alanna Mori, Rory O'Sullivan, Meredith Pressfield, Maya Prokupets, Laura Samuels, Jonathan Singer, Susan Sparrow, Marlies Talay, Ingrid Vidal, Michelle Yu, and Jonathan Zelig.

Introduction

The destiny of any nation, at any given time, depends on the opinions of its young persons under twenty-five.

—Goethe

Forty-seven-year-old Barack Obama won the 2008 U.S. presidential election against seventy-two-year-old John McCain, and several commentators at the time proclaimed that the Obama victory constituted nothing less than a generational watershed in our nation's history, ushering in a post-boomer epoch of youthful governance.[1] Young voters, eighteen to twenty-nine years old, had voted for the younger candidate by a 68 to 32 percent margin.[2] An estimated 23 million young voters overall cast ballots, an increase of 2 million since the 2004 election. Those voters turned out at the highest rate (est. 52–53 percent) since 1972, the year when the Twenty-Sixth Amendment (lowering the voting age from twenty-one to eighteen) went into effect.[3] Columnists variously branded these new-era, twenty-something voters the Generation O (for Obama), the Millennial Tidal Wave, or the Youthquake (to be contrasted in retrospect with Thomas Friedman's 2007 characterization of that age cohort as "Generation Q"—Q for "quiet").[4]

Whatever one calls it, the eighteen-to-twenty-nine-year-old demographic also seemed to define itself as a generational interest group of sorts. Extensive polls and studies—by the Harvard Institute of Politics, the Pew Research Center for Politics, the UCLA Higher Education Research Institute, and others[5]—had all consistently revealed that the eighteen- to twenty-nine-year-old "millennials"[6] held surprisingly similar and well-defined political views, particularly on the environment, health care, foreign policy, and gay rights.[7] Numbering about 43 million and constituting 20 percent of the registered voters and 18 percent of the total vote nationwide in 2008, the O-Gen voting bloc, one might surmise,[8] would also see its youthful surge and generational interests reflected in the halls of the newly elected 111th Congress.

The youngest electorate in history, however, elected the oldest Congress in our nation's history, continuing a record-setting trend with the previous five U.S. Congresses, each successively setting a new record for the average age of its members.[9] Only one senator was younger than President Obama (namely, Mark Pryor of Arkansas, who turned forty-six on January 10, 2009).[10] Only one House member, twenty-seven-year-old Aaron Schock of Illinois, was under thirty, and he was the one and only under-thirty member in several congressional sessions.

So let us ponder: How is it that the much ballyhooed 2008 "Youthquake" produced both the fourth-youngest president ever[11] and the *oldest* U.S. Congress ever? How should we evaluate the attendant paradox that only *one* out of the 535 elected congressional representatives can claim to be an age-appropriate spokesperson for those 23 million under-thirty voters (not to mention the 43 million eighteen- to twenty-nine-year-olds overall)? Should young voters be especially concerned, or just wait the situation out?

Of course one could dismiss the event—a virtual stampede of youthfully engaged citizens electing a bunch of graybeards—as little more than a demographic anomaly, or the insignificant by-product of a range of contingent variables, or another quirk of U.S. political history. I'd like to press the issue in a particular direction, however, drawing sustained attention to a structural issue of constitutional design, of which the outcome of the 2008 elections is, at least in part, symptomatic. To wit: one of the major obstacles facing eighteen- to twenty-nine-year-olds who might seek to rejuvenate the halls of Congress is that they must faithfully observe the minimum age requirements for elected federal office. These age limits harshly proscribe youthful governance and thereby also strongly discourage youthful candidacy. Yet the age of eligibility for office, as an issue, has drawn little attention and stirred scant controversy over the years in these United States.

The U.S. Constitution sets strict minimum age qualifications for our elected federal representatives: 25 for the House of Representatives, 30 for the Senate, and 35 for the presidency. Unlike the residency requirements for legislators and the requirement that the president be native born, which are subject to various ongoing interpretive challenges and accommodations, the constitutional age qualifications have been, in the modern period, strictly observed and enforced. Only three underage persons have ever been admitted to the Senate: Henry Clay (aged 29 in 1806), Armistead Thomson Mason (aged 28 in 1816), and John Eaton (aged 28 in 1818).

A few underage candidates for that body have run and been elected before they officially qualified: In 1934, Rush D. Holt Sr. of Virginia was elected to the U.S. Senate at the age of twenty-nine, but he had to wait six months, until his thirtieth birthday, to take his oath of office. Vice President Joseph Biden was first elected to the U.S. Senate in 1972 at age twenty-nine but turned thirty just two weeks after Election Day, about a month before his swearing in. Young Joe Biden had to explain to his constituents that he would be old enough in plenty of time to take office. In general, however, the constitutional age requirements for officeholding deter underage candidacy.[12] We the People can elect basically whomever we wish, but if they do not meet the constitutional age requirements for office, they will not be permitted to serve.

According to the U.S. Census Bureau, about one-quarter of the U.S. population, about 69,420,700 citizens, is between eighteen and thirty-four years old. Out of that pool of about 70 million adults, there are probably at least a few compelling individuals who might be electable to the U.S. presidency, or whose candidacy would prove strongly competitive and worthy of wide and serious consideration. Let us ask ourselves, Why did the framers of the Constitution create a system that forever bars even the possibility that charismatic and capable young adult candidates for office might emerge? What were the framers thinking? Why did they limit democracy in such a peremptory way? The quick answer is that the framers believed that only someone who had attained a sufficient level of maturity and experience was fit for elected federal office. But in that case, why didn't they decide to let the voters decide about any particular adult-aged individual's suitability for office? Why let process trump merit? Can it be that the framers designed a system that delivers, over time, a kind of prudential stability, even if it occasionally excludes exceptional individuals?

Surely most U.S. citizens take these requirements for granted; we simply accept them as the ground rules of our federal system. Perhaps it is time, however, to subject them to serious review. Only a bare handful of democratic governments the world over[13] has adopted this elaborate, multitiered system of age encumbrances (and the U.S. system is the second-most convoluted, next only to the Italian). The majority of the world's advanced democracies have no age restrictions on eligibility for office beyond the age of legal adulthood. Furthermore, almost every other field of meritorious endeavor—professional athletics, the music industry, higher education, Hollywood entertainment, the dot.com cyber-world, and gainful business generally—has become avidly opportunistic about recognizing and promoting talented individuals regardless of age. The military relies heavily on the ability and valor of the same age cohort (with no *official* age barriers to promotion). Only in politics do we see such structurally explicit constraints against greater formal involvement by the younger citizens among us.

In our country, eighteen- to thirty-four-year-olds can buy cigarettes, donate organs, play the lottery, drive cars, fly airplanes, shoot guns, start businesses, own homes, sign contracts, have consensual sex, get married, get divorced, have children, have abortions, join the military, serve as jurors, and be tried in court as full adults, but for some reason they are still branded, as an entire group, as somehow too immature and too inexperienced to run for one or more categories of elected federal office. With this book I want to propose that full constitutional adulthood should commence at the age of majority, which means that all U.S. citizens would become fully enfranchised at the age of eighteen. Thus I'm insisting that eligibility for office ought to be regarded in the United States as a fundamental right of the democratic franchise: all adult citizens should enjoy the right to run for federal office; that right is, I claim, as important to full civic enfranchisement as the right to vote. As an incidental yet by no means trivial matter, I suspect that the recognition of such a right is likely to lead to derivative consequences more beneficial than not: it may have the effect, for instance, of expanding the pool of office aspirants and thus enhance electoral competition. I happen to doubt that it would significantly reduce the overall age of Congress, but I submit that the existence of the right to be eligible to hold office ought to be assessed, as it were, independently of its consequences, that is, as a matter of *principle*. I don't want the argument that follows—which is essentially a normative case—to be staked on such consequences. I'm not making a causal argument contending that an increase in the numbers eligible for electoral office would lead to an increase in the number of younger candidates running for office, which would lead to an increase in the number of younger persons actually elected into office, which would lead to the passage of legislation beneficial to younger voters. I'm not contending that an age amendment can serve as antidote for all the generational ills and defects that may afflict our system. Instead, my attending to such on-the-ground concerns, when and where I do, is intended simply to draw attention to and sharpen awareness of the fact that the fundamental right to be eligible to hold office is not shared equally among adult citizens in the United States. And the absence of such a right, for so many, ought to make us pause. The average age of Congress rises every session, which means that our government is looking less and less like a truly representative democracy and more and more like a plutocratic gerontocracy. The framers explicitly rigged the system against younger citizens—and by doing so created a problem that has worsened in our lifetime. Knowing that these skewed demographics and the codified constraints are working effectively against them, why would a younger citizen, barred officially from holding the reins of power, even bother to vote? Would the O-Gen Youthquake voters have been as enthusiastic going into the election if they had realized that their collectively youthful efforts would result in the oldest Congress ever?

In the book that follows, I adopt a tone of cautious advocacy, dropping the academic convention or pretense that I have not yet drawn a judgment about the matters that follow. Truth be told, I have become convinced that the Constitution's minimum age requirements for the House, the Senate, and the presidency are anachronisms based on a superannuated form of age discrimination that, when identified as such, calls out for contemporary remedy. But the case that follows is not a simple one, and I hope my skeptical readers will think that I do justice to the counterarguments that complicate my presentation. If my extended brief appears in places to be imbalanced, my occasional tendentiousness probably indicates the difficulties of trying to meet a burden of demonstration sufficient to overturn the constitutional status quo: the default position, namely that inexperienced younger citizens ought to be excluded from the highest offices in the land, is a formidable and time-tested proposition. I concede as much at this outset, and ask from my captious readers only that they keep an open mind. The results of this quixotic investigation may not be, finally, convincing and conclusive. There are many facets to the issue, and many questions to be asked along the way, and the eventual answers may not always be obvious or beyond cavil. But such questions do start to accumulate. How did these qualifications get into the Constitution in the first place? The Articles of Confederation included no such strictures for delegates to the Continental Congress. Did the Constitutional framers thereafter present arguments pro and con, and what were they? Do such arguments now stand the test of time? Might there be a good political principle behind the apparent prejudice? Do these prohibitions actually constitute invidious discrimination? If so, why haven't we recognized it as a form of discrimination analogous to earlier constitutional prohibitions based on race, gender, property, and literacy—or can reasonable distinctions be drawn separating (youthful) age from the rest? Is running for office a fundamental right or liberty?

Does it bear on our notions of representative government? If age barriers represent an injustice, an abridgement of individual rights or a discriminatory practice against an entire class of persons, does that injustice rise to a level of urgency compared with other pressing or egregious issues? Does it actually warrant an amendment to the Constitution? How likely would it be for such an amendment to get off the ground and to wind through the maze of the amendment process? What good effects could be expected to obtain in fact as a result of removing such age requirements? Might such tinkering with the Constitution create unintended, undesirable consequences as well?

I write this inquiry as a political theorist, not as a public law specialist or as an empirical political scientist. The topic requires, however, that one pursue leads into different fields, subfields, and methods of analysis—democratic theory, normative theory, American historiography, constitutional law, analytic philosophy, comparative politics, and American political science. Such mingled methodologies will create certain shortcomings and frustrations. Specialists in any of the encroached areas will find that I've cut some corners in pursuit of an overview. I'm not sure my fellow theorists will be especially happy, either. While the prevailing conventions of political theory generally encourage such broad purviews and eclectic approaches, I must note as well that I am departing in this book from my usual modus operandi in the writing of political theory. My concern in this book is much more practicable, modest, and delimited than my own past efforts and those of many of my contemporaries. Herein I am not attempting to rewrite gender relations, restore first principles, reform patriarchal hegemony, undo colonial oppression, radicalize democracy, sabotage capitalism, challenge neoliberalism, revere the ancients over the moderns, instill global justice, save the planet, or unsettle logocentric heteronormativity. This is not an exercise in what Sheldon Wolin called epic political theory.[14] Instead, I am working from within the frame of the American system, which is to be properly named as a *constitutional democratic representative republic.* I am not trying to rethink the entire system from scratch, nor am I proposing sweeping reforms to representative government, such as eliminating the Electoral College, converting to proportional or parliamentary representation, or extending suffrage to children or noncitizens. I see the possibility of an AGE (All Grown-ups Eligible) amendment to the Constitution as a moderate, plausible, and potentially feasible way to improve the system from within.

The Case for an AGE Amendment

My main argument will be normative,[15] but not overly idealizing, romantic, moralistic, or utopian. I contend that passing a constitutional amendment to reduce the age restrictions for elected federal office to eighteen, the age of majority, is, speaking plainly, the right thing to do. I will point out possible beneficial consequences to such an amendment—but as I mentioned, my argument will not depend or turn finally on a consequentialist justification. This is a matter, not of effect or efficacy, but of justice. No less an authority than John Rawls, in his magisterial A *Theory of Justice*, lists the opportunity to run for public office as one of the "basic liberties" of citizenship (akin to the right to vote), to be distributed equally among all citizens.[16] Yet Rawls eventually mentions, albeit somewhat in passing and only briefly, that an age restriction on eligibility for office might be acceptable on certain grounds without undermining the basic principle of equal liberty.[17] We will need to scrutinize his reasoning, both the principle and possible qualifications, with care.

While concerns for fairness and equity in the American electoral system might present the most compelling reasons for the case at hand, we should emphasize as well that empirical circumstances also bear on the question and render the topic salient and timely. Developments in medicine, changes in life expectancy, and shifts toward an older population have altered the democratic calculus of politics since the national founding. Money, numbers, and power have been inexorably accruing to the aging "baby boomer" generation over the last few decades. As a result of these trends, certain political, economic, and cultural conflicts these days have become—sometimes conspicuously, sometimes incipiently—intergenerational in nature.[18] Militarism, environmentalism, global warming, budget deficits, transgenerational trusts and taxes, health care, stock market investment, savings rates, Social Security, and public education are all potential hot-button issues that can look quite different from short-term as opposed to long-term perspectives. Whether the elderly or the young actually or potentially constitute a coherent voting bloc or interest group on particular issues is really secondary. For now, what's becoming clear is that "the system" is inherently skewed in favor of older folks, a system that may even suppress the formation of younger generational groupings, and the situation is growing more and more acute. The AARP (formerly, the American Association of Retired Persons) has become one of the nation's most powerful lobbies, thanks to numbers, experience, organization, and wealth.

Even if younger voters could get their act together (beyond Obama-mania), recognize that they likely share certain generational concerns, then mobilize themselves into a voting bloc and raise sufficient funds to press for their concerns in a manner comparable to the AARP, the odds would still be stacked against them. The harsh fact would remain that younger voters cannot run for federal office or elect one of their own. To translate their group influence into legislative power, they therefore would still need to appeal to the good graces of a good number of older representatives—who, in many cases, would need to act against their own generational interests in order to do right by their younger constituents. Such younger voters would be, at best, *virtually* represented by their elders—which is much the same argument that many American (male) representatives once upon a time invoked to justify the delay and denial of female enfranchisement in the United States. We will need to examine whether the idea of *virtual representation*, or call it *generational guardianship*, for eighteen- to thirty-four-year-olds ought to be defended or discredited.

My own investment in the issue is as follows: As a professor of politics, I find it increasingly hypocritical to look my undergraduate students in the eye and encourage them to participate wholeheartedly in the American political system, as if their vote truly counted the same as the rest. The representative system puts them, as younger citizens, at a decided disadvantage, and many of them seem to know it. For instance, in the run-up to the Iraq War, twenty-seven women students from the Claremont colleges posed nude on the main campus quad, spelling out the word "PEACE" with their bodies. Frankly, I was embarrassed by the political lameness of their exhibitionist act. Did they really believe they were somehow the legatees of Lysistrata who could actually accomplish something by invoking the specter of female forbearance? At the time, I suppose I could have done my civic and professorial duty and instructed them to write their elected representatives instead; or I could have organized a teach-in on the theory and techniques of direct action, civil disobedience, and nonviolent protest. But I'm no longer sure that I can offer any of that political advice in good faith. For their age cohort, contacting or pressuring or voting for their (older) representatives seems to be an equally empty or desperate gesture. They might as well try to get what attention they can by taking off their clothes. But I think that their constitutional exclusion from front-row involvement in representative government should be seen—by all of us—as a more embarrassing display.

The fact of the matter is that our governmental system is *not* simply a "one person, one vote" democracy; rather, we are a *representative republic*, and it matters immensely that it is a system that is stacked against younger citizens. Exhorting younger citizens to vote, as many organizations do around every election cycle, is asking them to participate in something like a national Ponzi scheme, where earlier participants at the top become enriched through the contributions of later investors. Rock the Vote is one such get-out-the-youth-vote organization. Founded in 1990, it has attempted to raise youth turnout at the polls through high-profile registration and voter mobilization campaigns. It has spawned a bevy of other youth voter turnout organizations,[19] all of which, however well intentioned, are based on a common misconception, namely that the U.S. political system is a majoritarian democracy rather than a representative republic. They are based on the assumption that young citizens can work effectively within the existing framework of the representative system, if only they become sufficiently motivated to register and to vote. These groups do not seem to consider that the Constitution's representative structure, especially with respect to age, may need to be amended before their constituencies can make any real generational difference.

As Hannah Arendt emphasizes at some length, the framers did not inscribe the Constitution in stone, literally or figuratively. They intended that it could be, would be, and should be changed.[20] They made explicit provisions and procedures for such change, though they did not make the amendment process easy.[21] The amendments subsequent to the first ten (the Bill of Rights) express at least two ongoing themes of correction: Amendments 12, 17, 20, 22, 23, and 25 provide redress on problems relating to electoral and representational issues; Amendments 13, 14, 15, 19, and 24 provide redress for earlier discriminatory exclusions based on race, gender, and property. One of the most recent amendments, the Twenty-Sixth, which lowered the federal voting age to eighteen, provides ample precedent that the Constitution has not fully withstood the test of time with respect to its original assumptions and requirements about age. It may be time that those two recurring amending motifs in American constitutional history, corrections for representation and discrimination, converge into a joint impetus toward lowering the minimum age requirements for office.

The Constitution's age requirements present, however, a special problem of representation. Citizens not eligible to hold office *are* eligible to vote, and they enjoy formal representation in that sense of the term. It's not as if the youth today can unequivocally declare "No taxation without representation" and justifiably dump their chai lattes into the Boston Harbor. Rather, as citizens they fall into an ambiguous zone of classification: they enjoy some rights of citizenship, but not all, at least *not yet*. But, at least from the perspective of the history of group enfranchisement in these United States, they fall into an anomalous category. When the Fourteenth, Fifteenth, and Nineteenth Amendments effectively enfranchised Native Americans, African Americans, and women, they extended the rights of suffrage and eligibility for office simultaneously (if only tacitly)[22] to these respective groups; that is to say, these amendments contained no provision that would disqualify, or temporarily disqualify, these newly enfranchised citizens from running for office on account of their race or gender. All of a sudden, blacks and women—older ones, that is—could vote *and* run for office.[23] (The Fourteenth Amendment did bar from federal office any former federal or state official who served the Confederacy in the Civil War.) Younger voters in the United States—the separate yet partially overlapping underage blocs of 18 to 24 for the House, 18 to 29 for the Senate, and 18 to 34 for the presidency—fall into the awkwardly halfway category wherein these members have been granted the rights of citizenship, *but not yet fully*. The Constitution bestows on them the right to run for these various federal offices in a phased-in manner, rendering the polity overall into stratified categories of enfranchisement. Does that mean that they've been denied representation, or part of it, or only a kind of representation, or what?

Compounding the complexity of this problem, the word *youth* doesn't accurately describe the underage citizens that fall into these gradational blocs of ineligibility: A thirty-three-year-old voter doesn't quite belong to "youth" in the same way that an eighteen-year-old does. The term *youth* is thus misleading here, and there's no quick catchword to describe the eighteen-to-thirty-four-year-old bloc. Relatedly, it needs to be emphasized that the age requirements provide an exclusionary discrimination that redounds to the possible detriment not only of the excluded members but also of all citizens, since the requirements equally disable older voters from voting for younger candidates and thus limit every citizen's range of democratic choice. Thus this book isn't simply addressing a niche or special interest or an identity politics problem but, instead, is aiming at a *general* matter of the public good—the issue strikes at the heart of what it means to be living in a representative democracy at all.

Even as the issue potentially impacts citizens of every age, this book is nonetheless pitched especially to the young and young at heart in American political life. It is also directed especially to those who teach the young about the U.S. political system. The problem with changing the system on behalf of the young is that the young simply cannot do it by themselves (a point that shouldn't be construed as a reason to extend their original exclusion). First, they don't have a seat at the table, so the issue probably won't be raised or seriously raised unless they speak forth insistently.[24] But even before pressing for influence, inclusion, and power, younger citizens face a catch-22 of how to learn about and recognize the problem as a problem. The U.S. system of governance is complex. It generally takes a while to learn about it and to understand it. It especially takes some time to know its weaknesses and possible areas of reform and methods of reform. By the time most younger persons might recognize the Constitution's age requirements as unjust and as alterable, they may well have grown out of the very condition of their exclusion, or graduated from one stage to the next—thus incrementally divesting themselves of their stake in the matter. If the eighteen-to-thirty-four-year-old demographic represents a potential interest group, then its membership is ever changing. Yet here's one place where the experience and education of older folks can serve politics productively, in a proactive rather than reactive manner, and in a deliberative rather than factional manner. Civics teachers can and should assume, I propose, an influential role in eliminating this uniquely political form of age discrimination. Instead of eliding or ignoring the crucial differences between *representative self-government* and *generational guardianship*, educators should point out and insist upon this key distinction to their students—along with the fact that their students currently operate more under the latter system than the former. Political age discrimination is, alas, one of the last vestiges of early American prejudice. Yet once alerted to the problem, this enduring structural flaw in the Constitution, thoughtful educators, I suspect, will find it increasingly difficult to teach American government without raising the issue conspicuously, especially when we public-spirited teachers realize that the group of persons largely populating our classrooms has been constituted into an officially *second-class* category of citizenship for far too long.

As I see it, the potential ramifications for an AGE amendment do not boil down to a numbers game of how many previously underage candidates would in fact be elected into office and, thereupon, whether such a younger congressional presence overall would in fact translate into a significantly altered political landscape. Nor does it hinge on some speculation that voting rates of younger voters would necessarily rise. Rather, I think the bottom-line or end-of-the-day importance of such a proposal (in addition to its normative propriety) would issue foremost from its "signaling" effects. First, it would signal that all U.S. adult citizens should and do enjoy equal civic standing under the explicit terms of the Constitution—and equal civic standing, as Judith Shklar and Robert Dahl have both vigorously contended, *is* the institutional bedrock of the American polity.[25] Second, the immediate payoffs for younger citizens (as a whole) would likely result from their transformed status in *eligibility for office*, not actual *officeholding*. That is to say, I would expect that only a very few candidates would start to vie for national office at a younger age and that the overall electorate would continue to vote into office an overwhelming majority of representatives who remain well past the former age thresholds. I submit, however, that even hypothetically enlarging the pool of candidates eligible to hold office would alone deliver an important benefit, helping for one thing to make our federal elections more competitive, by now introducing age as a potential and explicit element of representation.

Such signaling—of democratic inclusion and expanded competition—could have ripple effects.[26] Surely the best way to alter our cultural assumptions and ingrained prejudices about the proper age for governing would be empirical: actual exposure to impressive younger candidates, who by their merits, ideas, charisma, and living presence would naturally dispel doubts about their viability for office. In comparison, an a priori theoretical case confronts some uphill obstacles. We could adduce considerable historical evidence showing that younger rulers have in fact assumed high office in the past: in Israel, China, Egypt, Rome, and Europe. We could point to prime ministers and elected parliamentarians in other contemporary democracies who would be age-ineligible under our system.[27] We could point to actual recent examples in our country where young persons have achieved extraordinary, mind-boggling success in other fields[28]—say, in business—that strongly suggests we are selling short our young political hopefuls.[29] One thinks of the entrepreneurial and precocious managerial leadership of, for example, Bill Gates and Paul Allen, who founded Microsoft at 20 and 22; or Steven Jobs and Steve Wozniak, who founded Apple at 21 and 26; or Sergey Brin and Larry Page, who founded Google at 22; or Pierre Omidyar, who founded eBay at 28; or Mark Zuckerberg, who founded Facebook at 20; or Jawed Karin, Chad Hurley, and Steve Chen, who founded YouTube at 25, 27, and 26. We could name all sorts of young actors and actresses, all sorts of young musicians and entertainers, all sorts of young athletes, all sorts of young decorated soldiers, all sorts of young artists, craftspersons, managers, and workers. Arguably, many of these young stars and heroes in other fields achieve their great successes precisely because they are operating at the very height of their physical and mental powers. Only in politics do we disqualify this bloc of humanity. If there is a potential "LeBron James of Politics"[30] waiting in the wings, the U.S. Constitution expressly prevents such a person from even running onto the court.

Lowering the age of eligibility for office would mean, at the very least, that younger candidates could gain valuable campaign experience on the federal stage at an earlier point in their careers. Studies show that the earlier the point of entry for candidacy, the greater the likelihood of a longer eventual career in politics.[31] We could probably expect that a number of young officials at the state and local levels would throw their hats into the national ring at an earlier age simply because they now could—and such early exposure would help position them for the next round of elections, even if they weren't successful on their first attempts. A patchwork of laws governs the various ages of eligibility for state and local elections,[32] but a number of young candidates are indeed routinely voted into office at subnational levels (the Young Elected Officials Network claims that 4.8 percent of all elected state and local officials in the United States are under thirty-five).[33] In 2003 the Eagleton Institute of Politics at Rutgers University issued a first-ever national study on Young Elected Leaders ("YELS") under thirty-five.[34] The study found 814 YELS in forty-eight states in 2002, including statewide elected legislators and executives, and elected mayors and council members in cities and towns with populations of thirty thousand or more. A sizable 86 percent of the YELS indicated that they aspire to offices beyond their current positions. Asked to name the highest elective or appointive office they hope to achieve, 58 percent chose a position at the federal level—including 14 percent who want to be president, 2 percent vice president, 24 percent U.S. senator, and 18 percent U.S. representative. The study pointed out that half of today's top federal officeholders were thirty-five or younger when they first won elective office. Of the 19 U.S. presidents in the last century, 12 held their first elective offices at thirty-five or younger. The same is true of 57 of the 100 current U.S. senators, 215 of the 435 U.S. representatives, and 25 of the 50 governors in 2003.

Other indicators hint that lowering the U.S. age of candidacy may not be entirely far-fetched and untimely. In a 2005 Greenberg Quinlan

Rosner survey of eighteen- to twenty-five-year-olds, respondents scored themselves "seven" on a ten-point scale as to how well the statement "I read a lot about politics" describes them.[35] The so-called Millennials also volunteer more than any other demographic: according to the Harvard Institute of Politics survey in 2006, a majority of eighteen- to twenty-four-year-olds had volunteered for community service in the previous year.[36] A 2007 Harvard Institute of Politics survey showed that 55 percent of eighteen- and nineteen-year-olds had discussed politics during the previous week.[37] A 2007 Pew Research Center survey found that 85 percent of eighteen- to twenty-nine-year-olds report they are "interested in keeping up with national affairs," a 14 percent increase over the 1999 findings.[38] The 2008 UCLA American Freshman survey indicated the highest interest in politics than at any other point in the forty years covered by the survey.[39] Perhaps as a sign of the times or of things to come, U.S. Representative Phil English (R-Pa.) in 2004 introduced a resolution to Congress (H.J.Res. 105) for a constitutional amendment to lower the age of qualification for the House and the Senate to twenty-one. While Representative English's bill attracted no cosponsors and was inauspiciously referred to the Subcommittee on the Constitution (where it sits), during that same year the British Parliament's Electoral Commission produced a report recommending that Britain lower its age of candidacy from twenty-one to eighteen.[40] For several years running, the British Youth Council had campaigned aggressively for such a measure. On the findings of its independent commission, Parliament lowered the age of candidacy when it passed the Electoral Administration Act of 2006, which went into effect on January 1, 2007 (for more on the British example, see chapter 3). Given these trends, one wonders how long young American citizens will remain content to lag behind their British counterparts.

Timely or no, why does it matter whether young adult citizens enjoy the right to candidacy? Some might dismiss out of hand the sheer idea of a twenty-three-year-old candidate for Congress, or a twenty-seven-year-old candidate for the Senate, or a thirty-three-year-old candidate for the presidency, on the grounds that "skateboarders shouldn't be officeholders." To which a quick reply might be: Maybe the best representative for a generation of skateboarders would be a fellow skateboarder, not some doddering old codger. Furthermore, maybe the ideas of a skateboarding generation won't be taken seriously until a skateboarding candidate is given the proper national

forum to speak his or her mind. And maybe the skateboarding generation should be able to vote for its own representatives, or to circulate
its own various views in the context of a competitive election, in order
to exert greater formal and informal influence on pressing federal decisions such as whether the nation ought to interrupt those skateboarding activities by sending its skateboarding young persons off to war.
The death and injury statistics from the Iraq War reconfirm the problem of political representation voiced in these 1965 antiwar song lyrics:
"It's always the old who lead us to war. / It's always the young to
fall."[41] Those who think the issue of eligibility for office is too obscure
or insignificant to warrant national attention may need to think about
the propriety of a democratic republic sending its young adults off to
war while denying them even the possibility of sitting at the table
where those decisions are reached and funded.

Without preempting the complexity of the case to come, I want to
be clear from the outset about the bare bones of my proposal for an
AGE amendment. Put in the language of positive rights, the main pillars
of my argument will be:

1. All citizens of the United States eighteen and older should enjoy
   a constitutional right to run for elected federal office, assuming
   they meet all other eligibility requirements (which is to say, age
   should not be a barrier to candidacy for citizens who have
   reached the age of majority).
2. All voters should enjoy the right (derived from the foregoing,
   even if not stipulated) to vote for candidates for federal office of
   their choosing, unrestricted by age (assuming such candidates
   meet other eligibility requirements and have reached the age of
   majority).
3. The foremost rationale for the foregoing is normative, not consequentialist, an appeal to the terms of justice rather than utility.
   Therewith, this book is mainly about eligibility for office, not
   election to office.

The historical, theoretical, and political arguments that follow in
this book may not convince every reader that an AGE amendment is a
just and worthy cause whose time has come. In the history of our
constitutional republic, we the people have rectified long-standing exclusions and codified discriminations only after protracted debate and
struggle. Recognizing and withstanding rank prejudice, then winning
over and converting hearts and minds, may not even rest, ultimately,

on scrupulous argument but something more like a leap of democratic faith—in this case, faith in some of the younger citizens among us, or faith in the idea of democracy itself.[42] I am not sure how to teach or to inspire such faith. By now I've presented and discussed this amendment proposal with many groups of mostly college-age citizens, and I take heart, and find further encouragement, in their thoughtfully enthusiastic responses (though I think some young persons secretly favor prolonging their adolescence into their adult years, as a kind of alibi for their political non-involvement).[43] By the same token, I've encountered at times a kind of negative reaction, beginning with shrug-of-the-shoulders indifference and perhaps developing into stodgy resistance, I must say largely from older folks, who seem to want to dismiss this idea out of hand. I wish this latter group would assess the U.S. representative system through the eyes of today's youth. But I think that's a big part of the problem: it's hard for some older folks even to recognize, let alone listen to, let alone take seriously, their younger cohort as political *equals*. They simply don't *see* the Constitution's age requirements as a *problem*.

Myself, I've benefited, as a scholar, from intellectual exposure to many rich and provocative theoretical studies that variously attest to the "unmarked" and seemingly "naturalized" hallmarks of hegemonic rule, a kind of rule, I've learned, that can be invidiously exclusionary without drawing special attention to its own terms of domination and privilege. Many feminists have unmasked "male privilege" and the unspoken masculinist rudiments seeming to inform many configurations of political authority and liberal contracturalism.[44] Race theorists have performed a similar exposé with respect to "white" privilege, queer theorists have interrogated "heteronormativity," postcolonial theorists have disclosed East-West dichotomies that turn on unspoken assumptions about "otherness" and "orientalism," and disabilities theorists have challenged long-standing assumptions about "normal" conceptions of personhood.[45] Yet *age*—even in feminist studies attending to paternalism—is seldom mentioned as one of the key, even if apparently naturalized and thus occluded, components of patriarchy.[46] Recent developments in the emerging scholarly field of "age studies" are just starting to challenge long-standing stereotypes about different age "groups." Yet in my own reading of these pioneering studies,[47] the main problem seems to be that ageist assumptions redound to the detriment of older persons. Work that might question debilitating preconceptions about younger persons tends to get short shrift.[48]

In politics, one repeatedly, almost incessantly, hears the undying refrain that young persons are "inexperienced." *Experience* thus becomes encoded as a not-so-cryptic synonym for *seniority*, an amorphously ennobling quality arising somehow out of sheer duration, a hallowed if indistinct aura achieved only over time, which younger persons almost *by definition* cannot possess. Few ever challenge the notion that experience is the exclusive province of oldsters. Hence it is apt to end this preliminary chapter with a passage from Randolph Bourne's essay "Youth" (circa 1913) that does precisely that, all to suggest that it may not be possible to sever constitutional analysis from a broadly ranging inquiry into cultural politics:

> Old men cherish a fond delusion that there is something mystically valuable in mere quantity of experience. Now the fact is, of course, that it is the young people who have all the really valuable experience. It is they who have constantly to face new situations, to react constantly to new aspects of life, who are getting the whole beauty and terror and cruelty of the world in its fresh and undiluted purity. It is only the interpretation of this first collision with life that is worth anything. For the weakness of experience is that it so soon gets stereotyped; without new situations and crises it becomes so conventional as to be practically unconscious. Very few people get any really new experience after they are twenty-five, unless there is a real change of environment. Most older men live only in the experience of their youthful years.
>
> If we get few ideas after we are twenty-five, we get few ideals after we are twenty. A man's spiritual fabric is woven by that time, and his "experience," if he keeps true to himself, consists simply in broadening and enriching it, but not in adding to it in arithmetical proportion as the years roll on, in the way that the wise teachers of youth would have us believe.[49]

 # History

Nothing is more incumbent on the old than to know when they should get out of the way and relinquish to younger successors the honors they can no longer earn, and the duties they can no longer perform.

—Thomas Jefferson

Chances are, if you ask almost any American citizen—young, old, or somewhere in-between—whether he or she thinks the Constitution's age requirements are fair, you are likely to draw a blank stare or a shrug of the shoulders. We don't think about them. We take them for granted. They aren't an issue. Yet if one examines the history of how they became inscribed into the Constitution, it is hard to avoid the conclusion that these rather cumbersome qualifications barely made it into that document. In retrospect, the original arguments for these requirements now look embarrassingly flimsy and hardly seem deserving of veneration. In view of this tenuousness, we should probably start asking questions about these age barriers rather than according them the benefits of doubt, indifference, and neglect. A good number of the advanced democracies have eliminated all age qualifications for elected officials (beyond the age of majority), and many stipulate in unequivocal terms that any citizen old enough to vote for federal offices is old enough to run for any of those offices. To be sure, several democracies include limited age requirements for one branch of government or another, but only a scant few emulate the U.S. Constitution's separate age requirements for each branch of elected federal office. In democracies the world over, younger adults enjoy much more political freedom to run for elected office than their American counter-parts. So how did the U.S. Constitution become such an outlier?

The Framers

A survey of early American history does not lend itself to the view that it was inevitable that the American framers would include age qualifications in the eventual U.S. Constitution. The Committee of the Whole at the 1787 Constitutional Convention voted 10 to 1 *not* to include age qualifications when the matter first came up. The Articles of Confederation had included no such strictures for delegates to the Continental Congress. Only two colonial state constitutions (Dela-ware's and Virginia's) included age qualifications for their legislatures that differed from the age of majority, both setting twenty-five as the minimum age for members. Only two (Maryland's and North Caroli-na's) included age qualifications for holding the office of governor that differed from the age of majority. Maryland set the governor's mini-mum age at twenty-five, and North Carolina set it at thirty. Most of the states had property requirements, and several of the states had graduated property requirements: Massachusetts, for example, re-quired voters to be twenty-one-year-old males who earned at least £3 from freehold property or held £60 in total property; members of the lower house had to own £100 freehold or £200 total property; senators, £300 freehold or £600 total; and the governor, £1000 freehold.[1] But no state constitution featured anything resembling the three levels of age qualifications that eventually found their way into the Constitution. Nor were the framers taking their cues from across the ocean, since England's law at the time required only that members of Parliament be twenty-one or older.[2] Instead, our Constitutional forebears pretty much concocted their elaborate age-graduated system on the spot in Philadelphia (albeit with undue influence from one Virginia delegate in particular).[3]

The American framers did not find the basis for establishing cate-goric age requirements by looking at their own collective body in the mirror. It is true that most of the revolutionary leaders and constitu-tional framers were middle-aged and older—so at least in terms of age, the decisions these groups made were *unrepresentative* of their national constituency. None of the fifty-five delegates to the Constitutional Convention of 1787 was under twenty-six, and most were middle-aged and older. Benjamin Franklin was the oldest at eighty-one.[4] What this means is that this insider's club enshrined in law and bequeathed to the future its own generational bias. Yet in other ways, the founders' actions reveal an enduring legislative hypocrisy, a "do-as-we-say, not-as-we-do" projection onto the future, since younger persons were always involved in the framing of the key documents of early American history.

Almost all of the 56 signers of the Declaration of Independence were over 40, yet there were key exceptions: Thomas Jefferson, the document's author, was only 33 at the time. Pennsylvania sent Benjamin Rush (31) and James Wilson (34). The entire South Carolina delegation was made up of relative youngsters: Edward Rutledge (27), Thomas Lynch Jr. (27), Arthur Middleton (34), and Thomas Heyward Jr. (30). Massachusetts's Elbridge Gerry (32), North Carolina's William Hooper (34), and Maryland's Thomas Stone (33 or 34) brought the total number of those under 35 to 10 of the signatories. In other words, about 18 percent of the signers of the Declaration of Independence would later be designated by the Constitution as legislatively unfit under at least one of the age qualifications.[5] This 18 percent "underage participation rate" is consistent with the participation rates at earlier key republican moments in American political history: Of the 53 delegates of the First Continental Congress who approved the 1774 Articles of Association, 9 were "underage" at the time (including 24-year-old Edward Rutledge, 25-year-old Thomas Lynch, and 28-year-old John Jay), for a 17 percent underage rate. Of the 48 delegates of the Second Continental Congress who approved the 1777 Articles of Confederation, 9 were "underage" at the time (including the 25-year-old Gouverneur Morris and 29-year-old Richard Hutson), for a 19 percent underage rate. Of the 345 delegates to the Continental Congress overall, 84 were "underage" at the outset of their service (including the 27-year-old Alexander Hamilton and the 29-year-old James Madison), for an overall underage participation rate of 24 percent.

At the 1787 Constitutional Convention, fourteen of the fifty-five delegates would have been ineligible for the Senate or the presidency under the age thresholds they imposed on posterity, a 25 percent "underage" participation rate. Of the thirty-nine signers of the Constitution, nine would have been too young to hold either senatorial or presidential office (Jonathan Dayton was 26 years old; Richard Dobbs Spaight, 29; Charles Pinckney, 29 or 30), for a 23 percent underage participation rate.

If anything, these numbers reveal that, as the founders turned from the business of revolution to governance, their "underage participation rate" *increased* from the period of 1774 to 1787. The numbers rise rather steadily (which means *more* younger persons were participating), from the Articles of Association delegates, to the Declaration of Independence signers, to the Articles of Confederation delegates, to the total number of delegates for the First and Second Continental Congresses combined (spanning 1774 to 1787), to the Constitutional Convention delegates, to the Constitution signers (17 percent, 18 percent, 19 percent, 24 percent, 25 percent, 23 percent). The *average* ages of the participants in these pivotal periods of American political history remain remarkably constant, however (45, 45, 45, 42, 44, and 45, respectively). The median ages correlate closely with the average ages (44, 45, 45, 41, 43, and 43).

Much as Hannah Arendt contended in her classic, *On Revolution*, that the American framers failed to incorporate the *spirit* of their own organizational activity into the *letter* of the Constitution,[6] so too do these numbers suggest that the American framers bequeathed an age bias unto posterity by which they themselves did not fully abide. Compare the age composition of the 111th Congress: out of 535 members, there are only 2 members under thirty-five: Aaron Schock of Illinois (at twenty-seven) and Patrick McHenry of North Carolina (at thirty-four). Hence the "underage participation rate" for the 111th Congress has dropped to a mere 0.37 percent (even lower than the 110th Congress's 1.3 percent rate), affording a strong contrast with the 17 to 25 percent rates of its early American counterparts. While several other demographical and political variables surely need to be introduced to account fully for this gerontocratic drift in the modern period, we nonetheless can conclude that the framers created a Constitution that would essentially guarantee that generations of Americans thenceforth would be governed by legislators older than these framers were themselves as a group.

The Constitutional Convention: George Mason Versus James Wilson

So how did those age requirements actually get into the Constitution? What were the arguments? Do they stand the test of time? The first way to approach these questions is to see the debate over the age requirements in its historical context largely as a clash of personalities, and thereafter as a clash of corresponding democratic theories.

The record of the debates at the 1787 Constitutional Convention reveals that the age requirements had one main advocate among the delegates, George Mason of Virginia, and one main opponent, James Wilson of Pennsylvania. Their clash on this issue is indicative of larger fissures running through the early American democratic project. In many ways Mason and Wilson, coming from different backgrounds, saw the world through different lenses and yet pursued sometimes overlapping, and sometimes diverging, interests. Wilson hailed from a lower-middle-class background—his parents were Scottish farmers— and he earned his living through the practice of law and through investments in land and manufacturing. Mason was the well-groomed, well-educated heir to a large tobacco plantation and thus led the life, much like fellow Virginians Jefferson and Madison, of a country gentleman. The more luminous stories of Washington, Jefferson, Franklin, Madison, and Hamilton have generally overshadowed Mason's and Wilson's respective roles in the formation of the Constitution, but these two were really key insiders, whose early cooperation on some matters and whose eventual bitter conflict on others ought to be better remembered by American historians and democratic theorists.

Chroniclers of the period note that Mason was the author of the Virginia Declaration of Rights and of much of the Virginia State Constitution, both of which were adopted about a week before the Declaration of Independence was declared in Philadelphia—which is to say (shortening a longer story), much of the authorial credit for the Declaration of Independence, the Bill of Rights, *and* probably much of the "Virginia Plan," which was the starting template for the U.S. Constitution, ought to go to George Mason.[7] Yet Mason also broke dramatically with the framers toward the end of the Convention, refused to sign the Constitution, and thereafter became a leading Antifederalist and opponent of ratification.

Wilson is also less heralded today but was nonetheless a pivotal figure at the Convention. He was one of only six persons to sign both the Declaration of Independence and the Constitution; and in the development of the latter, his influence, one scholar claims, was "second only to [that of] Madison."[8] After the Convention, Wilson became one of the leading proponents of ratification of the proposed, unamended Constitution, producing a pamphlet in its defense that one commentator calls "the ablest on that side"[9]—which meant that Wilson took a public stand very much in opposition to his former colleague Mason

(Wilson was so much identified as the leading proponent of ratification that Antifederalist crowds burned him in effigy).[10] In fact, a newspaper satire published at the time, "Recipe for an Anti-Federalist Essay," paired Wilson and Mason together as the rival leaders of the Federalists and the Antifederalists, respectively: "Take 'well-born' nine times; 'aristocracy' nine times; 'liberty of the press' thirteen times; 'liberty of conscience' once; 'negro slavery' once; 'trial by jury' seven times; 'great men' six times; 'Mr. Wilson' forty times; and lastly, 'George Mason's right hand in a cutting-box' nineteen times. Put all together, boil or roast or fry, and dish at pleasure. After being once used the remains of the same dish may be served a dozen times *ad libitum*."[11] Mason would eventually win the argument about the need for a Bill of Rights, as he did earlier in their dispute about age requirements, but as one historian concludes, "Even when Wilson lost battles during the constitutional convention, the future often affirmed his position. Today, the American constitutional system is closer to his vision than to that of any other founder."[12]

As delegates at the 1787 Constitutional Convention, Wilson and Mason both arrived in Philadelphia already predisposed toward a new federal government, sharing the view that the Articles of Confederation were defective in several areas. The main deliberations of the Committee of the Whole began on May 29, at which time Virginia governor Edmund Randolph presented fifteen resolutions drafted by the Virginia caucus, resolutions which collectively came to be known as the Virginia Plan and were attributed largely (and unofficially) to James Madison, the leader of the delegation. But it was Mason—again, chief architect of the Virginia Constitution—who became the first Virginian to stand up (in the ensuing debate, two days later) and defend the main sticking point of the Plan, namely the idea of popular election to federal government. And on this fundamental tenet of democratic republicanism, he teamed up with none other than James Wilson of Pennsylvania.

On May 31, Roger Sherman of Connecticut and Elbridge Gerry of Massachusetts spoke derisively about popular election. Sherman insisted that representatives to the first branch of a national legislature ought to be selected by the state legislatures: "The people should have as little to do as may be about the Government. They want information and are constantly liable to be misled."[13] Gerry added to this basic mistrust of unchecked democracy: "The evils we experience flow from the excess of democracy. The people do not want virtue; but are the dupes of pretended patriots" (1:48). Mason and Wilson responded with forceful arguments in favor of popular election to the proposed first branch of the legislature. Mason said that if the appointment to the legislature came directly from the people, the representation would be "actual," but if it came from the state legislatures, it would be only "virtual" (57). He envisioned this larger branch as "the grand depository of the democratic principle of the Government" and called it "our House of Commons." Such a house, he argued, "ought to know and sympathize with every part of the community; and ought therefore to be taken not only from different parts of the whole republic, but also from different districts of the larger members of it" (48–49). Even though Mason himself hailed from an American-style upper-crust background, he chided the implicitly aristocratic views of Sherman and Gerry: "We ought to attend to the rights of every class of the people," he said, wondering aloud how the superior and affluent members of society could remain indifferent to the needs and rights of the lowest classes. Wilson, following Mason's speech immediately, invoked the metaphor of a "pyramid." The most numerous branch of government should draw immediately from the people, he reasoned, providing the federal pyramid with as broad a base as possible. "No government can long subsist without the confidence of the people. In a republican Government this confidence is peculiarly essential," Wilson said (49). He shared Mason's view that popular election would help secure this confidence of the people and would also help destroy the rivalry between state and federal governments (56). Suffice to say that Mason and Wilson's arguments won the day on this point, by a vote of 6 to 2, with two additional state delegations divided.

This was not the last time during the Convention that Mason and Wilson would agree on a possible expansion of democracy—in July they would again join forces, this time to oppose restrictions on the future admission of Western states—but over the course of the summer of 1787 they found themselves disagreeing more and more. On closer inspection, their views on popular election to the House probably represented already divergent background views on a host of issues about democracy. Mason had drawn on his experience in Virginia, where democratic representation was needed, he said, to take into account the local differences of "produce" and "habits."[14] Eventually this concern for localism would fuel Mason's antifederalism, after he finally acceded to his gathering fear that the Constitution had centralized too many operations without explicitly guaranteeing the rights and liberties of individuals and local communities, but Mason would never abandon his early and baseline commitment to popular election in the House. There he had endorsed the idea of a "grand depository" of the "principle" of democracy, but his democratic endorsements always came with strong qualifications. He urged that members to the House be landowners and be free of debt to the United States. He was against the direct election of senators and strongly favored property qualifications as well as a fourteen-year citizenship requirement. (Plus, as we'll see, he was in favor of age requirements for *every* elected branch.) He was in favor of a very limited role for the judiciary. One of his pet projects was to insist on an anticorruption clause that would forbid congressmen from accepting any public offices for a year after their terms expired—indicative of his wider cynicism about the temptations of office with its lure of material gain for an upstart class. Yet Mason cannot be pigeonholed simply as a shill for the interests of the landed gentry. A slave owner, he nonetheless broke sharply with many of the Southern delegates who wanted to count slaves as freemen in order to boost Southern representation in Congress—because, he said, recognizing slaves only for that purpose would be tantamount to a tacit approval of slavery as a system.[15]

Mason was a passionate democrat, but only to a point.[16] His commitment to popular election, even for the House, was based largely on a protectionist view of the virtues of representation, and he was quick to hold democracy in check with other measures. Wilson, on the other hand, expressed an almost unmitigated enthusiasm for direct election at every turn: He was in favor of popular election to the House, the Senate, and the executive branch. In fact, he favored annual election of representatives to the House. He was the only founder who expressed unequivocal support for proportional representation (one person, one vote), against those, such as Mason, who would accept fractional compromises, such as counting slave populations at a three-fifths rate.[17] He opposed all property qualifications on voters (and, as we'll see, he opposed age qualifications for officeholders). Throughout the Convention, Wilson expressed an enduring faith in the people to make good decisions for themselves (although he did back Madison in Madison's pet idea of a national veto over state legislation); yet Wilson was neither unaware of nor naïve about the corruptions and tyrannies of power—one commentator attributes Wilson's broad democratic commitments to his general acceptance of natural law, universally and equally applicable to all parties.[18] Wilson had developed his theories of democratic representation in the years leading up to the Convention. He had gone beyond the view that representation ought to be actual, not virtual, to the point of espousing the position that representatives were properly to be considered the "creatures" of their constituents, duty bound by the people's instructions.[19] Putting Wilson at the center of the process, Bernard Bailyn describes a major transformation in the role of democratic government during this period:

> Where government was such an accurate mirror of the people, sensitively reflecting their desires and feelings, consent was a continuous, everyday process. In effect the people were present through their representatives, and were themselves, step by step and point by point, acting in the conduct of public affairs. No longer merely an ultimate check on government, they *were* in some sense the government. Government had no separate existence apart from them; it was *by* the people as well as *for* the people; it gained its authority from their continuous consent. The very nature and meaning of law was involved. The traditional sense, proclaimed by Blackstone no less than by Hobbes, that law was a command "prescribed by source superior and which the inferior is bound to obey"—such a sense of law as the declaration of a person or body existing independently above the subjects of law and imposing its will upon them, was brought into question by the developing notion of representation. Already in these years there were adumbrations of the sweeping repudiation James Wilson and others would make of Blackstone's definition of law, and of the view they would put in its place: the view that the binding power of law flowed from the continuous assent of the subjects of law; the view [i.e., James Wilson's] "that the only reason why a free and independent man was bound by human laws was this—that he bound himself."[20]

Thus Mason and Wilson's clash was a clash of competing democratic theories. Although the two men occasionally agreed, Mason endorsed popular election as a strategic check on government, to be deployed or abandoned as necessary along with other regulating mechanisms, whereas Wilson regarded popular consent as the very definition of democratic government, deserving of restriction and qualification only as a last resort. Although they were allies at the outset of the Convention, Wilson's affection for broadening democratic consent soon prompted not only Mason's rebuke but also his ridicule. And the parting of their ways came to a head with the age debate.

The Virginia Plan introduced on May 29 included age requirements for members of the House and of the Senate but left them temporarily unspecified, stating only that such members must "be of the age of _____ at least."[21] It included no age requirements for the executive or judicial branches. Two weeks later, on June 12, the Committee of the Whole voted 10 to 1 to abandon an age requirement for members of the House (Maryland was the dissent).[22] A proposal to require an age of thirty years for members of the Senate was passed 7 to 4.[23] The record doesn't reveal any debate over these votes. Two weeks later, on June 25, the delegates unanimously adopted the thirty-year requirement for senators, again without any debate. But the age for House members had become controversial. A few days earlier, on June 22, George Mason moved that an age requirement for House members be reinstated (revoking the 10 to 1 vote to abandon them)—and he proposed twenty-five years. Where or how did he come up with this idea? Certainly not from the British example, which at the time required only that members of the House of Commons not be minors. One scholar speculates that Mason was doing little more than drawing from his own convictions that earlier had found their way into the Virginia Constitution (again, most of which he drafted), which required members of the state legislature to be "upwards of twenty-five years of age."[24] Almost single-handedly, Mason had managed to inscribe age requirements into the Virginia Constitution; and thus emboldened, he was again single-handedly attempting to turn the tide at the Constitutional Convention back in this direction. Madison's notes record Mason's argument thus:

> He thought it absurd that a man to day should not be permitted by the law to make a bargain for himself, and tomorrow should be authorized to manage the affairs of a great nation. It was the more extraordinary as every man carried with him in his own experience a scale for measuring the deficiency of young politicians; since he would if interrogated be obliged to declare that his own political opinions at the age of 21. were too crude & erroneous to merit an influence on public measures. It had been said that Congs. had proved a good school for our young men. It might be so for any thing he knew but if it were, he chose that they should bear the expence of their own education.[25]

It should be noted that Mason was sixty-two when he delivered this speech, which proved to be a watershed moment in constitutional history. By way of an insinuating sarcasm (one of his trademarks), he successfully impugned the political abilities of all adult Americans, present and future, who were under twenty-five. Aside from the tone, the essence of his argument was that it is absurd to think that a person should be able to pass overnight from a condition of being too young to vote on one day to being qualified to manage national governmental affairs on the very next. Eligibility to hold office, in other words, should not coincide with the threshold age of suffrage: the former should be phased in over a span of time and experience.[26] Of course, Mason's invocation of a specter of woefully inept and presumptuous young politicians makes no mention of the voters' prerogatives—and on this point Wilson rose to take exception to Mason's resolution.

Wilson (who, for what it is worth, was forty-four at the time) said that he was against "abridging the rights of election in any shape." Madison's notes record the rest of his remarks as follows: "It was the same thing whether this were done by disqualifying the objects of choice, or the persons chusing. The motion tended to damp the efforts of genius, and of laudable ambition. There was no more reason for incapacitating *youth* than *age*, when the requisite qualifications were found. Many instances might be mentioned of signal services rendered in high stations to the public before the age of 25: The present Mr. Pitt and Lord Bolingbroke were striking instances."[27] In other words, the electorate should be entrusted with determining fitness for office, and neither youthful nor elderly citizens should be constitutionally barred (on those grounds) from holding office. Age should not be an impediment to running for office for an entire category of adult citizens. Moreover, youthful efforts in politics should be encouraged, not squashed or deterred—and actual individual cases of auspicious younger candidates, even if exceptional, should trump any categoric exclusion based on a blanket generalization. Today, we could call Wilson's argument an argument against discrimination based on age.

But Mason's motion carried, by a vote of seven ayes (Connecticut, New Jersey, Delaware, Maryland, Virginia, North Carolina, and South Carolina) to three nays (Massachusetts, Pennsylvania, and Georgia), and one divided delegation (New York). In late August and early September, the Committee of the Whole took up the question of an age qualification of thirty-five for the president (which, to repeat, had not been included in the original Virginia Plan), and by this time such qualifications apparently drew neither debate nor comment and passed easily.[28] By now Mason had apparently convinced the Convention delegates on this basic point about the political fecklessness of younger adult citizens. Mason's mistrust had clearly won out over Wilson's exuberance.

In the days following, Mason and Wilson would verbally spar on a number of key issues. Typically, Mason would find a rhetorical way to burst Wilson's bubble of democratic enthusiasm. Thomas Jefferson even characterized Mason's public speaking during these days as infected with a "touch of biting cynicism"—most of which was directed at Wilson.[29] On June 23, for instance, Mason and Madison were considering an anticorruption motion for the House. Mason could not imagine that a sufficient number of citizens could be attracted to legislative service without the inducements of emoluments, and thus such measures were unfortunately necessary. But along the way, he took a swipe at Wilson's wistful notion that men of genius and virtue simply ought to be encouraged into public service, as if genius were somehow immune to enticements: "Genius and virtue, it may be said, ought to be encouraged. Genius, for aught [I] know might; but that virtue should be encouraged by such a species of venality, is an idea that at least has the merit of being new."[30] On June 25, Wilson moved that the people should directly elect the electors for senators, thus producing proportional representation in both Houses (and also bypassing the influence of the states in the election of the president). Mason opposed the measure on the basis of states' rights (or, as he called it, "States-defense"), and many observers hail Mason's argument at this point as the crucial "stepping stone" to what became the doctrine of "equal representation" of small states and large states.[31] In mid-July Wilson returned to his proposal for direct election of the president (back on June 1, Mason had told Wilson that the idea was impractical and that he wished "Mr. Wilson might have time to digest it into his own form"),[32] and once again Mason shot it down with a caustic comment. Quoting Virgil, Mason said that he "conceived it would be as unnatural to refer the choice of a proper character for chief Magistrate to the people, as it would, to refer a trial of colours to a blind man. The extent of the Country renders it impossible that the people can have the requisite capacity to judge of the respective pretensions of the Candidates."[33] On July 26, in a long speech to the Convention, Mason became even more patronizing toward Wilson's proposals. A few days before, Wilson had suggested an alternative to direct election of the president, whereby the national legislature would assemble a committee of electors to choose the executive—with the twist that the committee be selected by a lottery.[34] About this proposal, Mason simply sneered: "Among other expedients, a lottery has been introduced. But as the tickets do not appear to be in much demand, it will probably, not be carried on, and nothing therefore need be said on the subject."[35]

Of course some of Wilson's offbeat proposals for the election of the president paved the way for the eventual adoption of the Electoral College as a compromise measure—which indeed mollified Mason for a short spell in September before he spurned the Convention altogether. Wilson lost out on several measures that have become more attractive with time. History has looked back favorably on his early preferences for broadening democracy albeit within the framework of representative government. Teaming up initially with Mason, Wilson won on the idea of direct election of representatives to the House, but lost on the proposals of direct election to the Senate and the presidency—and Mason decidedly parted company with him on these latter two proposals. Yet after the signing of the Constitution, several states on their own followed Wilson's lead on direct election to the Senate, prompting a movement that eventually culminated in the Seventeenth Amendment in 1913. Many people today question the need for the Electoral College and now share Wilson's earlier support for direct election of the president.[36] His advocacy of "one person, one vote" wasn't shared by his contemporaries but was belatedly affirmed in the 1964 Supreme Court decision in *Wesberry v. Sanders*[37] (and Justice Hugo Black cites Wilson's law lectures on this point).[38] Wilson successfully opposed property qualifications for voters and candidates, and Mason consistently lost these battles. But Mason, even while refusing to sign the Constitution, has exerted a lasting influence in at least one area, namely his reestablishing age requirements for members of the House, which seems (especially in the absence of any rival explanation in the record) to have galvanized support for, or preempted further opposition against, the age qualifications for the Senate and the presidency.

Post-Convention Commentary

The age qualifications did not attract much attention, let alone controversy, during the ratification period. Speaking to the Maryland House of Delegates in late November 1787 (and probably bearing in mind that Maryland had been the lone dissenting voice in the original 10–1 vote to abandon age requirements for representatives to the House), James McHenry said only this about the age qualifications: "And the

Period of Twenty five Years deemed a necessary Age to mature the Judgement and form the mind by habits of reflection and experience.—Little was said on this subject it passed without any considerable opposition and therefore I was not at the pains to note any other particulars respecting it."[39] George Nicholas, speaking to the Virginia ratifying convention (1788), associated age limitations with maturity in political judgment: "We find no qualifications required except those of age and residence, which create a certainty of their judgment being matured, and of being attached to their state."[40] Summing up the period, Joseph Story, the constitutional law and history professor at Harvard, wrote in 1851 about the age requirements, "In the state conventions it does not seem to have formed any important topic of debate."[41]

The rest of the record could be read, through contemporary eyes, as a catalog of an acquired eighteenth-century prejudice trying to pass itself off as ingrained wisdom about the folly of youth. In October 1787, the Pennsylvanian Tench Coxe, writing under the pseudonym "An American Citizen," justified the age requirement for the presidency by contrasting the proposed American republic with the British monarchy. But his first line of defense for the age requirement aimed pretty low: he said it was needed to prevent idiots from assuming office:

> In Britain their king is for life—In America our president will always be *one of the people* at the end of four years. In that country the king is hereditary and may be an idiot, a knave, or a tyrant by nature, or ignorant from the neglect of his education, yet cannot be removed, for *"he can do no wrong."* In America, as the president is to be one of the people at the end of his short term, so will he and his fellow citizens remember, *that he was originally one of the people; and that he is created by their breath*—Further, he cannot be an idiot, probably not a knave or a tyrant, for those whom nature makes so, discover it before the age of thirty-five, until which period he cannot be elected.[42]

This particular rationale for the presidential age qualification seems to be rather forced. It probably doesn't take thirty-five years to manifest one's "idiocy."

Coxe continues in the article to draw a sharp contrast between republicanism and royalty, whereby a fault of the latter, avoided by the former, is that monarchy is liable to install into office youthful presumption: "In all royal governments an helpless infant or an unexperienced youth, may wear the crown. *Our president must be matured by the experience of years*, and being born among us, his character at thirty-five must be fully understood. Wisdom, virtue, and active qualities of mind and body can alone make him the first servant of a free and enlightened people."[43] He repeats this theme, now expanding the discussion to the age qualifications for the Senate, in a second piece published two days later:

> No ambitious, undeserving or unexperienced *youth* can acquire a seat in this house by means of the most enormous wealth or most powerful connections, *till thirty years have ripened his abilities and fully discovered his merits to his country*—a more rational ground of preference surely than mere property.
>
> The senate though more independent of the people as to the *free exercise of their judgement and abilities*, than the house of representatives, by the longer term of their office, must be older and more experienced men.[44]

Royal governments honor hereditary privileges, says Coxe, whereas the U.S. system won't be assigning offices to persons merely because their fathers held them. Inherited wealth and inherited status will not be rewarded in this new government. Coxe's aversion to monarchy clearly is the main source of his animus against the prospect of young officeholders. Yet he does concede that some young men have acquitted themselves with distinction in Congress, provided that they earned their way into office rather than having it bestowed upon them: "If we recollect the characters, who have, at various periods, filled the seat of Congress, we shall find this expectation *perfectly reasonable*. Many *young* men of genius and *many characters of more matured abilities, without fortunes*, have been honored with that trust."[45]

A few weeks later Noah Webster published a pamphlet that explored in somewhat greater depth the rationale for the age requirements. Much of the first part of the pamphlet praises the proposed American system for its various checks and balances, such as a bicameral legislature. But Webster argues that the function of the Senate is not simply to check the House:

> Besides, the design of a senate is not merely to check the legislative assembly, but to collect wisdom and experience. In most of

our constitutions, and particularly in the proposed federal system, greater age and a longer residence are required to qualify for the senate, than for the house of representatives. This is a wise provision. The house of representatives may be composed of new and unexperienced members—strangers to the forms of proceeding, and the science of legislation. But either positive constitutions, or customs, which may supply their place, fill the senate with men venerable for age and respectability, experienced in the ways of men, and in the art of governing, and who are not liable to the bias of passions that govern the young.[46]

Because of the age requirement, says Webster, the Senate will be the repository of experience. He underscores the point with a speculative gloss: "Experience is the best instructor—it is better than a thousand theories." Immediately he attempts to draw on the actual experiences of Maryland, Connecticut, Pennsylvania, and Georgia to demonstrate the superior wisdom of an older and wiser upper house. In the Connecticut example he cites, the lower house had passed a resolution that would have "disgraced school boys"—and only the Senate's intervention, he says, saved the honor of the state: "All public bodies have these fits of passion, when their conduct seems to be perfectly boyish; and in these paroxysms, a check is highly necessary."[47]

Webster's next move in the pamphlet is to hark back to ancient Rome. He writes, "A man must be thirty years of age, before he can be admitted into the senate—which was likewise a requisite for a senator in the Roman government."[48] He also invokes the Roman example as a rationale for the age qualification for the presidency, but he concedes that there may be a need for latter-day updating to this requirement—and in the course of rethinking and renegotiating these requirements, he wonders aloud whether the age requirement for consulships was necessary at all:

The age requisite to qualify for this office is thirty-five years. The age requisite for admittance to the Roman consulship was forty-three years. For this difference, good reasons may be assigned—the improvements in science, and particularly in government, render it practicable for a man to qualify himself for an important office, much earlier in life, than he could among the Romans; especially in the early part of their commonwealth, when the office was instituted. Besides it is very questionable whether any inconvenience would have attended an admission to the consulship at an earlier age.[49]

Senatorial Privilege

Webster's essay is the only document from the period that explicitly traces the Constitution's age requirements to the ancient Romans. Yet it goes almost without saying that the founders more generally *must* have been drawing consciously from the Roman example merely in their naming the upper chamber "the Senate" while expressly rejecting the analogous British term, "House of Lords."[50] Furthermore, the choice of the name "Senate" alone would suggest that they must have been cognizant about age issues in the earliest stages of their preference for the Virginia Plan's bicameralism (and every state constitution at the time featured a divided legislature, except those of Pennsylvania and Georgia).[51] Recall that the Committee of the Whole voted to abandon age requirements for the House but never for the Senate. Designing a "senate" would necessarily entail thinking about minimum age requirements as an integral part of the design package.

"Senate" *means* a council of seniors. The root *senex* indicates an old man, and *senatus* thus means, literally, a council of old men. According to William Smith's 1843 *Dictionary of Greek and Roman Antiquities*, "A senate in the early times was always regarded as an assembly of elders, which is, in fact, the meaning of the Roman senatus as of the Spartan *gerousia*."[52] Of the Senate's earliest days when Rome was a monarchy, Smith's *Dictionary* says that we do not know the age at which a person might be elected into the Senate, but can surmise "no more than what is indicated by the name senator itself, that is, that they were persons of advanced age."[53] But he also writes that for both the Roman Republic and the Roman Empire, there exists abundant evidence that a minimum senatorial age (*aetas senatoria*) had been in force: "As regards the age at which a person might become a senator, we have no express statement for the time of the Republic, although it appears to have been fixed by some custom or law, as the *aetas senatoria* is frequently mentioned, especially during the latter period of the Republic."[54] He lists the probable minimum age at which a man during the Republic could become a senator as thirty-two. Another source concludes that the qualifying age during the Republic, when quaestors were regularly added to the senate, was twenty-eight.[55] Augustus eventually fixed the senatorial age at twenty-five, which it remained throughout the rest of the Empire. (One might speculate that Augustus was inclined to fix the *aetas senatoria* at a younger age because he himself had become a senator, albeit through force, at age twenty.)[56] As the Roman Senate became equally accessible to plebeians and patricians and grew in size, it gradually became an assembly representing the people[57]—which may account for the origin of the American framers' use of the Augustan age of twenty-five for the House, while harking back to an early period of the Roman Senate for the American Senate, selecting a number somewhere between the two main *aetas senatoria* on record, twenty-eight and thirty-two.

While Noah Webster cites a good bit of Roman history in his pamphlet, it's not clear where or how he arrived upon the claim that the *aetas senatoria* in Rome was thirty.[58] The exact reasoning for this number, however, is not important. What is important is that it reveals that the founders, some at any rate, presumed that the "upper chamber" in America ought to be populated not by lords, and maybe not exclusively by doddering seniors, but certainly not by those adults who have yet to reach (what we now might loosely call) middle age.[59]

Another line of political genealogy might help account for this attribution of the number thirty to the Roman senate, with an early American application. Many scholars have tracked Baron de Montesquieu's and David Hume's classical republican influence on the American founders. Montesquieu and Hume, throughout their political writings, quite readily apply the Roman term *senate* to the possibility of modern republican government. Hume, in his "Idea of a Perfect Commonwealth," names James Harrington as his source for his own conception of a senatorial enclave within bicameral government: "All free governments must consist of two councils, a lesser and greater; or, in other words, of a senate and a people. The people, as HARRINGTON observes, would want wisdom, without the senate: The senate, without the people, would want honesty."[60]

Harrington's seminal influence on John Adams's insistence that a "natural aristocracy" ought to be attracted into a senatorial body—and Adams's influence on this matter seems to have reverberated throughout many of the colonial states—has been well documented.[61] Yet if we look carefully at Harrington's reasoning in his utopian work, *Oceana*, a curious tale emerges. Harrington attributes the term *senate* to ancient Rome, but he also uses the term to describe various governing bodies in ancient Athens, Sparta, Carthage, Venice, and recent commonwealths in Switzerland and Holland. The oddity of his account is that he draws the most elaborate description of a senate from the Hebrew

Bible.[62] Strangely, he repeatedly refers to the "Seventy Elders" of the Old Testament—the Sanhedrin—as the "Senate of Israel." Biblically inflected notions of eldership patriarchy are interspersed throughout many of his age-based political recommendations for the Common-wealth of Oceana, showcasing an ongoing conflation of Talmudic, Roman, and Venetian sources on the matter. The second order of the Commonwealth "distributes citizens into youth and elders (such as are from eighteen years of age to thirty, being accounted youth; and such as are of thirty and upward, elders),'' and the text then goes on to establish thirty as the minimum age for holding senatorial office. That age threshold, dividing a militarized youth from an office-eligible senior class, surely echoes the general logic of Numbers (cf. 4:3), though Harrington adds that the Tullian law in Rome also established thirty as the official end of the period of youth.[63]

John Adams and other founders had a hard time ensuring that an "Upper Chamber" would necessarily attract Harrington's "natural ar-istocracy" of the virtuous, the wise, and the talented. Early "double-chambered" colonial state constitutions, such as Pennsylvania's, attached various eligibility requirements to officeholding—pertaining to, among other things, property ownership, military service, marital status, and age—all in the hope of attracting wisdom and talent into higher office, although indirectly, since none of those requirements was thought to be synonymous with the virtues sought. By 1787, all of these constitutional proxies for meritocratic worth, which had been featured in most colonial state constitutions, had fallen by the wayside, except for the age requirements (which, to repeat, had been featured in only two colonial constitutions). After 1787, then, the age require-ments, left pretty much on their own, seemed to take on a particularly heavy burden for attracting and justifying the entirety of the aristo-cratic element in American bicameralism, and many of the desired senatorial virtues had to be refracted through, and reduced to, the prism of age—bequeathing to us something of an amorphous history and an inexplicable textual provision.

We see evidence of this burden, and the explanatory difficulties attending to it, in the *Federalist Papers*. James Madison says offhand-edly in *Federalist* 62 that the nature of "senatorial trust" explains the need for advanced age requirements for the upper chamber, whose members must wield "greater extent of information and stability of character" than would be needed in the more democratic House.[64] But Madison offers no further argument to back this rather pat view about the superior knowledge and character of older men as a group.[65] Alexander Hamilton provides a clue in *Federalist* 68 as to the rationale for the presidential age restriction: the presidency is to be sought, he writes, only by citizens with "the requisite qualifications"; it should be a "station filled by characters pre-eminent for ability and virtue."[66] To those who don't question ageist assumptions and language, that scheme probably looks reasonably unobjectionable on paper. But Hamilton likewise provides no argument or evidence to back his wildly sweeping if tacit assumptions about the over-thirty-five crowd—wide, prejudicial assertions that necessarily impugn everyone under thirty-five. Constitutional apologists, following Hamilton's lead wittingly or unwittingly, have probably been too quick to equate prejudice with prudence on this score.

One might be inclined to look to Hamilton's argument in *Federalist* 35 for a theory of representation that would better justify such restrictions. Even though the House of Representatives in the proposed government is designed to be more numerous than the Senate, Hamilton points out that it can never be sufficiently numerous "for the reception of all the different classes of citizens in order to combine the interests and feelings of every part of the community, and to produce a true sympathy between the representative body and its constituents."[67] Such a view of representation—which echoes Mason's view of the assembly as a "grand depository" of the people—is seductive but specious, says Hamilton. In a diverse country, such representation would be impossible and impractical: "The idea of an actual representation of all classes of the people by persons of each class is altogether visionary. Unless it were expressly provided in the Constitution that each different occupation should send one or more members, the thing would never take place in practice."[68] The merchant can reasonably and naturally represent the interests of the mechanic and of all classes of the community. Substitute "youth" (or any age group) for "class," and Hamilton's response would probably be the same: "It is said to be necessary that all classes of citizens should have some of their own number in the representative body in order that their feelings and interests may be the better understood and attended to. But we have seen that this will never happen under any arrangement that leaves the votes of the people free."[69]

The problem with applying Hamilton's argument by analogy to youth, however, is that the Constitution does not explicitly bar mechanics *qua* mechanics from running for office. Conceivably it could *become* the case that if younger citizens were eligible to run for office.

Hamilton's brief against guaranteed proportional representation on the basis of occupation (or age) would then apply. *Federalist* 35 cannot be construed, however, as a blanket justification for almost any form of virtual, as opposed to actual, representation. It rather can serve only as an argument against codified proportionality. So it doesn't provide a theory of American representation that puts to rest the contemporary complaint about the Constitution's inherent discrimination against citizens from eighteen to thirty-four.

Primogeniture Concerns

Akhil Reed Amar, in his enormously learned book *America's Constitution: A Biography*, offers a global interpretation of the intent and effects of the age requirements in the Constitution, a theory that accords with his overall rereading of the Constitution as "more welcoming of mass democracy, more open to lowborn and unpropertied"[70] men than commonly understood (while also more tolerant of slavery and more biased toward the South than typically acknowledged as well). Amar's counterintuitive contention is that the Constitution's age limits embodied "republican principles" (69) and fit with a "larger egalitarian pattern" (163) of the framer's collective compromises in the 1787 Convention. Despite their obvious function as a restriction on electoral choice, the age limits, he insists, should be seen (in their context) as "populist" and "liberating," a roundabout way of "promoting a broader democratic culture of republican merit and equal opportunity" (160). In fact, he goes so far as to submit that the age requirements should be regarded as contributing to the original "radicalism" of the Constitution (473). While Amar adduces considerable evidence in support of his bold claims, the application of the book's general thesis to the particulars of the age requirements may be overstated and a bit forced. The evidence he cites needs to be carefully examined and weighed.

Amar's main contention is that, in requiring age limits, the founders were attempting to limit the influence of the rich and highborn, especially to check the influence of family dynasties. "Who other than the 'haughty heirs of distinguished names,'" Amar asks rhetorically, citing Tench Coxe's post-Convention "An American Citizen" article, "would be famous enough at a tender age to win a seat in the continental House or Senate?" (70).[71] But Amar doesn't explain that Coxe, in his piece, is referring only to the Senate, not the House (for which Coxe doesn't issue a broadside against youthful participation), and

Amar doesn't mention that Coxe admits that someone other than the "haughty heirs of distinguished names" have indeed earned their way into office at a young age. True, Coxe rails loudly against hereditary succession in this new government—but his arguments are all about ensuring that upper offices are held by those persons with merit, virtue, wisdom, and experience, all of which are best secured through age limits, he believes. Inherited privilege contravenes the benefits of seniority, but Coxe's main point in supporting age limits is to promote meritocracy—a position that should not be conflated with egalitarianism, as Amar apparently assumes. Curiously, Amar cites Pitt the younger as an example of the kind of British "favorite son" that the Americans were attempting to avoid.[72] Yet what record we have of the 1787 Convention debate over the age requirements shows James Wilson, in arguing against the age requirements, as citing "the present Mr. Pitt" as an exemplary, rather than cautionary, instance of public service at a younger age.

What's more, the record doesn't show George Mason, the main proponent for the age limits, as uttering a peep about their purpose as a structural check on aristocratic succession. One would think, if Amar were correct, that Mason would have drawn an explicit connection between the age limits and his concern to forestall youthful aristocratic entitlement, especially since Mason's first draft of his 1776 Virginia Declaration of Rights decried hereditary privileges as "unnatural and absurd" and since, at the 1787 Convention, Mason inveighed against those proponents of aristocracy who were indifferent to the rights of the "lowest classes."[73] Instead, the available record shows that Mason argued merely that youthful politicians are inexperienced and deficient in their judgments. To be sure, George Mason was a complicated fellow, but Amar's position on the allegedly populist drift of the age requirements would virtually require that Mason, as the leading and most vocal proponent of the age restrictions, be somehow an egalitarian advocate of the "lowborn" against their wealthy rivals, but then transmogrify into some other kind of beast altogether when he insisted upon property qualifications for every branch of federal government. In other words, Amar's thesis about the radicalism of the age limits works best as a speculative gloss, but it doesn't fit very well with the historical particulars of those articles. Similarly, while Amar attends to Tench Coxe's post-Convention publications, he overlooks Noah Webster's contemporaneous pamphlet about the rationale for the age limits—in which Webster merely associates advanced age with experience and wisdom, and youth with passion and bias, and says absolutely nothing about family favoritism. In his later writings, Wilson criticizes at length the reasons for the age requirements, but he never mentions the possibility that their genesis had to do with a republican concern for leveling the playing field of birthright.

Amar tries to strengthen his case about the Article I limits by looking at their immediate application, and he contends that cumulative data from the new Congress's first decade "provide further evidence that Article I's age rules probably did tend to dampen intergenerational aristocracy."[74] Younger officials in both the House and Senate seemed more likely to hail from families with political pedigrees than their older counterparts. But that data could attest to the relative success or to the relative failure of those age limits, and scant little can be inferred from those mixed results about the original purposes of the restrictions.

Amar's case about Article II's age requirements is somewhat more compelling. He draws heavily on Gordon Wood's extensive portrayal of the prevalence of political nepotism in the prerevolutionary colonies—a concern that seems to have informed and fueled the eventual animus against a reestablished monarchy in America, especially at the top of the executive branch. In the forty-year period before the Revolution, dominant families, writes Wood, monopolized political offices through successive generations. Wood and Amar both cite John Adams on this point: "Go into every village in New England and you will find that the office of justice of the peace, and even the place of representative, which has ever depended only on the freest election of the people, have generally descended from generation to generation, in three or four families at most."[75] Many of the revolutionary state constitutions had explicit language forbidding hereditary honors and positions. But the only solid evidence that Amar cites that links explicitly this general concern about dynasticism to the Article II age restrictions (besides the Tench Coxe piece) comes in a Federalist pamphlet published in April 1788:

> It is pretty certain that the President can never become the sovereign of America, but with the voluntary consent of the People: He is reelected by them; not by any body of men over whom he may have gained an undue influence. No citizen of America has a fortune sufficiently large, to enable him to raise and support a single regiment. The President's salary will be greatly inadequate either to the purpose of gaining adherents, or of supporting a military force: He will possess no princely revenues, and his

personal influence will be confined to his native State. Besides, the Constitution has provided, that no person shall be eligible to the office, who is not thirty-five years old; and in the course of nature very few fathers leave a son who has arrived to that age. The powers of the President are not kingly, any more than the ensigns of his office. He has no guards, no regalia, none of those royal trappings which would set him apart from the rest of his fellow citizens. Suppose the first President should be continued for life: What expectations can any man in the Union have to succeed him except such as are grounded upon the popularity of his character?[76]

Clearly the purpose of this passage is to allay anxieties about executive power vested in a single person. But nowhere in this pamphlet is there any hint of the idea that the constitutional limitations on the presidency, especially those inhibiting hereditary succession, are animated by a background egalitarian desire to give the underprivileged a fair shot at the office. Neither this pamphlet nor the procreative patterns of the early presidents that Amar inventories support his claim that the purpose of the age rules was to give "lower-born men a chance to outshine famous favorite sons."[77] The evidence mostly reveals merely blanket veneration about the benefits of senior statesmanship with a concomitant denigration of youthful involvement. While Amar may be correct that an underlying concern about hereditary presumption *contributed* to that prejudice against officeholding youth, he is too quick to draw the conclusion that the historical evidence "strongly supports an egalitarian reading of the seemingly bland words 'thirty five Years.'"[78] "Anti-aristocratic" is not synonymous with "pro-low-born"—which is to say, the age restrictions politically disqualified entire blocs of underage citizens in categoric fashion, drawing all young adults into disabling sweep, not simply the highborn. Attempting to recover a lost democratic logic lurking behind these requirements is probably a strained effort (and, to say the least, such an appeal to their originally radical intent shouldn't be construed into a contemporary rationale for their continued existence).

Post-Ratification Commentary

No matter what their original purposes, the age qualifications after ratification became a moot point, a complete nonissue. Most constitutional histories do not even discuss them. The exceptions are not particularly edifying, though they betray lingering prejudice about age.

St. George Tucker, in his 1803 *Blackstone's Commentaries,* observes that the British constitution has an age requirement for representatives of twenty-one, and expresses his simple preference for the American version: "Ours with more caution and perhaps with better reason, requires that he shall have attained to the age of twenty-five years."[79] Tucker later waxes eloquent about benefits of the senatorial age requirement thus: "Age must have matured the talents, and confirmed the virtues which dawned with childhood, or shine forth with youth. Principles must have been manifested, and conduct have evinced their rectitude, energy, and stability."[80] James Kent, in his 1826 *Commentaries on American Law,* says about the age qualifications for the Senate merely that "the superior weight and delicacy of the trust confided to the senate . . . required that a senator must be thirty years of age."[81] Joseph Story's 1851 *Commentaries on the Constitution of the United States* draws more attention to the age requirements only in an attempt, however, to dismiss any (imagined) objections to them. Of the age requirements for the House, he writes,

> The representative must have attained twenty-five years. And certainly to this no reasonable objection can be made. If experience, or wisdom, or knowledge be of value in the national councils, it can scarcely be pretended, that an earlier age could afford a certain guaranty for either. That some qualification of age is proper, no one will dispute. No one will contend, that persons who are minors, ought to be eligible; or, that those who have not obtained manhood, so as to be entitled by the common law to dispose of their persons, or estates, at their own will, would be fit depositaries of the authority to dispose of the rights, persons, and property of others. Would the mere attainment of twenty-one years of age be a more proper qualification? All just reasoning would be against it. The characters and principles of young men can scarcely be understood at the moment of their majority. They are then new to the rights of self-government; warm in their passions; ardent in their expectations; and, just escaping from pupilage, are strongly tempted to discard the lessons of caution, which riper years inculcate. What they will become, remains to be seen; and four years beyond that period is but a very short space in which to try their virtues, develop their talents, enlarge their resources, and give them a practical insight into the business of life adequate to their own immediate wants and duties.

Can the interests of others be safely confided to those, who have yet to learn how to take care of their own?[82]

Story continues this rather imperious tone in his brief on the senatorial age qualification:

The age of senators was fixed in the constitution at first by a vote of seven states against four; and finally by a unanimous vote. Perhaps no one, in our day, is disposed to question the propriety of this limitation; and it is, therefore, useless to discuss a point, which is so purely speculative. If counsels are to be wise, the ardor, and impetuosity, and confidence of youth must be chastised by the sober lessons of experience; and if knowledge, and solid judgment, and tried integrity, are to be deemed indispensable qualifications for senatorial service, it would be rashness to affirm, that thirty years is too long a period for due maturity and probation.[83]

Finally, Story's argument for the presidential age qualification is more of the same:

Considering the nature of the duties, the extent of the information, and the solid wisdom and experience required in the executive department, no one can reasonably doubt the propriety of some qualification of age. That which has been selected, is the middle age of life, by which period the character and talents of individuals are generally known and fully developed; and opportunities have usually been afforded for public service, and for experience in the public councils. The faculties of the mind, if they have not then attained to their highest maturity, are in full vigor, and hastening towards their ripest state. The judgment, acting upon large materials, has, by that time, attained a solid cast; and the principles which form the character, and the integrity which gives lustre to the virtues of life, must then, if ever, have acquired public confidence and approbation.[84]

One wants to say that Story's analyses, in retrospect, are self-betraying. His rhetorical questions probably reveal more doubts than answers. He claims that the subject does not warrant discussion, but then he proceeds to address exactly that topic and presses the issue using insistent, highly charged language. In the end, however, his "arguments" amount to little more than wanton stereotypes about various demographic groups.

Perhaps James Wilson deserves the last word from the nineteenth century. In his 1804 *Lectures on Law* he continues to question, even mock, the Constitution's age qualifications, again associating minimum age requirements with maximum age requirements—as he did in 1787—viewing both as age discrimination based on nothing more than cultural whims. His full remarks are reproduced below:

> We now proceed to examine the qualifications required from those, who are elected to that dignified trust.
>
> 1. A representative must have attained the age of twenty five years.
>
> It is amusing enough to consider the different ages, at which persons have been deemed qualified or disqualified for different purposes, both in private and in publick life.
>
> A woman, as we learn from my Lord Coke and others, has seven ages for several purposes appointed to her by the law. At seven years of age, her father, if a feudal superiour, was entitled to demand from his vassals an aid to marry her: at nine, she may have a dower: at twelve, she may consent to marriage: at fourteen, she may choose a guardian: at sixteen, marriage might be tendered to her by her lord: at seventeen, she may act as executrix: at twenty one, she may alienate her lands and goods. A man, also, has different ages assigned to him for different purposes. At twelve years of age, he was formerly obliged to take the oath of allegiance: at fourteen, he can consent to marriage: at the same age he can choose his guardian: at twenty one, he may convey his personal and real estate.
>
> The foregoing are the different ages allowed for different purposes in private life. In publick life, there has, with regard to age, been a similar variety of assignments; the reasons of some of which it is hard to conjecture; for the propriety of others, it is equally hard to account.
>
> In the government of the United States, it is supposed, that no one is fit to be a member of the house of representatives, till he is twenty five years of age; to be a senator, till he is thirty; to be a president, till he is thirty five.
>
> The duration assigned by nature to human life is often complained of as very short: that assigned to it by some politicians is much shorter. For some political purposes, a man cannot breathe

before he numbers thirty five years: as to other political purposes, his breath is extinguished the moment he reaches sixty. By the constitution of New York, "the chancellor, the judges of the supreme court, and the first judge of the county court in every county, hold their offices—until they shall respectively have attained the age of sixty years."

How differently is the same object viewed at different times and in different countries! In New York, a man is deemed unfit for the first offices of the state *after* he is sixty: in Sparta, a man was deemed unfit for the first offices of the state *till* he was sixty. Till that age, no one was entitled to a seat in the senate, the highest honour of the chiefs. How convenient it would be, if a politician possessed the power, so finely exercised by the most beautiful of poets! Virgil could, with the greatest ease imaginable, bring Aeneas and Dido together; though, in fact, some centuries elapsed between the times, in which they lived. Why cannot some politician, by the same or some similar enchanting art, produce an ancient and a modern government as cotemporaries? The effect would be admirable. The moment that a gentleman of sixty would be disqualified from retaining his seat as a judge of New York, he would be qualified for taking his seat as a senator of Sparta.[85]

Skipping to the present, I have found only two writers who have focused specifically on these age requirements,[86] and both challenge the earlier broad-brush assumption that these restrictions must necessarily amount to wise policy and ought not, therefore, to be reviewed and reformed. In 1988, William Cooper, in a short "Research Note" for the journal *Congress and the Presidency*, raised some unexplored constitutional difficulties regarding presidential succession posed by the different age requirements for members of Congress versus the presidency (I return to this question in chapter 3). But Cooper voiced an even greater worry that the age requirements have resulted in a lack of representation in Congress for young voters, which "might lead to a lack of generational balance in lawmaking itself": "Agenda items dealing with citizens under the age of twenty-five might not be given serious priority, and in current times, many pundits have wondered whether our national debt would have grown to such drastic proportion if the voters who must eventually pay for that debt were more appropriately represented in Congress."[87] The other wayward writer,

Matthew Michael, expressed concern that the presidential age requirement posed potentially "the greatest practical problem for current issues of American public policy." Much like Cooper, Michael thought such an age requirement makes it extremely difficult to address policy issues that are becoming increasingly "intergenerational" in our time: "With the growing importance and conflictual nature of intergenerational issues such as Social Security, the United States should level the presidential playing field by opening the possibility of presidential election to citizens under the age of thirty-five."[88] In sharp contrast to Story's claim, expressed about 150 years earlier, that "no one can reasonably doubt the propriety" of the age qualification, Michael contends that "there seems little substantive support for such a provision. Were a new Constitution to be drafted today, it seems exceedingly dubious that such an age restriction would be included."[89] Indeed, Michael in the piece calls on younger voters to mobilize in order to elect representatives to Congress who will emphasize intergenerational issues. But it doesn't seem as if many have yet heeded that particular call.

Although Cooper's and Michael's latter-day criticisms of the age requirements seem highly unusual, very much beyond the pale in view of two hundred years of constitutional commentary, their dissenting opinions probably can nevertheless be situated within a historical context (even as outliers for that period). Their critical views on constitutional age issues can be construed as emerging in the general (if somewhat protracted) aftermath of the passage of the Twenty-Sixth Amendment in 1971—an event indicating, if nothing else, that the Constitution has not completely withstood the test of time with respect to its original assumptions and requirements about age.

The Twenty-Sixth Amendment as Precedent

Section 1. The right of citizens of the United States, who are eighteen years of age or older, to vote shall not be denied or abridged by the United States or by any State on account of age.

Section 2. The Congress shall have power to enforce this article by appropriate legislation.

The history of the passage of the Twenty-Sixth Amendment is already contested.[90] Several analysts espouse the view, put forth most forcefully by political theorist Judith Shklar, that the Twenty-Sixth Amendment was nothing but a "frivolous exercise" that merely extended the

franchise to callow and ungrateful eighteen- to twenty-year-olds.[91]
Polls at the time showed neither demand for the measure among its
eventual beneficiaries, nor much if any support in the general population. Some commentators tend to attribute its passage to a purely technical conflict between the states and the federal government, and
thereby downplay its significance as a noteworthy episode in the
expansion of American democracy.[92] Some tend to belittle it as a mis-
guided response to the heightened passions emanating from the national conflict over the Vietnam War.[93] Still others point to the steady
decline after 1972 in voting among eighteen- to twenty-four-year-olds
as evidence that suffrage was a necessary but not sufficient condition
for sustaining young voter engagement.[94]

Many factors did indeed contribute to the passage of the amendment. But a broader retrospective would surely yield the view that the
entire issue was framed by wartime concerns. Most immediately, as
many have pointed out, the amendment was passed and ratified in the
midst of the Vietnam War and at the height of the antiwar protest
movement. The slogan "Old Enough to Fight, Old Enough to Vote"
was in wide circulation at the time, even if that sentiment didn't translate into significant polling numbers in support of the amendment.
Testimony to the Judiciary Committee at the time shows that senators
were alarmed by the demonstrations and violence on college campuses
and felt that lowering the voting age might "mainstream" and ultimately diffuse such dissent.[95] Some historians believe that President
Nixon's endorsement of the measure was a similarly crafted, calculated, co-opting response to the protest movement—but not a principled or heartfelt commitment to young voters as such.[96]

Yet the wartime origins of the amendment go back further, with
crucial touchstones in World War II and the Korean War, and suggest
deeper reasons for the slow but almost inexorable movement toward
the amendment. In 1942, Congress amended the Selective Service Act
to include eighteen-, nineteen-, and twenty-year-olds in the draft.[97]
From 1942 to 1943, thirty-one state legislatures introduced bills to reduce the voting age to eighteen. Georgia successfully lowered the voting age in 1943. In Congress, two senators and six representatives also
introduced resolutions proposing a constitutional amendment to do
the same. One of those representatives, Jennings Randolph of West
Virginia, would reintroduce a resolution to lower the voting age to
eighteen in *every* Congress through the ninety-second in 1971. Every
year, for thirty years without fail, Randolph felt it important to intro-
duce such a resolution, whether he was a member of the House or the

Senate. As he remarked at the time, "I am very firmly convinced, and I would not have sponsored this resolution were I not of the considered opinion, that young men and young women of 18 years of age today are in most instances more capable of deciding clearly and accurately the issues presented by candidates, or the theories advanced by the political parties, than the youth of the country, shall we say, 25, 50, or 100 years ago, at the age of 21."[98]

It is telling that Randolph began his quixotic but unrelenting quest during World War II, when many eighteen- to twenty-year-olds were off defending the nation with their lives. The idea of extending the vote next gained real momentum after the negotiation of the peace accords for the Korean War. At that time, President Eisenhower—who, as a former general, knew a thing or two about war—supported Randolph's proposal to extend the vote to those "old enough to fight and die for the United States."[99] "For years, our citizens between the ages of 18 and 21 have, in time of peril, been summoned to fight for America," Eisenhower said. "They should participate in the political process that produces this fateful summons."[100] Lyndon B. Johnson, no doubt feeling the heat of the antiwar movement, endorsed the idea before Nixon finally threw his measured support that way, too. Evidently Randolph had hit a nerve (and kept hitting it) that ran up and down the spine of U.S. representative government: How could older elected representatives continue to justify sending younger adult citizens off to fight and die in behalf of a country that would not allow those same persons to vote? In a morally acceptable democracy, shouldn't those persons who put their lives at risk for the sake of the nation be granted full standing as enfranchised stakeholders? Randolph had exposed a dirty secret about American democracy. He refused to stop pressing the case for eighteen-to-twenty-year-old suffrage until justice was done.

The moral passion and democratic principles informing Randolph's persistence have not been well chronicled—a full biography of Randolph has yet to be written[101]—but much of the rest of the story of the passage of the Twenty-Sixth Amendment is well known. Before Congress turned to a constitutional amendment to lower the voting age to eighteen, it first attempted to achieve that result through legislation. In 1970 Congress added to its Voting Rights Act of 1970 a rider that would enfranchise eighteen- to twenty-year-olds. At the time, Congress had viewed this extension of suffrage as properly belonging to its most important bill on civil rights, namely the five-year extension of the 1965 Voting Rights Act. The rider attached to the Voting Rights

Act of 1970 would lower the age for suffrage to eighteen beginning on January 1, 1971, for state and local as well as federal elections. Nixon expressed reservations about the proposal at the time, but did not veto it. He signed it reportedly with the hope that it would receive quick judicial review. Indeed, it received a prompt court challenge in *Oregon v. Mitchell*, and a quick decision as well. On December 21, 1970—that is, just a few weeks before the statute was to take effect—the U.S. Supreme Court ruled that because the Constitution gave the states the power to decide most voting qualifications, Congress had exceeded its authority in setting the voting age for state elections. The court declared unconstitutional that part of the statute while upholding the lowering of the voting age for federal elections. Most states at the time had a voting age of twenty-one, which meant that the court's decision would require separate ballots for federal and state races in the same election. Voting officials became very concerned that the presidential election of 1972 would become costly and chaotic, requiring in each state two sets of registration books; two sets of ballots, state and federal; and perhaps even separate voting machines. Congress then passed the Twenty-Sixth Amendment in good part to avoid this logistical mess. On March 23, 1971, Congress sent the proposed amendment to the states. The requisite thirty-eight states approved the amendment, in record time, by June 30, 1971. By now Nixon had jumped on the national bandwagon: although the Constitution makes no provision for the president to take part in the amendment process, Nixon held a purely ceremonial but very public "signing" of the Twenty-Sixth Amendment on July 5, 1971, even inviting three eighteen-year-olds to add their signatures below his to some official-looking document that was supposed to be the certified version of the Twenty-Sixth Amendment.[102] The amendment enabled 11 million new voters to participate in the elections of 1972, and turn out they did: 52 percent of the eighteen-to-twenty-four-year-old bloc of voters voted in that election, the highest rate ever.

Testimonies from the time seem to suggest that key supporters weren't just trolling for votes or outflanking pesky protesters, and they seemed aware of what it meant to be speaking on behalf of those unaccustomed to having a formal outlet for their views. In the Judiciary Committee hearings on the proposed amendment, Senator James B. Pearson (R-Kans.) said for the record,

> While some of our campuses may be torn by dissent, the fact remains that the great, indeed, the overwhelming majority of our

youths are responsible, hard-working, dedicated citizens with faith in our democratic process. They want to vote. They want to participate. They want to make our country a better place to live. Many of them join demonstrations simply because they feel it is the only way they can be heard. This is not to excuse the violence and complete disrespect for authority that some demonstrators employ. But the fact remains that many of the participants are involved because of their inability to find meaningful political outlets elsewhere to express their concern. For them, certainly, the right to vote is an opportunity for rewarding involvement in public affairs.[103]

Senator Birch Bayh (D-Ind.) added this endorsement:

No longer are young Americans content to sit idly by and watch the passing scene from the grandstand. They want to be down on the field. They have made it abundantly clear that they intend to participate in the game. No longer should older Americans be content to leave this vigorous and exciting force on the sidelines. This force, this energy, is going to continue to build and grow. The only question is whether we should ignore it, perhaps leaving this energy to dam up and burst and follow less-than-wholesome channels, or whether we should let this force be utilized by society through the pressure valve of the franchise.[104]

Jennings Randolph during the debate disputed the notion that young adults had nothing to contribute to the political process: "Young people are aware of the world around them and are familiar with the issues before government officials. In many cases they have a clearer view because it has not become clouded through time and involvement. They can be likened to outside consultants called in to take a fresh look at our problems."[105] Yet, to repeat, some political pundits, focusing on the short-term complications caused by the mixed decision in *Oregon v. Mitchell*, still characterize the passage of the Twenty-Sixth Amendment mainly as a quick-fix administrative measure. Others seem to want to dwell on the irony of having an extension of suffrage catalyzed not by a popular groundswell, but by a few forward-looking individuals and a handful of legislative elites. Such histories tend to eclipse the idea that the Twenty-Sixth Amendment should be viewed as a natural extension of a longer-running theme in the American project of extending enfranchisement belatedly to groups once constitutionally excluded. An exception is Louis Seagull, who (writing in 1977) viewed age as the last constitutionally inscribed barrier to full inclusion:

> It took a century and a half . . . before three kinds of barriers had been breached—those of property, race, and sex. Only the barrier of age remained. There was always an artificial quality to this barrier. The age of twenty-one as the threshold for civil majority owed its origin to medieval times. Obviously, the establishment of political majority at age eighteen does not remove the barrier of age; it merely lowers it. What is of immediate interest regarding this most recent change in the composition of the electorate is the rationale for it.[106]

Indeed, it has taken a good while for this last constitutionally inscribed barrier (putting aside the "natural-born" requirement for now) to be recognized as such. The passage of the Twenty-Sixth Amendment was symptomatic of a long-deferred need to address age issues with respect to American republicanism, but it must be said now in hindsight that the Twenty-Sixth Amendment was a flawed, incomplete, halfway measure in that regard. It was a missed opportunity. The proponents should have tackled the age issue tout court, addressing *both* the age of eligibility for office and the age of suffrage rather than focusing exclusively on the latter. Such myopia indicates a fundamental misunderstanding about the nature of the U.S. political system, a failure of civic understanding of the first order, even by senators and other uppermost officeholders. Ours is not an at-large democracy but a democratic representative republic. To be sure, suffrage matters, but only within and refracted through the terms of representation. The proponents of the Twenty-Sixth Amendment wanted greater political inclusion for young adults, rectifying an exclusion that became especially troublesome in times of war, when younger citizens were fighting and dying in behalf of their democracy but couldn't even vote although they had reached the age of adulthood (at least as far as the military was concerned). Political elites lowered the age of voting but didn't address the situation in which such newly enfranchised younger voters could vote only for older representatives. The wartime problem had not, however, been completely rectified: older representatives still held a virtual monopoly on the power to declare war (and thus to send younger citizens off to fight and die). We've seen lingering discontent as a result of the mixed legacy of the Twenty-Sixth Amendment: For

instance, during the protest leading up to the Iraq War, youthful demonstrators held placards that read, "No War without Representation."
At the outset of the 2004 presidential campaign, Urban Outfitters sold
a T-shirt that read, "Voting is for Old People" (later taken off the
market). It has taken another thirty years, and another war, to realize
that the Twenty-Sixth Amendment did not accomplish fully what its
designers originally intended it to.

Nonetheless, we can draw at least one instructive lesson from the
thirty-year period, 1942 to 1972, leading up to the passage of the
Twenty-Sixth Amendment. That lesson would be: Democratic change
does not always begin and proceed democratically. The means sometimes or in some ways belie the end, producing an unexpected trajectory toward change. The history of democratic inclusion in America
more generally shows that change in the name and spirit of democracy
often begins with a few agitated souls rather than a spontaneous
groundswell or outburst of popular support.[107] In the case of the
Twenty-Sixth Amendment, polls showed that neither youth nor the
general voting public pressed for its passage. It took a few movers and
shakers to get the ball rolling; and once the "elite-driven" legislation
got passed, everything else seemed to fall in place very quickly. *Pace*
some commentators' opinions, however, it ought instead to be under-
scored that the Twenty-Sixth Amendment was not merely triggered
by a technical conflict between the states and the federal government.
At the heart of that change, from its outset, was a normative vision, a
conviction about democratic principles and practices, about the way
America should treat its citizens. By the time the Twenty-Sixth
Amendment was ratified in record time, those norms, once occluded
and buried but then finally broached and exposed, had been rendered
almost indisputable.

Conclusion

Alexander Keyssar, in his extended study of the history of restrictions
to and extensions of suffrage in the United States,[108] suggests an in-
sightful way to frame, or to put into summary perspective, the somewhat parallel history of constitutional barriers to eligibility for office.
Namely, the pressures on suffrage have always involved *war*, claims
Keyssar: "Nearly all of the major expansions of the franchise that have
occurred in American history took place either during or in the wake
of wars."[109] Wartime demands created pressures to extend the right to

vote, often for the sake of military preparedness and national security, but at much the same time, those demands prompted and exposed related concerns about civic fairness and democratic inclusion. Most of the extensions of the franchise—eliminating or mitigating originally codified exclusions based on race and ethnicity, class, and gender—can be correlated to major U.S. war efforts. The Revolutionary War led to removing restrictions to the suffrage based on property; the Civil War, on race; World War I, on gender; World War II, on the civil rights of Native Americans and African Americans; and Vietnam, on age. Military considerations about the proper role of young adults giving service to their country, now under the active strain of war, were no longer to be simply and strictly cordoned off but, instead, gave rise to *political* concerns about the fundamental nature of democratic rights and republican justice. One would think, therefore, that extensions of eligibility to hold office, as one of the twin pillars of modern democratic enfranchisement in addition to suffrage, would also need to be correlated to wartime contexts and concerns.

As I have shown, the *documented* history of constitutional age restrictions does not reveal a clear-cut and well-founded rationale for their inclusion from 1787 on. The evidence, upon interpretation and analysis, suggests that these age qualifications were, in a negative sense, part and parcel of a wider founding animus against unchecked democratic majoritarianism; and in a more positive sense, they were the only remaining mechanism for promoting into office a ("naturally") aristocratic aspect in bicameralism as it developed in the United States. In the documents attempting to justify them after the fact, we see rather forced language brought into play, which crudely distinguished between the categoric callowness of "youth" and the sagacity and experience of "elders." That sharp, wholesale, and invidious distinction probably reflected and grew out of a combination of ambient cultural influences in the early American period, a cobbled-together concoction of various religious, philosophical, and political attitudes and practices in circulation at the time: one part Talmudic observance distinguishing between militarized youth and officeholding elders; one part Puritan-Presbyterian notion of eldership governance; one part classical-Aristotelian conception that women, slaves, and youth are nonpolitical animals; one part Roman-republican senatorial emulation, transmitted especially through latter-day European political sources; one part Anglo-American familial-paternalism.[110] Prominent patriarchal practices and attitudes of the day, informing both public and private spheres, surely contributed to and reinforced the legally inscribed view that old men ought to be officially and exclusively in charge.[111]

The Twenty-Sixth Amendment in particular challenged the assumed and long-standing, if sometimes only tacitly coded, association between militarized youth and office-eligible adulthood. Biblical sources had made this distinction clear—or at least it was a particular and widespread interpretation of those scriptural passages that supposedly rendered military service and governance as mutually exclusive and as age-specific. During the debate over the Twenty-Sixth Amendment, opponents came forth to rebut the slogan "Old Enough to Fight, Old Enough to Vote," and in the process reprised the strong wall of age-based separation between militarism and governance. House Judiciary Committee chair Emanuel Celler (D-N.Y.), who tied up the legislation for years, argued in response to the sloganeers, "To my mind, the draft age and the voting age are as different as chalk is from cheese. The thing called for in a soldier is uncritical obedience, and that is not what you want in a voter. To say that he who is old enough to fight is old enough to vote is to draw an utterly fallacious parallel. No such parallel exists." Celler went on, essentially, to smear an entire age cohort, and his inflated language clearly tended toward the hyperbolic and the hysterical. His sweeping stereotypes also became, in the same passage, mutually contradictory: the youth allegedly obey uncritically, and the youth are recklessly rebellious:

> The ability to choose, to separate promise from performance, to evaluate on the basis of fact, are the prerequisites to good voting. Eighteen to twenty-one are mainly formative years where the youth is racing foward to maturity. His attitudes shift from place to place. These are the years of the greatest uncertainties, a fertile ground for the demagogues. Youth attaches itself to promises, rather than to performance. These are rightfully the years of rebellion rather than reflection. We will be doing a grave injustice to democracy if we grant the vote to those under twenty-one.

Celler's conspicuously self-contradictory views did not ultimately prevail, since the Twenty-Sixth Amendment was indeed passed and ratified.[112] I want to add that the Twenty-Sixth Amendment (along with the elimination of the draft) obliterated the almost sacred assumption that young adults serve a nation primarily through military service but not through active participation in formal politics. On this antiquated view, they supposedly become full citizens not until and only after they pass unto an alleged age of proper eldership. With respect to voting, we no longer honor or abide by that dichotomous logic. With respect to eligibility for office, we may need another war-time exposé, if Keyssar's overall thesis still holds, in order to examine and to rectify many still deeply held prejudices about political governance.

Theory

You say you'll change the constitution
Well, you know
We all want to change your head
You tell me it's the institution
Well, you know
You better free your mind instead

—Beatles, *Revolution*

At first glance, the scholarly field of political theory does not give us much guidance in thinking about the particular issue of age qualifications for democratic officeholding. All that bookish erudition and all those words about the rudiments and the romance of politics seem to be of little use in this case—mainly because few have directly raised the issue. The various branches of and approaches to the field—classical, medieval, modern, or contemporary; liberal, radical, feminist, queer, postcolonial, or global; historical, analytic, or postmodern—simply do not engage the specific problem as such.[1] One could speculate on various broad reasons for this collective oversight. As Robert Dahl points out, before the twentieth century, the very idea that all adult permanent residents of a country should enjoy the full rights of citizens was unacceptable to almost all advocates of democracy.[2] The extension of participation, overcoming long-standing restrictions on enfranchisement, is a latter-day phenomenon, and democratic theory has lagged, like the owl of Minerva, behind democratic practice.[3] Aristotle's long-standing animus against young persons' involvement in politics may still inform wide-ranging and almost intractable, if almost undetectable, cultural prejudices. In America, no one before the 1960s, as several commentators have noted, was much interested in the topic of young people in politics in any regard.[4]

Yet several prominent contemporary theorists have given us strong arguments in support of the idea that all adult citizens of a democratic representative republic ought to enjoy, and enjoy equally, the basic rights of citizenship—which entails the elimination of age restrictions for holding office for all adult citizens. John Rawls contends that the right to run for office is a basic liberty, a bedrock on which a theory and practice of justice is to be erected.[5] Robert Dahl lists the right to run for elective office as one of the key aspects of inclusive citizenship, which he hails as an essential "political institution" of modern representative democratic government.[6] Judith Shklar cites the right to participate in politics as a necessary condition not just for personal freedom but as a matter of political standing and equal respect. Hanna Pitkin, in her landmark study *The Concept of Representation*, navigates deftly through the various senses of the term *representation* along with their practical implications, from which one could logically infer that American representation ought to be more age-inclusive. These theorists help us tremendously to think carefully about basic democratic rights, notions of political equality, intergenerational justice, and representative government—all topics which touch upon the particular issue of age restrictions for holding office. But none of these thinkers takes the extra step to say explicitly that eliminating such requirements would be a natural extension of their arguments. We may need to take that extra step for them, aided, however, by their efforts and the benefit of hindsight.

Classical Ageism and Machiavelli's Rebuttal

A survey of the Western canon can help us gain a sense of the inertia that runs *against* the prospect of full republican rights for all adult citizens (and specifically young adult citizens). Put generally, Plato, Aristotle, and Cicero similarly appeal to (what they purport to be) an intuitively normative hierarchy, allegedly inscribed in nature and confirmed in practice, which supposedly enshrines eldership as the basis for superior political rule. Given their prominence at the outset of the Western tradition—a tradition that can be tracked as directly influencing early American constitutional designs in favor of seniority—it behooves us to look critically at their stipulations and arguments to that end.[7] Much of what they wrote on the matter of political seniority presumably still provides a justificatory background for many such patriarchal *cum* generational beliefs and practices today.

Plato

Plato famously begins *The Republic* by framing the pursuit of justice from the explicit perspective of age. Socrates asks an old man named Cephalus about his views on justice, which he wants to know precisely because Cephalus is old. Cephalus responds that when he gets together with his old friends, many of them complain about old age because they miss many of the pleasures they enjoyed in their youth. But he, Cephalus, doesn't see old age as the cause of their miseries. He himself feels liberated from the raging tyranny of youthful desires; and so he declares to Socrates that if one has an orderly character, neither youth nor old age will be a burden. Character is what counts, he proposes (rather self-servingly). Socrates humors Cephalus but asks pointedly whether his graceful consolations may be due to his inherited wealth rather than his orderly character. Eventually Socrates twists Cephalus's views around until Cephalus contradicts himself on his definition of justice, and so Cephalus's son Polemarchus must step in and "inherit" the argument from his father. To the reader who attempts to read between the lines of Socratic-Platonic irony,[8] neither generation of these wealthy businessmen provides a satisfactory answer to the question of what justice is—and thus this opening to the *Republic* raises the question of age with respect to just governance but coyly leaves it unanswered. Still, we can discern and appreciate Cephalus's larger point, one that Plato probably wants us to ponder, namely that the propensity for pursuing justice ought to be attributed to character rather than to age, even if Cephalus himself isn't a perfect spokesperson for that elusively exalted principle.

An ironic deconstruction and clever exposé of the political biases of wealth doesn't, however, prove by default that the propensity for pursuing justice transcends all age considerations. Later in the *Republic* Plato seems to return to this opening theme and to fill in some of the gaps, since he makes some very definite, very cut-and-dried recommendations about the proper age for holding political office—and some of these recommendations are then echoed and elaborated or else modified in the *Laws*. Still, we probably ought to bear in mind that these apparently down-to-earth specifics may be an extended way of ironically begging certain points.

In book 3, Socrates and Glaucon take up the question of which of the guardians should rule over the city, and Socrates states that it is obvious that the rulers must be the elder and the ruled must be the younger (412c). But later (536d) he explicitly retreats from this point, saying that in educating for wise guardianship, old men must not be favored over younger men. The dialectic must be presented to them while they are still relatively young. Yet young persons may treat dialectics too playfully and "lawlessly" (539b). So, let the guardian class-in-training play around with dialectics from the ages of thirty to thirty-five (539e), and then they are to be marched back down into the cave and compelled "to rule in the military and in offices fit for the young" (540a). After fifteen years of such lowbrow governance, they will be allowed at age fifty, if they have survived all tests, to bask in the higher realms of philosophy, and thereafter to take turns holding office in service of the state (540b). Hence in the *Republic*, thirty-five and fifty are stipulated as the minimum ages for different forms of officeholding, lower and higher, though it again bears repeating that the *Republic* in general, and these passages in particular, seem to lend themselves to highly skeptical, comedic, or ironic renderings and readings.

The *Republic*'s minimum age requirements for office do not quite square with those enumerated in the *Laws*, and the particulars, especially in the latter, are flatly asserted rather than argued. The minimum age for official appointments for men, states Socrates, shall be 30; for women, 40 (785b). Military service for a man shall be from ages 20 to 60; for women, post-childbirth to 50. The ultimate curators of the law must be at least 50 years old (755a). Certain watchdog positions are to be occupied by younger men 25 or over, but under 30 (760c).

At several junctures in the *Laws*, Socrates reiterates the apparent naturalness of eldership rule, usually drawing it from analogy: the well-born have a title to rule over the baseborn, just as elder men ought to rule over the younger, or slave owners over slaves, or the stronger over the weaker, or the wise over the ignorant (690a–c); parents claim authority over their offspring, just as older men over younger, just as the wellborn over the baseborn (714e); good men are the superiors of worse, just as the aged are of the youthful, just as parents are of their offspring, just as husbands are of their wives and children (917a). While these passages seem to suggest that Plato subscribes to a strict naturalism that invidiously separates a ruling class from a subservient class, inasmuch as the wellborn, the slave owners, and fathers hold natural authority over the baseborn, the enslaved, and the wives and children, a naturalist division can neither abide nor fully account for the operational distinction between the aged and the young, since the latter will eventually evolve into, and replace, the former. Hence in one place in the *Laws* (762e), Plato explains that a key to successful ruling is having first experienced submission to the laws and to one's elders: "It must be strictly binding on all to believe that no man whatsoever will prove a creditable master until he has first been a servant, and that less pride should be taken in successful ruling than in loyal service—service, in the first place, of the laws—since to serve them is to serve heaven—and after the laws, of a young man's honorably distinguished seniors."

Aristotle

Perhaps Plato meant for his age proposals to be taken with a grain of interpretive salt, or perhaps for the whole feast to be chewed over rather than fully consumed. If Plato in fact influenced Aristotle on his notions of eldership rule in particular, we don't see much evidence in Aristotle's subsequent reception that Plato's ostensible naturalism was to be taken other than at face value. If anything, Aristotle extends and deepens those stark distinctions between rulers and those to be ruled. It is thus that Aristotle becomes the original source, the *locus classicus*, for much subsequent age discrimination against younger adult citizens. Aristotle most clearly and most adamantly provides the classical case against youthful participation in politics: "A young man is not equipped to be a student of politics; for he has no experience in the actions which life demands of him, and these actions form the basis and subject matter of the discussion."[9] Young persons, Aristotle rails, are deficient in living and are too easily swayed by emotions (*pathos*) and are thus incapable of regulating their actions by a rational principle. Note that Aristotle's complaint against youth is two-pronged: the youth are immature and inexperienced. Their immaturity is a result of their inability to curb their emotive, bodily, pleasure-seeking tendencies by way of self-controlling reason. Aristotle returns to this sweeping critique against the young throughout the *Nicomachean Ethics*, issuing wholesale slurs on several fronts: the young cannot control their appetites for sexual gratification (79); their excitable natures make them pursue wanton pleasures like drunkenness (211); their friendships are craven and superficial (219); shame is the only form of restraint that can temper their emotional selves (109); they eschew virtue because it isn't fun (296). Aristotle doesn't think young persons can even *study* politics, let alone do it, because they simply don't care about knowledge and understanding: "Knowledge brings no benefit to this kind of person" (6). To be fair, he qualifies that his critique of youthful indiscretion isn't confined to the biologically young only: "Whether he is young in years or immature in character makes no difference; for his deficiency is not a matter of time but of living and of pursuing all his interests under the influence of his emotions" (6). Note, however, that Aristotle's qualification doesn't work the other way: whereas some older persons may well be immature despite their age, he doesn't observe that some younger persons may escape the alleged follies of youth prematurely.

This blanket disqualification seems to suggest that all youth are averse to all knowledgeable pursuits. But elsewhere in the *Nicomachean Ethics*, Aristotle complicates that portrait of youth (160). Someone who engages in politics, he argues, must be capable of exercising practical wisdom—a kind of mental comportment that understands the "particulars" of a situation, the various complexities, contingencies, and circumstances involved. In contrast, young men are indeed capable of becoming good geometricians and mathematicians, he allows, attaining what he calls "theoretical wisdom," a kind of abstract knowledge that is oriented toward universals rather than particulars. But knowledge of particulars derives from experience, and experience is the product of some extended interval of time—hence the young, because of their youth, have insufficient experience, and therefore are incapable of grasping and exercising practical wisdom, and therefore are unfit for politics. A boy, Aristotle observes, can become a mathematician but not a philosopher. Young men can assert scientific principles, but can have no genuine convictions about them. You might consult a young math whiz prodigy about how to differentiate a polynomial equation, but you would not ask that person to make judgments about character, or to deliberate about affairs of state.

Aristotle thus entertains two distinct complaints about youth with regard to politics. On the one hand, their basic bodily immaturity is politically debilitating, because they are simply not mature enough to be rational actors. On the other hand, a few exceptional young persons might display precocious rational abilities, but those mental operations are not yet, and cannot yet be, tempered by experience. These are separate complaints, that the young lack self-control and that the young lack experience, but a biologically informed naturalism animates both: the young have yet to grow and to develop sufficiently.

Aristotle almost always mentions the young in his naturalist hierarchy of those who rule versus those who must be ruled. In the *Politics*, he makes a common complaint about the rational deficiencies of slaves, women, and children—all three groups are unqualified for ruling, he contends. But he also claims that each of these groups has a different kind of rational deficiency; thus they are politically unfit for separate reasons; "For rule of free over slave, male over female, man over boy, are all natural, but they are also different, because, while parts of the soul are present in each case, the distribution is different. Thus the deliberative faculty in the soul is not present at all in a slave; in a female it is inoperative, in a child undeveloped."[10] Because women are unthinking, it is best that they be silent and take orders, repeats Aristotle. Slaves ought to perform menial tasks—though some slaves are slavish by circumstance rather than by nature. Such semirational slaves, thinks Aristotle, are to be treated more like one would treat children, that is, by suggestion and advice rather than by fiat (as one would treat a woman and a true slave). As for children, Aristotle says, "Take the child: he is not yet fully developed and his function is to grow up, so we cannot speak of his virtue as belonging absolutely to him, but only in relation to the progress of his development and to whoever is in charge of him."[11] Thus one must adopt an evolutionary, developmental view of a growing (male) youth.

To most contemporary ears, Aristotle's analysis of the inherent rational deficiencies in women and slaves sounds more than merely suspect; his derogatory remarks are now widely regarded as pernicious and offensive. With a bit of background research, one quickly discovers that Aristotle's infamous claims about the rational shortcomings of women and slaves provided some of the American framers with a classical justification for the country's most regrettable constitutional exclusions, to wit, against women, Native Americans, and African American slaves.[12] While today such charges about women and slaves are read with general embarrassment, political theorists, constitutional scholars, and American historians have not yet taken Aristotle to task for his similar broadside against the young (and certainly not the "young" who fall into the eighteen-to-thirty-four-year-old bracket). Something about the general callowness of youth still resonates or else escapes detection. It may be that most commentators don't recognize Aristotle's animus against politicized youth as a categoric prejudice, a form of unwarranted and invidious discrimination, because they tacitly accept Aristotle's developmental account as valid. After all, the immediately affected parties—young persons—will grow out of their condition, unlike exclusions based on race or gender. Aristotle even seems to anticipate an eventual apathy regarding age requirements for office and offers an explanation for it:

> Again it cannot be disputed that rulers have to be superior to those who are ruled. It therefore becomes the duty of the lawgiver to consider how this distinction is to be made and how they shall share in government. We noted earlier that nature herself has provided one distinction: that class which in respect of birth is all the same she has divided into older and younger, the former being more fit for ruling, the latter for being ruled. No one really objects to this method of command by seniority or thinks himself too good for it; after all he knows that once he reaches the required age, he will get what he has earned by waiting.[13]

Over the course of a normal life span, young persons who would otherwise be eligible for office will eventually get their chance—so an age disqualification isn't unfair. Aristotle thus successfully "naturalizes" such discrimination, folding it into an evolutionary, developmental account of the expected life course of a supposedly typical human specimen. His inductive, generalizing approach concerning women and slaves we now view, in retrospect, as gross stereotyping—but we haven't quite extended the same skepticism to his broad-brush claims about the impetuousness and shortsightedness of all youth. Moreover, even though he presents a developmental account of political maturation, a coming-of-age narrative separating the *oikos* from the *polis*, he doesn't invoke a clear line of demarcation between childhood and young adulthood—thus anyone who could be plausibly labeled as "youthful" is liable to be drawn into his critique. In Aristotelian terms, a tag of "youthfulness" in politics is far more likely to be insulting than complimentary, and one of his enduring legacies may be that the slur can be applied very broadly, that is, even to adults who are well into the age of responsibility. Recall Ronald Reagan's famous putdown of Walter Mondale in their second presidential debate in 1984, a dig that humorously but effectively deflected attention from Reagan's advanced years: "I will not make age an issue of this campaign. I am not going to exploit, for political purposes, my opponent's youth and inexperience."

Cicero

Marcus Tullius Cicero, in various works and writing under various assumed identities in his dialogues, consistently expresses an obvious preference for a senate—an advisory body of wise old men—as a crucial component of an exemplary commonwealth.[14] He also strongly endorses the Roman practice of minimum age requirements for particular public offices[15]—a preference commingling Aristotelian, Platonic, and Roman influences that eventually was to inform strongly the development of the U.S. Senate. But his most elaborate paean to eldership is to be found in his essay "On Old Age." Writing in the voice of "Cato the Elder," Cicero rebuts common prejudice against old people: old age is bearable and not necessarily miserable, despite diminished capabilities, pleasures, and memories. Yet Cicero doesn't stop there. He makes a case that old age is *preferable* to one's younger years in several respects. One's virtues have, with time, become more practiced; one's intellect can now apply itself more powerfully. In matters of governance in particular, old age is a definite advantage over youthfulness:

> Granted that an old man does not do what young men do: still, the things he does are vastly more significant and more worthwhile. . . . Naturally he wouldn't be running and jumping over the fields, or practicing the javelin-throw or the sword-duel; no, he'd be sitting in council, debating, speaking in support of his opinions. If these activities were not within the purview of the old, our ancestors would not have called our highest deliberative assembly "The Elders." . . . You will discover that it is young men who have sent the most powerful governments crashing to ruin, and the old who have either kept them strong or restored their strength.[16]

Cicero then quotes a question from a play: "Your State was a great one: tell me, how / did you lose it in so short a time?" And the answer, he says, is this: "New politicians stepped to the fore, / the lot of them foolish and brash young men."[17]

Machiavelli

Niccolò Machiavelli directly challenged Cicero's preference for senatorial governance along with Cicero's general views about youthful versus elderly rule. That particular "Machiavellian moment," namely Machiavelli's views on the proper age for eligibility for republican office, has not been well remembered in American historiography, even as a road not taken.[18] Cesare Borgia, the object of Machiavelli's fascination, became the duke of Valentinois at age 23, subdued the cities of Romagna before he turned 25, and became something of the model of a Renaissance prince before dying at the age of 31—yet his youthful contributions to ruling were hardly virtuous. Perhaps because he pays so much attention to Borgia, Machiavelli in *The Prince* is nuanced in his judgment about young political actors, contending infamously that "Fortuna is well disposed toward young men"—but we ought quickly to note that Machiavelli's reasons for this assessment provide a backhanded compliment for younger politicos: "they" (young men) are "less circumspect, more violent, and more bold to command" Fortuna.[19]

Yet in his *Discourses on Livy*—sometimes described as the founding document of modern republicanism—Machiavelli is very clear that every republic ought to follow the example of the ancient Roman consulship, election to which was open to all citizens, regardless of age. In fact, Machiavelli devotes an entire chapter to the topic: Chapter 60, "How the Consulship and Every Other Magistracy in Rome Were Bestowed Without Respect to Age." The Roman Republic, he says, always sought to attract *virtú* into its governing offices, accommodating merit regardless of age (or birth). He cites the testimony of Valerius Corvinus, who was made consul of Rome at age twenty-three and claimed that "the consulate was the reward of ability, and not of birth." Cities that desire glorious and virtuous governance, Machiavelli insists, should *not* include minimum age (or birth-based) requirements for office:

> Given that this is the case [that offices shouldn't be granted on the basis of family ties or class background], the distinction based on time has nothing to be said for it, and on the contrary must be disregarded, and when the multitude elects a young man to a position which needs the prudence of an older man, some illustrious action on his part should be the cause for elevating him to that rank. When a young man has such exceptional ability that he makes himself known through some illustrious deed, it would be a most damaging thing if the city were not able to avail itself of his talent, and if it had to wait until age has affected that strength of mind and readiness of his early years of which at that age his native city could have availed itself, as Rome availed itself of Valerius Corvinus, of Scipio, of Pompey, and of many others who triumphed while still very young.[20]

Machiavelli's decided rejection of minimum age requirements has not been well heeded, even by subsequent republicans. In fact, it would eventually be explicitly repudiated, an outright rejection that would directly influence early American constitutionalists.

Anglo-American Legacies for the Politics of Age

Harrington

James Harrington, the author of *Oceana*, is one of the few canonized political theorists who recommend set ages for holding political office. Concerned about attracting a "natural aristocracy" into a modern senate, Harrington basically writes a foundational (if fanciful) book about, among other things, the primacy of eldership governance. In the imaginary Commonwealth of Oceana, the "youth" (those 18 to 30 years old) belong to the military, whereas the "elders" (those 30 and older) occupy the "standing garrisons of this nation."[21] Harrington does consider the case of ancient Rome, which, he reports, distributed "her magistracies without respect to age," and he notes, "Machiavel . . . commends this course."[22] Yet he explicitly rejects Machiavelli's advice on this score: "The opinion of Verulamius is safe: 'The errors,' says he, 'of young men are the ruin of business; whereas the errors of old men amount but to this, that more might have been done, or sooner.'"

As I pointed out in chapter 1, John Adams chose Harrington's, rather than Machiavelli's, view of the propriety of minimum age requirements in Roman republicanism as a way of attracting a naturally meritocratic class into office; and Adams's influence on this particular matter, drawing explicitly from Harrington and reflecting a Ciceronian preference for the Roman senate over the Roman consulship, reverberated throughout the American colonies in the early writing about bicameral state constitutions. But the Cicero-Harrington-Adams trajectory cannot serve as the last word on the intellectual history of the matter of U.S. age restrictions; we need to draw upon other theorists for cumulative insight into the cultural politics animating (or undermining) such constitutional designs.

Locke

John Locke in *Two Treatises on Government* spends a great deal of time distinguishing paternal from political authority, as a rebuttal to Sir

Robert Filmer's presumption that children are naturally subject to a father's patriarchal authority for the duration of their lives. Locke rather insists on the distinction between minors and those who have reached the "full Age" of being free, rational adults (he mentions in passing the age of "one and Twenty")[23]—and once one passes the appropriate age threshold, one should enjoy, according to Locke, the full consensual rights of citizenship, now entering into full freedom and equality with others. Commonwealths take notice, observes Locke, of a certain time "when Men are to begin to act like Free Men," no longer subject to the absolute dominion of the father and capable of exercising independent rights.[24] Even with his emphasis on childhood, Locke does not provide the foundational theory for an American-style system of graduated, phased-in categories of free adult citizenship beyond the age of consent, and instead would seem to provide arguments in the direction against protracted political dependency and guardianship. Yet he never speaks directly to the point. Still, one wonders how, whether, or to what extent the early American constitutionalists rejected or consciously qualified Locke's notion of a clear demarcation, a threshold, between the age of minority and the "full age" of free and equal citizenship.

Paine

Thomas Paine, rejecting Edmund Burke's cross-generational "partnership" among the living, the dead, and the yet-to-be-born,[25] pointedly argued that every generation must be free to fend for itself: "Every age and generation must be as free to act for itself, *in all cases,* as the ages and generations which preceded it. . . . Every generation is, and must be, competent to all the purposes which its occasions require. It is the living, and not the dead, that are to be accommodated."[26] In *Rights of Man,* Paine doesn't differentiate one living generation from another; he approaches the political question of generationalism as an issue of the dead versus the living, which he sees as the primary rub in the debate over hereditary versus democratic government. In *Dissertations on the First Principles of Government,* Paine asserts that the living comprise separate generations ("The father, the son, the grandson, are so many distinct generations").[27] One living generation can't be sharply defined and distinguished from the next, since the overall process of being born, aging, and dying in a nation is an ongoing flux. But Paine maintains that for political and legal purposes, a strong generational distinction can be observed between those who are minors and those "in whom legal authority resides," namely those over twenty-one. The latter group ("the aged") must observe and protect the rights of minors as a "sacred guardianship." Those minors, after all, will soon come of age. Yet for all practical purposes Paine recognizes the democratically enfranchised as an undifferentiated whole. Still, it wouldn't take too much tweaking of Paine's thinking to recalibrate his concern for the vitality of rights with greater generational specificity among the living: each generation, however defined, should be empowered politically to legislate in its own behalf.

Mill

One might expect that John Stuart Mill, accomplished at an early age, would take up the subject of youthful engagement in politics. But his remarks in his major works are scattered, fleeting, and inconsistent on the subject. In *On Liberty* he compares underage youth to the "barbarians" of a backward society, none of whom is yet fit for politics.[28] "Liberty," he says, "has no application to any state of things anterior to the time when mankind have become capable of being improved by free and equal discussion."[29] One might thereafter scan the rest of the essay looking for remarks about the potential of adult-age persons, no matter what their age, to think freely, but one would search in vain.

Mill's "Considerations on Representative Government" deserves closer inspection, however. Therein we find a classic case in behalf of representative government and Mill's explicit defense of "universal, but graduated suffrage."[30] Controlling the government is not the same as administering the government, asserts Mill, and a popular assembly is "as little fitted for the direct business of legislation as for that of administration" (277). Sovereignty is vested in the people, and all adult citizens should be guaranteed the right to vote. Yet the hard business of legislation and administration should be performed by "experienced and exercised minds." Mill thus limits the proper function of a representative body to that of making good administrative appointments. Moreover, as the means of electing representatives to the assembly, he recommends a scheme of "plural voting"—departing from the standard "one person, one vote" model—such that persons whose occupations indicate greater intelligence (banker, merchant, or manufacturer as opposed to an ordinary laborer or tradesman [336]) would each receive a vote that would count double or triple that of an ordinary person's single ballot. If we could reliably test for intelligence, Mill proposes, that would be the best way to weight the ballot.

Barring that, a voter's occupation is the next best indicator of intelligence, he believes. He explicitly excludes property, wealth, skin color, hair color, height, and gender as relevant restrictions on political rights (341); suffrage should be universal, even if graduated on the basis of occupation (as a marker of intelligence). Hence we see in Mill's case for representative government a combination of inclusive and exclusionary elements—but at least in this section of his essay, he remains silent on age as a valid or invalid restriction.

Elsewhere in the essay Mill mentions youth in passing. The business of drawing up legislation should be delegated to a small commission appointed by the Crown and whose members should serve fixed terms of five years—and the reasons for fixed terms, Mill says, is to get rid of underperforming commissioners and to infuse "new and younger blood into the body" (224). He cites the same advantages of fixed-term appointments in the military and executive branches, since they bring in "highly qualified persons of younger standing, for whom there might never be room if death vacancies, or voluntary resignations, were waited for" (347). More generally, any political body, he proposes, should feature a variety of temperaments and character types; a government should include, for instance, minds that are cautious and others that are bold. Mill throws age considerations into this mix, though he qualifies that the right balance between old and young shouldn't be achieved through regulatory mechanisms: "The natural and spontaneous admixture of the old and the young, of those whose position and reputation are made, and those who have them still to make, will in general sufficiently answer the purpose, if only this natural balance is not disturbed by artificial regulation" (166).

On the basis of these remarks one might suppose that Mill would not be in favor of age restrictions, especially if they systematically barred intelligent young adults from holding office. Yet in his reflections on Indian government, he tends to look favorably on the old Civil Service order that promoted the right persons upward on the basis of experience and competence: "The safety of the country is, that those by whom it is administered be sent out in youth, as candidates only, to begin at the bottom of the ladder, and ascend higher or not, as after a proper interval, they are proved qualified" (420). Competitive entrance examinations are helpful, but they cannot be relied on exclusively for staffing such administrative bureaucracies. For such (appointed) offices, Mill sees nothing wrong with strict eligibility requirements: "It is in no way unjust, that public officers thus selected

and trained should be exclusively eligible to offices which require spe-
cially Indian knowledge and experience. If any door to the higher appointments, without passing through the lower, be opened even for
occasional use, there will be such incessant knocking at it by persons
of influence, that it will be impossible ever to keep it closed" (420).

Mill's view of the limited legislative ambit of representative government doesn't really apply to the American model, and so it may be
inapt to look to his writings for authoritative insights or conclusions for
our particular issue. Suffice to say, however, he is no radical democrat
who would want to open up eligibility for office to all comers. He is,
after all, an explicit proponent of a graduated voting scheme. Yet he
also believes strongly in universal suffrage: his entire argument in favor
of representative government (actual, not virtual) is that if, for example, the working classes are denied suffrage, no one in government is
likely to speak for them or to question matters through their eyes or
interests (188). That basic point about groups such as workers could
easily be extended to generational representation; and in key places,
Mill does appreciate explicitly the contributions of intelligent persons
regardless of age as well as younger appointees. Perhaps more important, he is quick to invalidate exclusionary criteria that he thinks are
politically irrelevant, such as gender. But nowhere does he take the
next (logical?) step to say that once citizens cross a key threshold of
political maturity, age considerations thereafter should be deemed
largely irrelevant to the electoral process (although they may indeed
be immensely important in particular cases or for particular voters).

Whitman

A few of the American transcendentalists reveal a hint of a favorable
estimation of youthful political involvement and seem to speak very
generally to the issue. Walt Whitman would certainly be the best example of someone who writes enthusiastically for and about youthful
participation in politics. His (mostly) exuberant essay "Democratic
Vistas" casts American democracy itself in youthful terms and metaphors. The "real gist" of democracy, he writes, still sleeps in America,
"quite unawaken'd"; its history remains unwritten because it has yet
to be enacted. Democracy lies in repose as some sort of "younger
brother" to Nature, whose history also has yet to be written because it
remains at an early stage of formation.[31] Whitman presents a vision of
a capacious democratic sentiment that binds all nations, fuses all persons into an interconnected fraternity—and he almost always mentions

explicitly young persons in this ecstatic gesture: "It is the old, yet ever-modern dream of earth, out of her eldest and her youngest, her fond philosophers and poets" (381). He lists "young persons" in his unsung panorama of the American people (388), and imagines that he can "see there, in every young and old man, after his kind, and in every woman after hers, a true personality" that exemplifies the highest traits of selfhood yet which are not elitist but instead "in buoyant accordance with the municipal and general requirements of our times" (402). Yet Whitman descends from the clouds to give very pointed political advice, which he directs squarely at young men: "To practically enter into politics is an important part of American personalism" (399). He implores "every young man, north and south" not to fall into a cynicism about American politics that decries the whole enterprise "as beyond redemption, and to be carefully kept away from." He admonishes his young male reader, "See you that you do not fall into this error." Given Whitman's scathing critique of American politics in the essay up to that point, it is significant that Whitman goes out of his way to tell young persons, "As for you, I advise you to enter more strongly yet into politics. I advise every young man to do so. Always inform yourself; always do the best you can; always vote" (399). Whitman, by the way, doesn't confine his political purview to young men, either. In the section immediately following his political call to arms for young men, he proclaims his conviction that the democratic entrance of women into all arenas of "practical life, politics, the suffrage, &c." is inevitable (400–401).

Throughout his poetry and prose, Whitman returns to youthfulness as a trope for democracy's future. Yet in his essay "The Eighteenth Presidency! Voice of Walt Whitman to each Young Man in the Nation, North, South, East, and West," Whitman explicitly calls upon a "new race" of young men to replace the ossified and corrupt politicians who currently hold office at all levels in the nation. In particular he envisions a day when a young man (from a working background) need not go through the party structure, or be vetted by antidemocratic screening processes operating "under the name of respectability," in order to ascend to high public office:

> I expect to see the day when the like of the present personnel of the governments, federal, state, municipal, military, and naval, will be looked upon with derision, and when qualified mechanics and young men will reach Congress and other official stations, sent in their working costumes, fresh from their benches and

tools, and returning to them again with dignity. The young fellows must prepare to do credit to this destiny, for the stuff is in them. Nothing gives places, recollect, and never ought to give place except to its clean superiors. There is more rude and undeveloped bravery, friendship, conscientiousness, and practical genius for any scope of action, even the broadest and highest, now among the American mechanics and young men, than in all the official persons in These States, legislative, executive, judicial, military, and naval, and more than among all the literary persons.[32]

Emerson

Ralph Waldo Emerson, on the other hand, was not so kind on the question of the suitability of young citizens for politics. In his essay "Politics" he refers repeatedly to "youth" in condemnatory terms. In fact, the main part of the essay draws an invidious distinction between callow youth and wise elders. "Society is an illusion to the young citizen,"[33] Emerson begins. Young persons are taken in by all of the official names and degrees and procedures and institutions; young persons thus believe in the solidity, integrity, and durability of the political and social apparatus. The old guard, however, knows better and can see through and beyond these will-o'-the-wisps: "But the old statesman knows that society is fluid; there are no such roots and centres; but any particle may suddenly become the centre of the movement, and compel the system to gyrate round it" (335). Emerson escalates his rhetoric against young citizens' political misconceptions (note that Emerson is referring here to young citizens and not underage youth): "Republics abound in young civilians, who believe that the laws make the city, that grave modifications of the policy and modes of living, and employments of the population, that commerce, education, and religion, may be voted in or out; and that any measure, though it were absurd, may be imposed on a people, if only you can get sufficient voices to make it a law" (335). In contrast to such youthful, democratic folly, Emerson again invokes the voice of the "wise," who reportedly "know that foolish legislation is a rope of sand" (335). The character and culture of citizens come first, and the state must follow rather than lead. Yet "tender poetic youth" dream and pray and agitate for human affairs to be conducted by way of politics and law (336). Emerson casts his sweeping indictment of "society" almost entirely in terms of a parallel indictment of young citizens' views of politics: "Society always consists, in greatest part, of young and foolish persons. The old, who have seen through the hypocrisy of courts and statesmen, die, and leave no wisdom to their sons. These believe their own newspaper, as their fathers did at their age. With such an ignorant and deceivable majority, States would soon run to ruin, but that there are limitations, beyond which the folly and ambition of governors cannot go" (338). Of course, if Emerson had his way, there'd be little need for government at all ("Hence, the less government we have, the better,—the fewer laws, the less confided power" [344]), so his hyperbolic animus against *both* youth and politics probably cannot serve finally to adjudicate the issue of age barriers to office—though we could surely surmise that he'd propose the more barriers, the better.

Thoreau

Henry David Thoreau turns Emerson's young-old distinction on its head. Thoreau regards old persons as holding suspect, unexamined, and ossified views. This passage from *Walden*, which stands out as uncommon advice, is worth quoting at some length:

> It is never too late to give up our prejudices. No way of thinking or doing, however ancient, can be trusted without proof. What everybody echoes or in silence passes by as true to-day may turn out to be falsehood to-morrow, mere smoke of opinion, which some had trusted for a cloud that would sprinkle fertilizing rain on their fields. What old people say you cannot do you try and find that you can. Old deeds for old people, and new deeds for new. Old people did not know enough once, perchance, to fetch fresh fuel to keep the fire a-going; new people put a little dry wood under a pot, and are whirled round the globe with the speed of birds, in a way to kill old people, as the phrase is. Age is no better, hardly so well, qualified for an instructor as youth, for it has not profited so much as it has lost. One may almost doubt if the wisest man has learned anything of absolute value by living. Practically, the old have no very important advice to give the young, their own experience has been so partial, and their lives have been such miserable failures, for private reasons, as they must believe; and it may be that they have some faith left which belies that experience, and they are only less young than they were. I have lived some thirty years on this planet, and I have yet to hear the first syllable of valuable or even earnest

advice from my seniors. They have told me nothing, and probably cannot tell me anything to the purpose. Here is life, an exper-
iment to a great extent untried by me; but it does not avail me
that they have tried it. If I have any experience which I think
valuable, I am sure to reflect that this my Mentors have said
nothing about.[34]

Emerson might indeed have written the classic essay on self-reliance;
but in *Politics*, he in effect counsels the young to rely on the old, since
he questions their ability to rely on their own judgments, impaired as
those judgments are as a function of their youth. Thoreau, in this passage, shows himself, compared with Emerson, to be the real voice of
self-reliance for younger persons.

Contemporary Theory

Arendt

Hannah Arendt spoke to the issue of eligibility for office in one place
in the corpus of her prolific writings. In her controversial essay "Reflections on Little Rock," Arendt argues (notoriously, for some) against
government-mandated integration as well as against using underage
schoolchildren in service of a political cause. Her argument turns on
her well-known distinction between the social realm and the political
realm. All sorts of discrimination persist in the social sphere, she contends, and governmental legislation can do little about that kind of
discrimination—and ought to leave it largely alone—though discriminatory segregation enforced by law surely deserves to be abolished.
But legislators cannot force equality upon society; in fact, private or
civil discriminatory attitudes and practices will flourish and, on the
whole, contribute productively to the plurality of the human condition.
But equality is required, she insists, in the political sphere, and legislators ought to enforce equality scrupulously within the body politic.
Arendt at this point in her discussion digresses just a bit into the terms
of political equality that, while restricted to the political realm, ought
to be observed and strictly enforced therein:

> Under modern conditions, this equality has its most important
> embodiment in the right to vote, according to which the judg-
> ment and opinion of the most exalted citizen are on par with the

judgment and opinion of the hardly literate. Eligibility, the right to be voted into office, is also an inalienable right of every citizen. . . . Eligibility, therefore, is a necessary corollary of the right to vote; it means that everyone is given the opportunity to distinguish himself in those things in which all are equals to begin with. Strictly speaking, the franchise and eligibility for office are the only political rights, and they constitute in a modern democracy the very quintessence of citizenship. In contrast to all other rights, civil or human, they cannot be granted to resident aliens.[35]

Although Arendt writes in apparent disparagement of certain key aspects of the civil rights movement and, elsewhere, of the student movement of the 1960s—so one might unfairly presume or conclude that she would be averse to younger citizen mobilization—these remarks demonstrate unequivocally that she believed that eligibility to hold office was an inalienable right of citizenship, applicable to all citizens without qualification, that is, as an extension of the most fundamental terms of political equality. One could easily take that position one step further, construing it to mean that the constitutional terms of American representative democracy, specifically the age requirements for federal office, place too many restrictions on the political rights of equal citizenship and would not receive her approval. But she never commented explicitly on the matter.

Foucault

Michel Foucault, in *The Use of Pleasure*, volume 2 of *The History of Sexuality*, takes up the issue of the political status of the young man in ancient Greece—a topic that bears on our discussion, since Foucault analyzes the age of governance as the product of a longer legacy of power politics. Foucault submits that for the ancient Greeks the boy on the verge of manhood was the focus of a great deal of uncertainty, combined with intense interest: "The young man—between the end of childhood and the age when he attained manly status—constituted a delicate and difficult factor for Greek ethics and Greek thought."[36] While the moral education of women was surely important, that of male children was even more so because it bore directly on the formation of future citizens who would participate in the government of the city.[37] In light of Aristotle's grouping in the *Politics* of (freeborn) boys along with women and slaves, Foucault asks how boys could graduate from an "inferior" status in society to assume eventually a role of authority, not only in the household but also in the public sphere. A boy's honor was attached not to his future status in marriage in the private realm, as it might be for a girl, but to his future role in the public business of the city. Foucault sketches an intergenerational male-to-male dynamic of how young men became eventual patriarchs, officials, and citizens. Young men, mindful of keeping their honor, conducted themselves with an eye toward their future as eventual citizens and patriarchs, while the older men in good standing made it their business to look after the honor of the boys-to-men. This "transitional age" constituted a trial period, a test (*agon*), at the completion of which young men would be admitted to certain magistracies. Foucault's main claim is that, during this transitional period, boys won their reputations and upheld (or ruined) their honor precisely in the arena of sexual relations, specifically male-to-male relations. Foucault cites an ancient text titled *Erotic Essay* to show this connection between homoeroticism and political development: "I think [says the author of the text] . . . that the city will appoint you to be in charge of some department of her business, and in proportion as your natural gifts are more conspicuous it will judge you worthy of greater responsibilities and will the sooner desire to make trial of your abilities."[38] But what exactly was the test, asks Foucault, what constituted suitable honor that made one worthy to hold office? While Foucault cites a host of materials indicating that amorous male-to-male relations with young boys was certainly not proscribed in the ancient world and cites further evidence suggesting that moralists of the day were not recommending to maturing boys that they forgo or forsake all overtures from their older male admirers, he nonetheless concludes that ambitious Greek boys demonstrated their honor by exercising certain forms of sexual restraint and forbearance. Writes Foucault, "By not yielding, not submitting, remaining the strongest, triumphing over suitors and lovers through one's resistance, one's firmness, one's moderation (*sophrosyne*)—the young man proves his excellence in the sphere of love relations."[39] Thus Greek men drew an analogy between sexual and political forms of excellence: one's refusal to accept a position of inferiority, subordination, or humiliation in sexual relations indicated one's suitability for political office. Boys worthy of leadership positions should not behave "passively," letting themselves be manipulated and dominated; in contrast, one would demonstrate one's manly authority through sexual scrupulousness and selectivity.[40]

Foucault thus limns a possible legacy from ancient Greek cultural politics that might be applied, with some interpretive license, to the early American constitutional prohibition against young men holding political office. Foucault's analysis suggests that patriarchal systems characteristically feature a transitional period in which maturing young males must negotiate their short-term civil inferiority and dependency upon the men they will eventually replace. Foucault attends to the ancient Greeks because theirs was a cultural-political system that admitted and celebrated its intergenerational homoeroticism while at the same time marking future leaders by their sexual restraint. Superior (older) men respected only superior (younger) men, and vice versa, which meant that both parties had to exercise a kind of sexual asceticism toward their objects of greatest sexual attraction, a mutual courtship yet mutual forbearance all encoded and refracted in the language of honor. Some might find Foucault's broadside psychosexual analysis unconvincing, and its application to American constitutional history a bit far-fetched—but Foucault's treatment does provide one possible explanation of not only why older males would insist upon a politics of self-enclosed seniority that keeps the younger men at bay, but also why capable, younger men would willingly defer to and uphold such a system for the time being.

John Rawls: Political Liberty

Foucauldian insights notwithstanding, we're probably not at a stage of American constitutional history such that an amendment proposal could successfully wind its way through the labyrinth of ratification procedures via a public relations campaign announcing that the American system of federal age requirements constitutes a complex interplay between homophobia and homoeroticism. In the various genres of contemporary political theory, we probably need to turn as far away from Foucauldian cultural analysis as we can get, looking instead at the "normative-analytic" tradition in political philosophy, whose star proponent has been John Rawls. There we are more likely to find the most compelling case for amending the Constitution, drawing on clear, principled arguments regarding important public concerns about issues of justice, equality, and representation.

John Rawls provides the philosophical tools for eliminating age restrictions to holding office, yet he himself does not apply his own theory to that end, nor have his interpreters made that case. But the case should be made in Rawlsian terms, namely as a matter of justice and, thus, as a fundamental issue concerning the equal rights of citizenship.

At the very outset of *A Theory of Justice*, Rawls states two principles of justice. Throughout the book he will clarify, amend, and restate them, but the preliminary version goes as follows:

> First: each person is to have an equal right to the most extensive basic liberty compatible with a similar liberty for others.
>
> Second: social and economic inequalities are to be arranged so that they are both (a) reasonably expected to be to everyone's advantage, and (b) attached to positions and *offices open to all.*[41]

The two principles are sometimes referred to as the "liberty" principle and the "difference" principle. Rawls says that the first has precedence over the second. He defines the "basic liberties" pertaining to the first principle: political liberty, liberty of conscience and freedom of thought, freedom of the person along with the right to hold property, and freedom from arbitrary arrest and seizure as defined by the rule of law. He stipulates that these basic liberties must be applied equally to every citizen, since "citizens of a just society are to have the same basic rights."[42] Of the first basic liberty of citizenship, political liberty, Rawls mentions first and foremost "the right to vote and to be eligible for public office," referring to suffrage and eligibility in the same breath; and then he adds to the list of political liberties, freedom of speech and assembly. Here is one of the rare moments in the history of Western political thought (along with Arendt's passing comment above) where a seminal thinker states unequivocally that eligibility for (public) office is a basic right of citizenship that must be applied equally. The liberty to run for elected office is to be understood as a centerpiece of a democratic conception of justice.

Following Rawls's order of explication, we will first look to his discussion of the second principle for insights about the details of eligibility for office. Rawls explains that these two principles are special subsets of a more general conception of justice that can be expressed as follows: "All social values—liberty and opportunity, income and wealth, and the bases of self-respect—are to be distributed equally unless an unequal distribution of any, or all, of these values is to everyone's advantage."[43] Departures from a strictly egalitarian distribution of rights and primary goods are permitted, he says, but only if they can be shown to be ultimately to everyone's benefit—and Rawls's famous depiction of the original position elaborates how the principle of equality might be fairly reconciled with a difference principle in society. This is not the place, however, to offer yet another encapsulated discussion of Rawls's original position.[44] For now, I want to turn to his discussion of the phrase "open to all" in the second principle, a phrase that he admits is ambiguous. Rawls examines several different possible interpretations of the phrases "equally open" or "open to all" and settles on a "democratic" conception as the best way to balance equal liberties and justifiable differences—so that the phrase "equally open" ought to be understood as "equality of fair opportunity." He thus modifies the second principle of justice to read, "Social and economic inequalities are to be arranged so that they are both (a) to the greatest benefit of the least advantaged and (b) attached to offices and positions open to all under conditions of fair equality of opportunity" (83). He explains that the reasons for requiring open positions are not those of efficiency. It might be the case that restricting access to office would work to the overall advantage of everyone in certain instances. But the principle of open positions, he declares, forbids the consideration that restrictions might encourage better performance. Rather, the argument for openness "expresses the conviction that if some places were not open on a fair basis to all, those kept out would be right in feeling unjustly treated even though they benefited from the greater efforts of those who were allowed to hold them" (84). Rawls says that persons excluded from such offices would be justified in their complaints not only on consequentialist grounds (that is, because they had been denied the external rewards of office, such as wealth and prestige) but also on grounds of personal dignity (because they were "barred from experiencing the realization of self which comes from a skillful and devoted exercise of social duties"). Such a deprivation, Rawls insists, is a denial of "one of the main forms of human good" and undermines the most basic pillar of justice, namely, equal citizenship.

These are strong words, and one would think that Rawls would apply the second principle to the U.S. Constitution and declare outright that the age restrictions violate the principle of equal citizenship and therefore are patently unjust. But he does not take that next step. He does, however, explicitly take up the question of age restrictions with respect to the first principle of justice in the section of *The Theory of Justice* titled "Political Justice and the Constitution." Rawls begins the section by fleshing out the meaning of "equal liberty" (the first principle of justice) under terms of constitutional (or call it political) justice. The question of political justice is one of procedure (as opposed to outcome): what amounts to a fair procedure? Rawls answers that fair procedures must be guided by the principle of equal liberty, and equal liberty in a constitutional setting necessarily entails the idea of equal participation. The principle of equal participation "requires that all citizens are to have an equal right to take part in, and to determine the outcome of, the constitutional process that establishes the laws with which they are to comply" (221). The entire idea of translating concerns of justice into fair practicable procedures begins, says Rawls, with an understanding of equal participation in the process. But whereas equal participation in the original position entailed a kind of direct democracy, a face-to-face bargaining session, equal participation in a constitutional setting will need to be translated into the rules of representative-democratic government (Rawls here references Benjamin Constant's distinction between the ancients and the moderns to signal the difference between direct and representative democracy).[45] So the question becomes, what are the fair procedures to assemble a representative body so that we can designate a particular constitution as just? Rawls examines (very quickly) various conventional hallmarks of modern representative government: universal suffrage, "one person, one vote," fair and free elections, a constitutional bill of rights, equitable territorial representation and fair procedures for districting, and so on.

Whereas Rawls moves rather precipitously through the inventory of procedural requirements (entire books have been written on each of them), it is perhaps telling that he next pauses long enough to devote a separate (albeit short) paragraph to another aspect of the principle of equal participation: equal access to officeholding. He begins by stating, "The principle of participation also holds that all citizens are to have an equal access, at least in the formal sense, to public office."[46] The phrase "in the formal sense" means that no person or class of persons is explicitly barred from access to public office; conversely, no one enjoys a substantive guarantee of election into and occupation of such offices (for instance, it could be the case that for a period of history only white males actually get voted into office, which of itself wouldn't amount to a violation of just procedures if all others could run for those offices as well). Such formal proceduralism is the crux of the idea of equal opportunity for participation. Rawls further explains that equal access in the formal sense means, "Each is eligible to join political parties, to run for elective positions, and to hold places of authority" (224). But then Rawls introduces a major qualification to this principle of equal access: "To be sure, there may be qualifications of age, residency, and so on." How could Rawls, so adamant about the principle of equal access, justify any such departures based on invidious criteria involving social standing? He quickly provides his rationale for legitimate departures from equal access: "But these [qualifications] are to be reasonably related to the tasks of office; presumably these restrictions are in the common interest and do not discriminate unfairly among persons or groups in the sense that they fall evenly on everyone in the normal course of life" (224).

To put it baldly, I think Rawls errs at this point. He basically opens the door to post-age-of-majority age requirements for office (by shutting the door on only some, that is), even against all of the provisions of his first and second principles of justice that demand open and equal access to office as a fundamental liberty and as an integral component of fair procedure. We need to look carefully at his rationale for these qualifications. My contention is that they do not hold up under scrutiny.

The first point to note is that Rawls's rationale seems to apply only to age requirements and not to the residency requirement, or to the other (unspecified) possible qualifications. For the presidency (to take one instance) a residency requirement in the sense of a "natural born" requirement does in fact "discriminate unfairly among persons or groups" in the sense that it falls *unevenly* on persons in the normal course of life. Residency requirements can be justified as reasonably related to the tasks of office and as serving the common interest (as a rational mechanism to ensure single-state citizenship and undivided allegiance), but immigrants who become naturalized citizens can never become president; this is a permanent exclusion. And within the confines of a country's borders, it's not clear that a residency requirement for other offices, even with the prospects of interstate or interdistrict mobility, can be said to "fall evenly on everyone in the normal course of life." That phrase seems applicable only to an age requirement, and then only to a minimum age requirement. For that matter, would Rawls really deem as justifiable a maximum age requirement on such a fundamental principle of justice—wholesale discrimination against the elderly as a class depriving them of a basic liberty—if only it could be argued that such exclusion is "reasonably" related to the tasks of office and serves the common interest?[47] Or would he condone such deprivation by saying that earlier in their lives, old people had their chances—even if they missed them or passed over such opportunities—and therefore the denial of this opportunity to those who have reached a certain age is something that falls "evenly on everyone in the normal course of a life?"

What, then, might Rawls mean by the qualification "reasonably related to the tasks of office?" The U.S. Constitution's three different age requirements for eligibility for office seem rather arbitrarily drawn, and thus applying Rawls's normative analysis to that document begs questions of the standards and thresholds of "reasonableness." If we attend quite strictly to those specific age limits, the burden would seem to fall on Rawls to show convincingly that and how one *must* be twenty-five or over to perform adequately the tasks of a representative, that and how one *must* be thirty or over to perform the tasks of a senator, and that and how one *must* be thirty-five or over to perform the tasks of a president. Such an articulated justification would probably need to draw upon empirical criteria that clearly distinguish those above and those below those age limits and connect those criteria to the tasks of the different offices—criteria that supposedly trump and thus need to preempt the criteria of a democratic electorate. If we try to read that level of "reasonableness" into the Constitution's age requirements, Rawls would surely fail to meet the requisitely high burden of proof. If we loosen the standard of demonstration, however, so that one need argue only that it is generally helpful to be "experienced" as an officeholder, and that minimum age requirements—at whatever age stipulation—are reasonably helpful to ensure that the pool of aspirants all meet a minimum threshold, then Rawls is on safer grounds, namely because the "reasonable" nexus between age and tasks of office is left ambiguous. We could still strongly object, of course, to Rawls's hypothetical "life expectancy" model of fairness that stakes the claim about "equal opportunity" on a postulated "normal course of life" that assumes that all persons may well live beyond thirty-five—a fallacy of a "life-course imaginary," as one age-studies author puts it.[48] Such crude one-size-fits-all modeling doesn't differentiate at all among other empirically based actuarial models of life expectancy; one could point out that Rawls's method is a virtual formula for blatant discrimination against certain disabled persons,[49] or those afflicted with certain life-threatening illnesses at a very young age, or those whose family or genetic life expectancies fall far short of the statistical norm. Rawls's signature method of thinking through these issues as if from behind a "veil of ignorance" about such real lives makes his way of philosophizing extremely susceptible to such oversights and to the attendant charges of insensitivity or even discrimination. In any event, if we grant Rawls a looser standard on age as it relates to the "tasks of office" requirement, what might that do to the "and so on" cases?

In U.S. constitutional history, the major "and so on" qualifications for office, in addition to residency and minimum age requirements, have involved property, literacy, race, and gender (other ballot access requirements at the state and local levels have included requirements involving educational levels, mental capacity, noncriminal standing, and party affiliation). The problem with a looser standard for the "related to office" requirement is that one could make a reasonable case for making an analogy between minimum age requirements and requirements pertaining to race or gender. By a loose standard one could conceivably argue that, for instance, white males are generally deemed in our society to be more authoritative and experienced, and thus limiting the pool of office applicants to white men might be a rational mechanism to ensure such political authority and experience (this example would fail Rawls's second test, however, for it would discriminate unfairly in the sense that it would fall unevenly upon persons in the normal course of life). The point is that the grounds for attaching age to the merits of political officeholding are as weak as attaching "white maleness" to such tasks.[50]

Rawls runs into greater trouble with property and literacy qualifications. The main arguments throughout history in favor of property and literacy requirements have been that those traits can indeed be tied directly to the tasks of the office. The propertied, it is said, are stakeholders; only those who pay taxes should be allowed to vote on how tax revenues ought to be distributed. Literacy, many have argued, is a baseline educational standard that should apply to all voters and officeholders. Yet I think it is fair to say that most Americans would now view an explicit property or literacy qualification as violating some basic democratic tenet of equal participation (and not just as a cover for racist practices). Moreover, I'm not sure that Rawls's second test can save him from this analogy, as it might in the cases of race and gender. If a penniless or illiterate person is not formally barred from gaining property or literacy, it is hard to say conclusively that a property or literacy requirement discriminates "unfairly among persons or groups in the sense that they fall evenly on everyone in the normal course of life." You may not have property now, but you can be reasonably expected to gain property in the fullness of time—or at least nothing is officially preventing you from acquiring property; it is not a "permanent exclusion" or "immutable" characteristic. So, too, with a

literacy requirement: unless something is formally or physically barring you from learning to read, you cannot charge unfair discrimination
if a political system enforces that modest standard—at least not according to Rawls's time-projected notion of normative personhood ("in the
normal course of life"). In fact, it would probably be asking less of an
unpropertied or illiterate person that he or she acquire some modest
property or basic reading skills than it would be to ask a twenty-year-
old diabetic quadriplegic to wait five or ten years before running for
federal office if that is his or her ambition. Moreover, Rawls's argument is further complicated by the fact that the U.S. Constitution includes not one minimum age requirement, but three. Imagine if
property or literacy requirements were to be phased-in in a similarly
graduated manner. Suppose that anyone with $10 in his or her pocket
and the ability to sign his or her name would be eligible to run for the
House, but running for the Senate would require a net worth of
$200,000 and a bachelor's degree, and running for the presidency
would require a net worth of $1,000,000 and a postgraduate degree.
(The idea isn't so absurd: before the ratification of the Constitution
several of the states had graduated property qualifications.)[51]

Rawls's analysis simply does not give us consistent, clear, and compelling criteria for distinguishing fair from unfair departures from the
principles of equal opportunity to hold office. That curious proviso
in that key passage—"reasonably related to the tasks of office"—is
something of an analytic legerdemain, subtly changing the question of
a "fundamental liberty" into a question of fair procedure. Charles
Beitz, in his book *Political Equality*, takes Rawls to task on precisely
this point, addressing specifically Rawls's discussion of eligibility for
office as a fundamental liberty and insisting that that notion be severed
from the idea of political equality. All of this suggests that we may
need a more focused analysis of the normative principle of political
equality as distinguishable from the normative ideal of an individual
right: maybe the case for a constitutional amendment on age should
be viewed first and foremost as a fundamental issue of equality, not
liberty.

Robert Dahl, Charles Beitz, and Judith Shklar: Political Equality

One, if not *the*, preeminent democratic theorist of our time, Robert
Dahl, in his many writings on the subject, associates the history and
norms of democracy not just with the virtues of liberty, but necessarily
with the virtues and claims of equality. In his book *On Democracy* Dahl

explains that a push toward democratic participation develops out of what he calls "the logic of equality."[52] In ancient Athens, for instance, all citizens felt themselves entitled to participate in the assembly, and the assembly elected key officials (even military generals) by lottery. An ordinary citizen, says Dahl, "stood a fair chance of being chosen by lot once in his lifetime to serve as the most important presiding officer in the government."[53] The right to participate in governing the Roman Republic was at first restricted to patricians, but after much struggle, eventually extended even to plebeians. Throughout eighteenth-century Europe, the logic of equality stimulated, he says, the creation of local assemblies, a practice of participation that gradually fostered the claim that laws generally should be based on consent. Consent in the laws, moreover, required representation in the regional or national bodies that made the laws. The idea that the consent of free citizens would require elected representative bodies at several legislative levels became a baseline presumption for all subsequent democratization, in Europe and elsewhere.

Dahl points out that democratic participation always attracted critics along the way. He calls the main rival to participatory, democratic, representative government "political guardianship." Proponents of guardianship typically base their opposition to democratic equality and participation through supposedly preemptive claims about superior expertise and higher competence. Government, they contend, ought to be based on knowledge and expertise, and therefore officeholding ought to be the exclusive province of the uniquely qualified. While experts are certainly needed in government, Dahl counters that the business of governing should not be handed over to them exclusively, especially since that negates the benefits of participation. In the ongoing rivalry between democracy and guardianship, the democrats have won, he says. In rejecting the case for guardianship, we have concluded, writes Dahl (his italics), "*Among adults no persons are so definitely better qualified than others to govern that they should be entrusted with complete and final authority over the government of the state.*"[54] The principle of "full inclusion" now reigns—so much so that Dahl insists that "inclusive citizenship" needs to be recognized as a requisite political institution for modern representative democracy. He defines the "political institution" of inclusive citizenship as follows:

> Inclusive citizenship: No adult permanently residing in the country and subject to its laws can be denied the rights that are available to others and are necessary to the five political institutions

just listed. These include the rights to vote in the election of officials in free and fair elections; to run for elective office; to free expression; to form and participate in independent political organizations; to have access to independent sources of information; and rights to other liberties and opportunities that may be necessary to the effective operation of the political institutions of large-scale democracy.[55]

In *Democracy and Its Critics* Dahl goes to greater lengths to justify this principle of inclusiveness—which he now describes as a categorical principle for democracy. He explains that the broad criterion of inclusiveness issues from a Strong Principle of Equality that undergirds modern democracy itself. Modern democracies no longer sanction internally exclusionary practices: "Experience has shown that any group of adults excluded from the demos—for example, women, artisans and laborers, the unpropertied, racial minorities—will be lethally weakened in defending its own interests. And an exclusive demos is unlikely to protect the interests of those who are excluded."[56] The Strong Principle of Equality, says Dahl, provides "reasonable grounds for adopting a criterion that approaches universality among adults."[57] He insists that the democratic process must include "all adult members," with the only exceptions being "transients and persons proved to be mentally defective." Yes, we could quibble, he says, over the precise definition of adulthood, and no definition of the term will ever be completely watertight. But the legal test should suffice: "If a legal system assigns burdens, obligations, and punishments to persons when they reach an age at which they are legally presumed to have achieved the minimum threshold of reason and responsibility for their actions, then that age might also serve as the threshold at which the right to inclusion in the demos ought to begin." The meaning of that categorical criterion, Dahl underscores, ought to be clear enough: "A demos that permitted the concept of adulthood to be manipulated in order to deprive certain persons of their rights—dissenters, for example—to that degree would simply fail to meet the criterion of inclusiveness."[58]

Put some of the pieces of Dahl's very clear account together—no manipulation of the term "adulthood"; no restrictions on inclusion for adult citizens; the right to run for office as one of the fundamental criteria for inclusive citizenship—and you have a strong, unqualified case for eliminating age qualifications for elected representatives (beyond the age of majority). But Dahl himself does not take that extra step. In his recent book, *How Democratic Is the American Constitution?*

he examines many of the lingering obstructions for achieving a more democratic republic here in these United States—but nowhere does he mention the constitutional age provisions. Earlier, in his discussion of the lottery system in ancient Athens, Dahl remarks that the Athenian system of selecting citizens for public duties by lot never became an acceptable alternative to elections as a way of choosing representatives.[59] But it should be pointed out that the framers included no age qualifications for federal judges or jurors—and to this day jurors are routinely summoned and selected for that public duty by lot. Notwithstanding these few oversights, Dahl makes a formidable, if finally incomplete, case for viewing age qualifications for holding elected office as a fundamental affront to democratic institutions.

In similar fashion, Charles Beitz calls for a theory of political equality for constitutional democracies. He contends that most democratic theorists (he names Carole Pateman, Amy Gutmann, Jane Mansbridge, Ronald Dworkin, Robert Dahl, John Rawls, Jack Lively, and David Miller) would not see the need for such a theory, because they would basically agree with Rawls that political (that is, constitutional) equality means distributing the opportunities for participation equally among all citizens. Such an egalitarian view of participation also entails that any departures or restrictions on equal opportunity must meet an extraordinary burden of justification (and Rawls's own exceptions to his theories, as we held above, probably fail to meet that strong test). But Beitz takes exception with what he calls the "simple view" of political equality, namely that "political equality is the requirement that democratic institutions should provide citizens with equal procedural opportunities to influence political decisions (or, more briefly, with *equal power over outcomes*)."[60] That simple view is usually outcome-based, designed to produce desirable representative results of one sort or another. A democratic theorist might call, for instance, for greater female participation in order to change legislation in a particular way or else simply to have women gain more legislative seats in Congress. But Beitz objects that the "simple view" of political equality is deficient because it equates the abstract ideal of political equality with the institutional standard of procedural equality. In contrast, he proposes a theory of "complex proceduralism" that attempts to institutionalize the norm of political equality not by translating it into the requirement of equal weight in decision making but instead via a conception of procedural *fairness* (as opposed to strict procedural equality). Fair democratic procedures, he says, should treat persons as equals, but that general (and noninstrumental) notion of equal citizenship shouldn't be identified with equal treatments of their welfare or their preferences. Fair procedures are fair "when they are reasonably acceptable from each citizen's point of view, or more precisely, when no citizen has good reason to refuse to accept them" (23). Hence, Beitz's theory of political equality as procedural fairness allows for departures from equal participation; but, like Rawls, who insists that departures from uniform distributions of justice must be justified as working in principle to the advantage of the least well-off in society, Beitz requires that departures from procedural egalitarianism must be justifiable according to a democratic conception of "reasonable acceptance from each citizen's point of view."

Beitz does not directly apply the political virtue of fairness to the question of age restrictions, but he does address the general question of the fairness of "agenda-structuring" provisions that restrict opportunities for contending for public office. First, however, he rejects outright Rawls's claim that eligibility for office is a "basic liberty" that is to be restricted only with extraordinary justification and only in a manner that distributes the burden equally. If it were a basic liberty, then Beitz says he would agree that restrictions could be justified only if distributed equally. But Beitz sharply disagrees with Rawls that it is as fundamental as the right to vote and the right to participate in public political deliberation. He argues that these latter rights are exercised by "everyone, or nearly everyone" and thus are "basic"—but the right to run for office "is not basic in this way" (174). He elaborates, "Arguably, voters may have an interest in being able to vote for positions close to their own, and citizens may have an interest in the representation of their concerns in public deliberation and in the legislative process, but neither of these concerns implies that every willing candidate should have equal access to the competitive political process. The right to have one's position represented or taken into account is not the same as the right to represent one's own position" (174). He claims that the "right to represent one's own position" is something like the (social/personal) right to choose a career—but that notion of choice cannot be construed as a "basic liberty." And a personal right to choose does not distinguish eligibility for office from a host of other social goods, he contends. Moreover, the individual's right to run for office has to be weighed against the structural benefits that restrictions might bring. The main point of fair restrictions, Beitz submits, is that "these mechanisms should ensure public presentation of positions responsive to the needs and interests of all significant portions of the citizenry"

(176). He proffers some qualities he believes are indicative of an appropriately wide-ranging democratic agenda: completeness, coherence, and range. But in the remainder of his book he works out the details of these qualities by way of applications other than age qualifications, so we're not sure exactly what follows from his critique of Rawls except that eligibility for office isn't a basic liberty (and thus the question of whether that Rawlsian liberty should be distributed equally is moot). Certainly on the basis of his discussion of agenda-structuring provisions we can surmise that Beitz would probably not deem age restrictions as patently unfair and a necessary affront to political equality—as long as they are arguably justifiable from an informed conception of democratic reasonableness.

Yet Beitz's passing dismissal of Rawls on the notion of eligibility for office as a basic liberty shouldn't go without critical comment. Beitz's first point that eligibility for office isn't "basic" because few actually run for office is weak: the principled existence of a right shouldn't be conditional on its exercise. But more, he seems to be smuggling in unacknowledged cultural/historical considerations, referring implicitly to contemporary (mass) democracy, under the terms of which very few persons in fact can and will run for office. Further, his point about some necessary divide between eligibility and exercise doesn't pertain to democratic examples drawn from Attic Greece, Rousseau's Geneva, or many contemporary Swiss cantons. Even in the American mixed-republic case, the same ideal of eligibility for office underlies the Madisonian innovation of rotational offices for various representative levels (as in *Federalist* 39). Notwithstanding the restrictions written into the Constitution, many of the American founders saw officeholding to be the revolving-door province of amateurs and commoners rather than that of a predetermined or self-perpetuating elite. The right to run for representative office surely couldn't be exercised by everyone and certainly not by all at once, but in principle and over time it could be exercised by a great many citizens and not just a few. Rawls may be right to intuit and abstract a "basic liberty" to eligibility for office from the implicitly American context, even if the American founders weren't always true to their aspirations to democratic participation when it came time to commit their beliefs to writing. Still, Beitz's hyperbolic insight that not all citizens can in fact compete for office in any given election—hence some restrictions must always apply—does not sabotage Rawls's contention that eligibility for office is a basic liberty.

Beitz's second point in arguing against Rawls's notion of eligibility for office as a basic liberty turns on a questionable notion of representation that deserves review ("The right to have one's position represented or taken into account is not the same as the right to represent one's own position"). Beitz construes this "basic liberty" to be merely a matter of an individual right or choice rather than as a choice already imbued with collective dimensions. If a person who is (also? inextricably?) a woman asserts her right to run for office as a "basic liberty," she may not be asserting that right simply in her own behalf; she may in fact see herself as a spokesperson for a larger, perhaps female-based constituency. She may already have a group or political or collective dimension incorporated into that "choice," and thus her running for office cannot be reduced to a mere personal preference akin to a "career choice." Beitz's argument—which at this point evidently considers individuals as abstract persons rather than as engendered or acculturated beings already implicated in interpersonal identities, investments, and obligations—runs the risk of justifying "virtual representation" as sufficient to satisfy the terms of his fair proceduralism. Imagine how Beitz's notion of political equality might have worked in a nineteenth-century American context: One would have to reject arguments in favor of women's suffrage and the eligibility of women for office on the "simple view" of outcome-based schema. If it could then be argued as "reasonable" that society would be better off with only male citizens in charge, and if it could be argued—or at least not well rejected—that such patriarchy still respects women as equal "persons" notwithstanding their obvious exclusion from participatory representation, then Beitz's theory of political equality could somehow be mobilized to justify such patently unfair and unequal restrictions (and he admits that his use of the phrase "political equality" does not square with ordinary uses of the term). At the time, a "reasonable" nineteenth-century convention might hold, for instance, that a good many women defer willingly to men and do not want equal standing as active participants (only an outlying minority of suffragettes would be clamoring for that liberty). To be fair, Beitz spends some time arguing against "elite" models of democratic competition, and he expresses sympathy for arguments in favor of measures that place before voters a broad range of "alternatives" to "programmatic" competition such as two-party models. But he says nary a word about how group identities per se might undermine or be reconciled into his complex conception of fair proceduralism—and such oversights are conspicuous by their absence in a book devoted to issues of political equality and democratic representation.

In the end, Beitz retreats too far from a commonsensical conception of political equality (to the point of almost obscuring it) in favor of an overly abstract conception of reasonable fairness. Still, we want to agree with him and draw from his theory on several basic points: The argument in favor of a constitutional amendment eliminating age barriers cannot be staked exclusively or primarily on an "outcomes-based" or instrumentalist theory of political equality. That is to say, the elimination of these age restrictions cannot be justified by a utilitarian argument asserting either that society will necessarily be better off if more youth are in fact elected into office or that there will be a salutary benefit that accrues to youth themselves if they run for and hold more elected seats. If we put Rawls's claim about eligibility for office as a basic liberty into abeyance for a moment, then an argument for such an amendment based on political equality will need to be pitched in normative terms that nonetheless resemble Beitz's quasi-Kantian conception of equal personhood. Beitz's conception of procedural fairness, however, abstracts too far from the real world of democratic social roles and lived identities—even though he claims that his theory doesn't operate from behind a veil of ignorance about such matters. Or perhaps another way of criticizing and recuperating Beitz's argument is to say that he needs to observe and insist upon a distinction between *equal personhood* and *equal citizenship* as an adjudicating norm for democratic theory (and too frequently he conflates the two). On this particular point Judith Shklar makes an important contribution.

In her book *American Citizenship*, Judith Shklar insists that a theory of political equality must be contextualized, situated explicitly in its particularly American setting and undertaken by way of "a historically rich inquiry."[61] Her purpose in the book is to call attention to the notion of American citizenship as a matter of equal *standing*. American politics, she begins, has always been democratic, "but only in principle." Freedom and democracy were championed in America always against the background of chattel slavery and cultural misogyny; the celebration of democratic virtues was always fraught with internal contradictions, hypocrisies, and exclusions. She quotes the historian James Kellner on this defining paradox of the American political character: "In truth, from the nation's beginnings as an independent republic, Americans were torn by 'glaring inconsistencies between their professed principles of citizenship and their deep-seated desire to exclude certain groups permanently from the privileges of membership.'"[62]

She adds a curt comment to this quotation from Kellner: "These tensions constitute the real history of its [America's] citizens."[63]

Shklar emphasizes that the story of political equality in America was similarly one of antagonism in the face of obtuseness: "The equality of political rights, which is the first mark of American citizenship, was proclaimed in the accepted presence of its absolute denial" (1). Thus, for Shklar, the significance of political equality in America can never be examined simply as a freestanding norm but must be set against a fitful history of exclusion, struggle, and extension: "These essays are meant to recall that the disenfranchised and the excluded were members of a professedly democratic society that was actively and purposefully false to its own vaunted principles by refusing to accept these people or to recognize their right to be voters and free laborers" (14). Overcoming exclusion, attaining citizenship and equal standing with others, was always something that required protracted struggle—and thus the unique character of American citizenship owed much to the fact that citizenship for many was something *attained* after having been denied for so long. But it was also forged against a background of an ongoing national master narrative that feigned ignorance about such exclusions and struggles: "What gave citizenship as standing its historical significance is not that it was denied for so long to so many, but that this exclusion occurred in a republic that was overtly committed to political equality, and whose citizens believed that theirs was a free and fair society" (17).

In laying out the case for the centrality of standing in the history of suffrage reform, Shklar immediately turns to a contrastive, contemporary example involving youth, namely the circumstances that surrounded the passage of the Twenty-Sixth Amendment in 1971. Polls at the time, she points out, indicated that eighteen- to twenty-year-olds were not clamoring for the right to vote. They didn't feel demeaned by their exclusion from the national charter. They didn't ask for this amendment, nor did they rejoice at its passage, nor have they, as a group, accepted responsibility for the franchise since its ratification. Shklar disapproves, and reproves accordingly, "When there is no standing involved, the franchise is simply not valued" (18). She calls this episode of suffrage extension "a frivolous exercise" based on a "complete misunderstanding of the value of enfranchisement." Whereas Beitz largely discounts the value of "outcome-based" approaches to evaluating the importance of political equality, Shklar contends that the real-world precedents and antecedents to the equalizing distribution of political rights matter tremendously.

Noteworthy for our purposes in Shklar's discussion of the Twenty-Sixth Amendment is her examination of "youth" as a group and her comparison of its political coming of age with the experiences of blacks and women in gaining the franchise. She is one of the few contemporary political theorists (Foucault is the other) to focus on this Aristotelian trilogy of the traditionally excluded in politics (based on race, gender, and age), even though her point is to distinguish youth from blacks and women—in an odd though unacknowledged reversal of Aristotle's estimation of the political potential of each of these groups. Her reasoning for denigrating the extension of the franchise to eighteen- to twenty-year-olds is as follows: "The utter indifference of the young stands in stark contrast to the intensity with which blacks and women, only too fixed in their physical and social condition, have fought for the vote and for their political standing" (19). But cracks start to show in Shklar's presumption to be able to speak so sweepingly on behalf of these "groups." She qualifies that many young persons at the time of the passage of the Twenty-Sixth Amendment were indeed politically active, though she dismisses such activity as mainly war protesting (as if that can be cordoned off). She claims that the young didn't rejoice at the passage of the amendment, and she relies on a few polls to make that claim about their supposed disinterest—but then she fails to note that the eighteen-to-twenty-four-year-old bloc voted in great numbers in the 1972 election. She doesn't address the question of how numerous members of a previously disenfranchised group may have become, over time and many indignities, resigned to their second-class condition and cannot see a way out—call that false consciousness, bad faith, or internalizing one's oppressor. Or at least she doesn't extend this possibility to the youth in America in 1971, but she does apply this possibility to early American blacks and women—which complicates and qualifies her portrayal of those groups as struggling and grateful for their eventual standing as full citizens. American women did not universally support the suffrage movement, she admits—in fact, a fair number "were content with their existing condition, disliked any radical social change, and, worst of all, feared that they would lose the support of their husbands and other male family members if they left their 'proper sphere'" (19). Many objected to the comparison with slavery—a perceived misanalogy that continued into the twentieth century, accounting for much female resistance to the Equal Rights Amendment, according to Shklar. And she adds that while no black leader ever expressed a comparable hostility to the right to vote, some, such as Booker T. Washington, thought that other priorities should come first, putting economic progress ahead of political equality, thus deferring the latter indefinitely. Some Northern free workers, she contends, thought that they were better off before they had become wage workers—a view sometimes complicated, she notes, by the talk in the air "about the good life enjoyed by black slaves on the Southern plantations" (21). Shklar still comes down on the side of the view that "blacks" on the whole struggled for their inclusion, both politically and economically—but a reader of her account might still raise the question whether her more nuanced reading of women and blacks in American history could also be extended to her rather brusque treatment of American youth in the period leading up to the passage of the Twenty-Sixth Amendment. Her dismissal of youth gaining the vote ("a frivolous exercise") could well be seen as overdrawn and even patronizing.

Yet elsewhere in her writings on American political history, Shklar focuses again on youth (that is to say, young adults), albeit this time with a bit less obvious rancor. In an essay, "The Boundaries of Democracy,"[64] Shklar poses the question of what "We the People" actually means. Defining who constitutes "the people" in a democracy is the question most "vexing for modern democratic thought." What boundaries, she asks, mark a democratic people off from others? What exactly marks a citizen from a noncitizen within certain geographical confines? Democracy raises all sorts of territorial conundrums, but the question it raises "above all," according to Shklar, is, *How are generations to be sorted out?* "How are the dead and the living, the old and the young, and the past and the present to be divided or joined? Consent, after all, occurs only here and now" (127). Many writers attempted to draw on the past for answers to American democratic identity, she notes—but Thomas Paine urged Americans to stop looking to the past for counsel and direction. Paine thought that "ancestor worship" could be of little use to such a new nation, and he thought that "youth" should instead serve as the guide: "Youth is the seed-time of good habits" (136). Paine radically envisioned a democracy without boundaries "between ruler and ruled, citizen and emigrant, old and young." Youthful, forward-looking democratic citizens, unencumbered by past memories and baggage, could imagine a capacious democracy that would need little government and that promised an intermingling of democratic nations the world over.

Shklar withholds critical comment about this vision of democracy without borders and says only that Paine's "greatest single achievement was the profound impression that his writings made upon

Thomas Jefferson" (138). Paine's views accorded with Jefferson's deepest beliefs about one set of boundaries, says Shklar, namely those between generations. Following Paine's conviction that the living owed nothing to the dead, Jefferson believed that each generation must be autonomously self-ruling: "One generation is to another as one independent nation to another." He calculated a generation to last for about nineteen years—so it followed, explains Shklar, that all existing laws should be revoked at the end of twenty years. Jefferson was absolutely serious about the phrase "consent of the governed": democracy, based on consent, had to be government by, for, and of those living, those alive in the present. One immediate, practical consequence of such a view for Jefferson was that America should not incur foreign debts and saddle future generations with such obligations (which such future citizens need not heed anyway). But Shklar points out that Jefferson's view of generational independence (arising out of his insistence on democratic consent by and for the living) held implications far beyond issues of international indebtedness. It cast doubt on whether any democratic law or constitution could be valid beyond a twenty-year sunset clause. Laws would therefore need to be constantly reviewed and renewed—such legislative flux would be the necessary consequence of government based on consent. Shklar interjects that Madison objected to such instability and inefficiency only on prudential, not philosophical, grounds.

Genuine democracy, for Jefferson, would thus not be easy to arrange. But according to Shklar, Jefferson was absolutely committed to pursuing an unmitigated version of it: "The barriers between generations, between those majorities that could consent and dissent and those that could not, must be absolute. There could be no abridgment of the rights of the living" (139). The vehicle to this hopeful, if ever changing, scheme-of-things would be education. The young could become superior to their elders, one generation could improve upon its predecessors, via greater and greater learning and insight. But the proper form of education, while building on the past, had to be such that it cultivated intellectual self-reliance as well. The young were in the best position to remain skeptical of earlier generations and staid conventions; and retaining their derring-do and upbeat innocence, the young would be more inclined to break free from accepted arrangements and to approach democratic possibilities with a spirit of innovation, novelty, and most important, self-determination. In truth, for Jefferson, youth—educated youth who might become yeoman farmers and the like—would be the quintessential exemplars and practitioners of a vitalized American democracy. Shklar in this essay doesn't refract her disparagement of the Twenty-Sixth Amendment through her sympathetic Jeffersonian lens, so we can only ponder that evident disparity when we read her two treatments of youthful politics side by side.

The point of Paine and Jefferson's joint passion for generation-specific legislators was that genuine consent—the backbone of democracy itself—can never truly be delegated. If, for practical purposes, democracy cannot be direct but need be representative (a commonplace in American political theory), then legitimate representatives must emerge somehow directly on the basis of the consent of those for whom they claim to speak. In her book *American Citizenship*, shortly after her diatribe against the Twenty-Sixth Amendment, Shklar takes up the issue of actual—as opposed to virtual—representation in the early American republic. She charts a historical development by which white American males ceased to be satisfied with British parliamentary schemes of virtual representation and started demanding the right to elect their own representatives—and she explains that this original demand for universal white manhood suffrage and equality of representation paved the way for blacks and women eventually to demand that *their* representation must similarly be actual, not virtual. In the debates over universal (manhood) suffrage, Shklar contends that no name was invoked more than Jefferson's. She traces how the Jeffersonian legacy applied to blacks and women—but somehow, in this discussion of equal representation for groups, Jefferson's concern for youth and generationalism drop out of Shklar's purview and picture altogether.

America's revolutionary generation, she writes, rejected the practice of "virtual representation"—though it took a while, and the idea of equal rights always had its enemies. Earlier, some Americans seemed content with the English system of highly unequal representation; they claimed that they would be satisfied if American Englishmen were represented in Parliament on the same "virtual" terms as Englishmen. This was because, Shklar explains, representation under the British Empire was viewed as a means to an end, the pursuit and protection of one's interests. Having a direct voice in Parliament was merely a matter of prestige, but wasn't a necessity nor viewed presumptively as a right for far-flung colonists. But the Americans soon favored the idea of popular election, she says, and from then on, there was no turning back. They demanded that they be heard and served. In the colonies themselves, representation was actual, not virtual—

though there were property (and other) qualifications for voting. Shklar elaborates,

> Most white men had the vote, and to be represented meant to be spoken for, but it was also a matter of being there, being heard, counting, having a sense of "somebodyness" as a black voter was to say many years later.[65] Certainly virtual representation by Europeans could not accomplish that for Americans. Englishmen were too remote from them culturally and politically to understand them fully or to speak for them. In any case, by then they had rejected the old system in the name of the rights of man. They wanted not merely to be represented, but to be electors.[66]

After the Civil War, Shklar says, "race and gender replaced property" as the disqualifications that gave white males the exclusive privilege of voting—but again, though she invokes Jefferson throughout this exposition, Shklar fails to mention anything about marginalized youth under the explicit terms of the Constitution. She observes an irony about democratic reform in the name of equality: many of the beneficiaries of earlier such reforms, once they become club insiders, often resisted further extensions of such rights. Even after property qualifications for voting had become widely discredited as a latter-day form of enslavement, it still took a while for the complete abolition of that restriction. But the claims of democracy prevailed over fears about the expropriation of property: "The republic was an association of persons united by a contract, not a business corporation, and citizens had an equal claim to their rights."[67]

Shklar's overall point about subsequent black and female enfranchisement is that the right to vote removed a stigma—which, to be sure, was a significant accomplishment—but voting on its own accomplished little else.[68] For blacks, winning the vote, according to Shklar, meant that many war-weary abolitionists could now forget about the black man, since enfranchised blacks were now supposed to look after themselves. Democratizing the vote also shifted the scene of prejudicial obstruction onto other mechanisms in the representative structure: "The vote could not protect the black Southerner against grotesque registration requirements, literacy tests, poll taxes, grandfather clauses, white primaries, and more chicanery than they could possibly defeat."[69] The impediments to voting and representation weren't lifted, Shklar adds, until the Voting Rights Act of 1965 and by various court cases along the way. Shklar's conclusion is that the significance of universal suffrage for blacks—one person, one vote—can be easily overstated: "In actuality the right is not fundamental because it secures benefits or other rights directly for the individual voter acting alone; it does so only if he or she votes as a member of a group."[70] She makes a similar point about female enfranchisement: "When women finally went to the polls, it turned out to be the biggest non-event in our electoral history."[71] The vote, Shklar says, did not alter women's social lives significantly—mainly because women did not vote as a bloc.

Shklar's analysis thereafter rather peters out. She doesn't follow through on the problem she broaches, namely how the extension of democratic suffrage (the principle of one person, one vote) to individuals qua their identity as a member of a group can translate into effective group representation. Instead, she frames the failures of effective black and female representation as a problem of aggregate (that is to say, individualized) decision making. And again, while Jefferson as the "Saint of Monticello" informs every page of her writing about democratic reform, Jefferson's own concern with generational representation doesn't seem to occur to her at all. Clearly we need to clarify the concept of representation and how it bears on the question of youth representation.

Hanna Pitkin: Political Representation

Hanna Pitkin's *The Concept of Representation* provides an analytic yet panoramic investigation into the meaning(s) of the term *representation*, especially as it has been applied to politics. The book has become a classic in political science literature and deserves a full reading for the many nuances and implications of this contested concept. For our purposes, however, a few summary observations and lessons can be selectively drawn. Pitkin goes a bit further back into English history than Shklar does to trace the early modern origins of the concept of political representation, especially as it was eventually conveyed to America. Early notions of parliamentary attendance did not hold any connotation of a right or privilege, she says; only with the passage of time did parliamentary representation acquire the sense that such a body could serve as a device to further local interests or check the power of the king. By the seventeenth century the right to elect a member of Parliament could be claimed for even the poorest—a precarious claim that hardened into a venerable tradition, which eventually informed the rallying cry of the American Revolution, the famous

"Taxation without representation is tyranny." Pitkin writes, "Representation had become one of the sacred and traditional 'rights of Englishmen,' worth fighting for; with the American and French revolutions it was transformed into one of the 'rights of Man.'" Thus representation came to mean popular election of representatives and became linked with the idea of self-government, "of every man's right to have a say in what happens to him."[72]

Yet Pitkin contends that we don't pay much attention to the word *representation* and thus are prone to use it sloppily. John Stuart Mill wrote an entire book on representative government but nowhere in it explained what he meant by the term. On careful inspection, however, the concept of representation reveals many different meanings and various implications that attend to those respective meanings. Pitkin lays forth a helpful typology of the major uses of the concept of (political) representation: formalistic, standing for (descriptively), standing for (symbolically), and acting for. Formalistic views of representation (she cites Hobbes as a quintessential formalist) concentrate on the process or transaction out of which a representative is officially authorized to claim the right to act or speak as a political representative.

"Standing-for" theorists of representation try to answer the question of what representative persons or bodies actually should be or do. True representation, they argue, "requires that the legislature be so selected that its composition corresponds accurately to that of the whole nation."[73] Typically such writers advocate that the representative body ought to resemble the composition of the nation in some significant manner(s); it ought to be a "mirror" or "map" of the community. John Adams (at least during the revolutionary period) argued that a representative legislature "should be an exact portrait, in miniature, of the people at large, as it should think, feel, reason and act like them."[74] James Wilson contended at the Constitutional Convention that "the portrait is excellent in proportion to its being a good likeness," so "the legislature ought to be the most exact transcript of the whole society," "the faithful echo of the voices of the people."[75] Algernon Sidney and Beatrice Webb invoked the same reasoning when they condemned the British House of Lords as "the worst representative assembly ever created, in that it contains absolutely no members of the manual working class; none of the great class of shopkeepers, clerks and teachers; none of the half of all the citizens who are of the female sex."[76] Most often, the rationale for producing a representative body as an "accurate reflection" of the community or nation turns on a view of the function of the legislature first and foremost as a discursive,

deliberative body. Having the diversity of community opinions reflected and represented within the legislature is seen as crucial to the
(deliberative) operation of that body. Different schemes of representation may lay claim to such descriptive reflection (random sampling,
proportionality according to various ascriptive characteristics). Representatives serve, then, not just as formal proxies but are viewed as
"standing-for" some specific group constituency. Pitkin says that
"standing for" theories of representation tend to emphasize the talking and deliberating functions of representative government rather
than the "acting" or "governing" features of government.

"Acting-for" theorists of representation put primary emphasis not
on how one is elected (formalistic) or who is elected (standing for), but
on "what" is to be done by way of governmental action. Government
exists, they posit, in order to fulfill certain functions and purposes, and
representatives are impaneled in order to further those objectives. In
the name of those objectives, representatives see themselves as properly authorized to take action to those ends, now claiming to act on
behalf of others or for the sake or protection of their interests. Such a
view of representation lends itself to near-synonyms for the representative official: deputy, delegate, ambassador, envoy, emissary, commissioner, trustee, or guardian. These terms suggest that the political
representative is dispatched from a local community with a mission to
do something. Many such proponents see representative government
as a form of trusteeship, serving the "larger" purposes of the community or nation. Often the notion of trusteeship is linked with the idea
that "the beneficiary is incapable of acting for himself, or at least that
the trustee is far more competent than he."[77] As one moves in the
direction of an "acting-for" and trusteeship view of representation,
Pitkin warns that one may be moving away from on-the-ground democratic justifications: "The implications of calling government a trusteeship are thus by no means democratic ones. It is implied that the
government must then act for the benefit of the people, but it is
equally implied that this does not require consultation or responsive-
ness to their wishes."[78]

Edmund Burke explicitly defended a theory of representation as a
form of elite trusteeship, so much so that proper representation could
exist without even holding elections. Pitkin calls such a view "virtual"
representation. She explains that the justification for bypassing actual
elections is that certain elites, for Burke, could supposedly better grasp
and look after the higher or common interests of the national constituency. The more a theorist sees an "objective" interest animating the

purposes of government, the more it is possible, says Pitkin, to further that interest without actually consulting one's constituents. The more one sees interests as definable only by the people who feel them, the more consultative one will expect "representatives" to be and accordingly will put directly interactive institutional mechanisms in place.[79]

Pitkin apparently agrees with Shklar that American liberalism in its postrevolutionary period quickly and continually divested itself of lingering vestiges of Burkean views of virtual representation. "In America," Pitkin writes, "representation was clearly to be of persons"[80] as well as their interests—with their interests to be tamed by a well-constructed government. Earlier theorists of liberalism generally thought of representation as being of individuals rather than corporate bodies or classes or (economic) interests. Yet the American founders concocted a scheme of representation based on "representation by population" as situated within different geographical districts—in good part to safeguard property interests against possible majoritarian redistributions. The authors of the *Federalist Papers*, Pitkin observes, describe representative government as a device adopted instead of direct democracy, mainly because an extended republic cannot assemble so many people in one place. Representative government is a substitute for direct participation, as well as a desired check on majoritarianism. The legatees of the slogan "Taxation without representation is tyranny!" viewed participation in government as a personal right—thus they viewed representation as representation of *persons* (that is, more in accord with a "standing-for" theory). But they also saw government as the pursuit of interests, especially as a check on factionalism and majoritarianism—and thus representation would be delegated to a small number of citizens in the name of these statesmanlike interests and the public good (that is, more akin to the "acting-for" theory). Yet Pitkin points out that Madison believed the delegatory aspect of federalism did not require more "enlightened statesmen" at the helm—so any tacit notion of trusteeship fell far short of Burkean elitism.

Pitkin's book is a work of scholarly analysis, not partisan advocacy, so we probably should not expect to find an explicit answer to the normative question about what America's representative structure ought to be now. Suffice to say that one could reasonably conclude from her exposition that America's system is best *described* as featuring over time a mix of "standing-for" and "acting-for" components—and yet one could also extrapolate a few steps beyond the trends she identifies in American history. White manhood suffrage was soon regarded as an inalienable right, as early Americans quickly abandoned colonial schema of "virtual representation" in favor of "actual representation"—a demand that led to nothing less than a war for independence. These bold assertions of sacred political rights and declarations of natural equality could hardly be contained within the exclusionary framework in which they were first pronounced: such rights were eventually extended to Native Americans, African Americans, and women. Some Madisonian check-and-balance mechanisms do resemble "acting-for" restrictions on direct participation—but, as Pitkin points out, these were "secondary devices," imposed on top of, as it were, fundamental and expanding commitments to fully participatory enfranchisement.

Whatever hints in favor of our case at hand we might glean from Pitkin's book, we must also note that she does not address the particular issue of age qualifications. Age qualifications present a peculiar "halfway" problem regarding representation. One may gain "active representation" in the sense of suffrage but then will be, as a younger citizen, explicitly barred from running for office (and everyone is thereby barred from voting for certain potential candidates from those underage groups). Pitkin uses the term "popular election" to mean "suffrage" alone, that is to say, the right to vote for representatives—though it could be argued that in the history of American enfranchisement, eligibility for office was assumed and embedded in the right to vote (with the age qualifications as the explicit constitutional exception). The idea of descriptive representation ("standing-for") in which a legislature serves as a "mirror image" of the electorate—or almost any form of proportionate representation—tacitly requires that suffrage already include eligibility for office as a package deal. Otherwise, the right to vote would mean nothing more than the right to vote for a person whose only "resemblance" to you, as a fellow constituent, is geographical. Imagine if in American constitutional history, at the times of the passage of the Fifteenth and Nineteenth Amendments, provisions had been included that granted the right of suffrage but explicitly barred Native Americans, African Americans, and women from running for office (or even barred them from running for an interim period of ten years or so). Surely we would regard such restrictions as an affront to full enfranchisement—and I doubt that anyone, then or now, would try to justify halfway forms of enfranchisement as a wise Madisonian check on direct democracy. If, for instance, blacks could vote but only for white candidates, or if women could vote but only for men, that would surely be seen, and rightly so, as a patronizing and prejudicial form of trusteeship.[81]

Yet few seem to recognize that the constitutional age restrictions are just as prejudicial. The Constitution offers citizens in those respective federal categories—18 to 24, 18 to 29, 18 to 34—suffrage but not eligibility for office. Following Pitkin, however, one wants to say such restrictions partake more of the theory of "virtual representation"—or guardianship along generational lines—rather than "active representation" precisely because elected representatives would be unable to "resemble" or "mirror" or "stand for" younger citizens in any meaningful sense. Such older representatives could "act for" younger citizens' causes or generational interests, but they cannot truly speak or stand for these younger voters except as virtual representatives.[82]

Brian Barry: Intergenerational Justice

Brian Barry and John Rawls have each tackled the thorny normative problem of how to distribute justice across generations.[83] Strictly speaking, justice cannot be conceptualized as a conversation only among the living (Paine notwithstanding), since society is always in the process of population replacement. To talk of a "generation" is merely to abstract away from this continuous process—yet despite all of the difficulties defining and addressing the issue, the problem nonetheless remains of how to conceptualize a just polity over time. Both Rawls and Barry are concerned about their customary contractarian approach as it is applied to the issue of intergenerational justice, since successive generations necessarily have a one-way relationship to each other; thus one generation's bargaining power over another will always be asymmetrical. Yet both Rawls and Barry still recommend deploying Rawls's famous "original position" for imagining how diverse generations might converse with one another and strike agreements in principle upon a just distribution of resources over time. Barry takes issue, however, with Rawls's provision that all parties to the original position are generational contemporaries, even though they do not know the specific (post–original position) generation to which they will all eventually belong. Barry's response is that the original position must feature representatives from all generations, even though a veil of ignorance would conceal from them the identity of the generation to which each belongs. The point, for Barry, is to produce a level playing field among the generational representatives by avoiding situations in which "an earlier generation would always have the whip-hand over a later one in the negotiations."[84]

Neither Rawls nor Barry applies his lofty considerations about inter-generational justice to the particular issue of age qualifications for office, and one may wonder why neither of them examines age qualifications as a practical laboratory for the question of intergenerational justice. Both tend to treat the matter of political generationalism as a question of succession and inheritance passed from the dead to the living and then to the not-yet-living. They do not frame the question, not even as one aspect of the question, as how one living generation should treat another living generation. Both Rawls and Barry clearly regard the matter of intergenerational justice to be immensely important, and both think the solution is to get representatives from various generations, as it were, to the same bargaining table, either through random chance generational selection (Rawls) or through proportional representation (Barry). The problem from our perspective is that they both prefer an imaginary bargaining table for expanding this intergenerational discussion, and thus overlook the prospect of a real one, at least among the generations of the living. Eliminating the age barriers to federal office would, however, open the way to bringing more generational representatives to the real-world bargaining sessions about political justice.

Constitutional Coming of Age: Eligibility for Office as a Fundamental Right

Drawing critically on the works of the theorists I have mentioned, we can now collect and clarify the theoretical case for eliminating the constitutional age restrictions to elected federal office. The classical case for age restrictions—from Plato, Aristotle, and Cicero—was based on an ingrained elitism attributable to and supposedly fixed by nature. That classical naturalism influenced Harrington's, and in turn Adams's, belief that a "natural aristocracy" could be vested in a legislative body, namely a senate, that would be defined almost entirely by way of age requirements—though they distinguished "natural aristocracy" from "hereditary aristocracy," thus insisting on a difference between earned and unearned distinction. Machiavelli's rebuttal of Cicero was not based on some normative appeal to justice or republican equality; rather, his rejection of age restrictions was based simply on a different prudential calculation (eschewing on empirical grounds the wisdom of blanket naturalism) about how best to attract merit into office. Yet even as they shared Machiavelli's political regard for earned merit, Harrington, Adams, and then most of the American framers rejected Machiavelli's recommendation for expanding the applicant pool of political talent, perhaps because, following Harrington in particular, they wished to reconcile biblical notions of eldership election with republican virtue.

The Anglo-American tradition of political-theoretical commentary reveals other significant qualifications to and departures from the Cicero-to-Harrington-to-Adams intellectual trajectory that resulted in a proliferation of constitutional age restrictions. John Locke's broad arguments against divinely inspired patriarchy and his focused insistence on full and equal citizenship at the age of twenty-one perhaps did not prevail completely at the Constitutional Convention of 1787, but Locke's breakthrough contribution to the notion of political adulthood provides a countervailing resource to the propriety of the U.S. age restrictions. We also can detect wayward rumblings about such restrictions, a counter-tradition of sorts, in the writings of Paine, Whitman, and Thoreau. Heeding that extraconstitutional but parallel tradition, Hannah Arendt pointedly concludes, "Strictly speaking, the franchise and eligibility for office are the only political rights, and they constitute in a modern democracy the very quintessence of citizenship."[85]

A few contemporary scholars have attempted to make sense, to give an updated account, of these two "political rights" that Arendt contends are the very quintessence of citizenship in a modern democracy: the franchise and eligibility for office. As we've seen, John Rawls agrees with Arendt on this very point. He declares open access to office to be a "basic" liberty that must be distributed equally among all citizens, and such equal ground rules for citizenship are nothing less than a matter of "justice." Rawls, we noted, makes a strong normative case for eligibility for office as a fundamental (individual) right, while making an extremely weak case for exceptions. Similarly, Robert Dahl, Charles Beitz, and Judith Shklar assert the need for procedural considerations about political equality and civic standing, even though all three authors express certain reservations about strictly egalitarian models—yet much of what they write reinforces Rawls's original normative outlook. Shklar and Hanna Pitkin, contextualizing such claims to normative justice, both read U.S. constitutional history as the assertion and extension of the presumption of a right to actual, as opposed to virtual, forms of (group) representation. Deferred claims for political equality have resonated and cut deeply in American history, and many of the Constitution's amendments are testaments to an expanding spirit of American equality in sharp rebuke to the initially codified exclusions and restrictions. Modern representative democracy would seem now to favor procedural equality and direct representation over classical elitism or even the later, amended version of a "natural aristocracy" as the key to effective republican representation. In short, gathering together these threads of commentary, we might conclude that eliminating the U.S. Constitution's age requirements, distributing the right to eligibility for office equally to all adult-age citizens, and eliminating the vestiges of old-world guardianship and group-based discrimination would seem to accord quite easily with modern conceptions of democratic justice as such principles and practices have evolved in the U.S. context. Such a measure would also serve the purposes of intergenerational justice, as variously promoted by Thomas Paine, John Rawls, and Brian Barry. Overall, we might want to declare confidently that completing the franchise by granting eligibility for office to all adult citizens is an appropriate, timely, and just thing to do.

Yet I'm not sure the argument made thus far is adequate. It draws upon a linear logic of progress, momentum, continuity, and extension: The age barriers were largely the result of old-fashioned prejudices and naturalized exclusions, which we can now begin to recognize as antiquated and unfairly discriminatory. Thus enlightened, we ought to actualize our principles of just representation in much the same way that we have rectified other constitutionally codified forms of political disability. But I think many readers might rightly resist that narrative logic of principled extension. Were we to eliminate these age restrictions, I suspect many citizens and commentators, young and old, would apprehend (at least initially) the prospect of a twenty-two-year-old running for federal office as something rather *new* and jarringly so, and not merely as a belated episode in the noble evolution of equal citizenship in the U.S. republic. Instead of repairing simply to the established language of positive rights, we need to speak to the sense of novelty that such a measure introduces, an appeal to emergent, unsettled, and new (or rather new) rights claims. Heretofore we citizens in these United States—Arendt and Rawls notwithstanding—have *not* recognized that eighteen- to thirty-four-year-olds have an as yet unrealized right to eligibility for office; and maybe such a form of exclusion, based on age, isn't wholly analogous with previous exclusions and identities based on property, religion, race, or gender. So how do we account for such a *break* from the past, and would acknowledging such a break undermine the case for establishing this right with an amendment to the U.S. Constitution?

Bonnie Honig, adapting William Connolly's analyses of emerging rights,[86] contends that rights campaigns typically draw upon a "chrono-logic of rights," alluding to and invoking for legitimacy a transhistorical universalism that allegedly eluded the full grasp of earlier epochs: "For the chrono-logic of rights puts us into its temporality: 'We are rationalizing and extending this system of rights,' its proponents say. 'This right is like the others that came before it. If you supported equal suffrage for women and blacks, how can you get off the bus here? This is the next stage of the same project.' "[87] The inspiring story that such proponents customarily tell is that of law's anticipated forward progress and the eventual prospect of legal triumphalism and the vindication, once finally codified into law, of a right's claim to universality. Those who don't share the progressive chronological outlook are forced into a reactive conservatism or a reluctant and maybe panicked submission ("I don't feel good about the likely ramifications of this new right, but I have to support it because not to do so is to cast in doubt the legitimacy of all the rights we supported until now").[88] Honig contends that a chronological case for emergent rights rests on a false or overdrawn dichotomy between unwieldy democratic politics and orderly constitutionalism. Instead of looking at new claims to rights as legitimate only if they can be subsumed under older, established, already codified ones—as if the law stood "outside" the people who brought it into being—Honig invites emergent-rights movements to acknowledge the newness and precariousness of their claims (as well as to invite legal scholars to see the ongoing performativity of constitutional law). Their rights claims *will* be experienced, she says, as fragile, contingent, and unsettled. But an ethos of embracing novelty and provisionality can also advance a productively transformed understanding of the relationship between politics and constitutionalism. It can shift perspective, submits Honig, to the political/juridical actor's vantage in the present rather than evaluating political/legal action—as just or not—from the vantage of "time's normativity."[89] Such actors are trying to change the way we see the world, are trying to change the terms of that world, are forming new political identities and forging new political alliances; they are not, in contrast, simply trying to ape their forebears and adhere to an already written script.

What might Honig's analysis mean for the AGE amendment proposal? Overlooking some complications and remainders, I nonetheless remain attracted and attached to the language of positive rights for forwarding the case for reducing the constitution's age requirements for office. Such a right seems best stated, first and foremost, as an individual right: the right of any adult-age citizen to run for elected federal office—as an article of equal citizenship. Next it makes sense to speak in terms of an aggregate of individual rights, a matter of popular sovereignty: the right of voters at large to vote for candidates of their choosing without regard to age (beyond eighteen)—which is another way of saying that the age restrictions eclipse the democratic rights or democratic interests of *all citizens*, namely to vote for the best possible representatives as they see fit. To my mind, it makes less sense to speak of the proposal as an interest-group right, a repair on behalf of "the young" as such. The age restrictions, in other words, do not partially disenfranchise only the young; they partially disenfranchise everyone, young or old, who might prefer to vote for a young candidate in a given election. The nature of the problem an amendment proposal would address, therefore, isn't a question of "youth politics" per se but instead implicates every U.S. adult of voting age. Nevertheless, I do still find compelling the particular story of extending group rights in the history of the United States, from originally codified exclusions and schema of virtual representation to expanding notions of the franchise and equally inclusive citizenship. That said, I take very well Honig's cautionary tale about making a case for extending rights based on "chrono-logic"; moreover, I accept her thoughtful counsel that divesting oneself of such temporalized universalisms, and in turn embracing the contingency of one's claims, can open up helpful resources for seeing the political world anew. It's true, we must concede, that we haven't regarded eighteen- to thirty-four-year-olds as fully enfranchised political actors. It's also true, we must concede, that we don't regard eighteen- to thirty-four-year-olds as members of a coherent identity group. What we are proposing *is* rather new. Asserting a rather new right isn't simply a form of belated recognition, a codification into law, a reflection after the fact, of preexisting democratic wills and energies; it also can be a way—following Honig—of using the law to enact and help produce a more fully just democratic world. In that sense, the AGE amendment, the articulation of an emergent right, would be something of a call to arms, a dare or challenge or summons, directed toward all citizens, a high-minded exhortation that the younger adult citizens among us ought to count and be included as our civic equals, becoming fully enfranchised political actors not simply to ape their elders but to renew the world in possibly unforeseen ways.

A final note: The democratic theorists I have discussed emphasize the normative value of procedural equality in a modern representative republic, and I want to underscore that point here. An AGE amendment would assert the democratic value—a matter of justice—of extending eligibility for office to all adult-age citizens. Younger citizens, previously prohibited from candidacy, would now enjoy a constitutional right to run for elected federal office—or at least they wouldn't be restricted from candidacy on the basis of age. The value of that procedural right implies nothing, however, about outcomes. The "justice" of the proposal does not depend on whether younger candidates actually get elected into office, or whether their voting rates increase, or whether the overall age of Congress declines, or whether youth-friendly legislation starts to pass. The proposal does not presume or vest or assign some special political virtue to "youth" as such. If that were the intent, then it would make more sense to call for generational quotas in Congress or an urgent campaign to get younger voters necessarily elected into office. But that's not the argument here. Earlier extensions of the franchise were never staked on the utility of outcomes: the moral prospect of granting suffrage to African Americans and women did not hinge upon calculations about their eventual voting rates and patterns.

 Politics

In the context of a minimum voting age of 18, we can see no reasonable argument why the candidacy age should not be brought into line with the current voting age.

—The Electoral Commission (UK), 2004

The overall arguments of the preceding chapters could be encapsulated as follows: both the history of the age qualifications in the Constitution and the principles on which they were based are now to be viewed as questionable and maybe even objectionable. In short: the historical record of American constitutionalism and the preponderance of democratic theory reveal decided, albeit geologically slow, movement away from these original kinds of invidious restrictions and preemptory exclusions. Those inclined toward constitutional reform might want to hasten it on the grounds that the citizens of a democracy are equal before the law and thus ought to enjoy as a fundamental liberty the right to vote *and* to run for public office as well as the general right and the freedom to vote for those candidates they think best for elected public office. The bare notion of opening eligibility for elected office to all adult citizens—put very generally—accords quite easily with liberal principles and intuitive tendencies toward procedural fairness, just representation, democratic equality, and electoral competitiveness.

The proposition becomes more complicated, however, when we leave the rarefied realm of normative theory and enter what John Rawls refers to as "the non-ideal" world, a real-time venue of contestable practice that Hannah Arendt associated precisely with politics as such.[1] Under those messy and pluralized conditions, the wisdom of lowering the U.S. age of candidacy may not be as clear as the normative argument might seem to imply. Practical questions, prudential concerns, and matters of implementation now come into play: Why an AGE amendment *now*? What is the right (age) to run, according to U.S. courts? What would the state and local implications be? Is a temporary exclusion from office a form of "discrimination"? Is this a liberal or a conservative proposal? Shouldn't vested stakeholders be given a pocket advantage in politics? Do the age restrictions warrant constitutional repair?

Why an AGE Amendment *Now*?

Demographic Change

Times have changed since the Constitution was ratified. Life expectancy rates in the United States rose dramatically in the twentieth century owing to improvements in public health, nutrition, and medicine. The average life expectancy in 1900 was 49.24; in 2002, it rose to 77.3.[2] In contrast, most of those living in George Washington's America never reached age 65, and the median age of the population was a mere 16.[3] A child born in 1776 in America could be expected to live to 35 on average.[4] Since the founding, the normal human lifespan has thus more than *doubled* (although falling infant mortality rates account for a good part of the dramatic doubling). In light of that altered age variable, one might be tempted to conclude that, if anything, age qualifications should be *raised* instead of lowered, indexed upward to stay tracked with the increase in life expectancy. Conversely, if the original age limits stay in place, their political significance attenuates as overall life expectancy increases. That point about *relative* deprivation, however, misses the real problem with rise in the median age. Namely, dramatically increased life expectancy means that twenty-first-century America, compared with eighteenth-century America, will be in fact populated by many more older persons, both as an increased percentage of the overall population and in absolute numbers. Such rates and numbers likely translate, in a democracy, into greater political clout overall—a compounding variable that now even further reduces the representative significance of younger generational cohorts. The original *de jure* disadvantage, in other words, has become exacerbated (rather than relieved) by *de facto* demographic developments.

In our own time, the postwar "boomer" generation, those 76 million people born between 1946 and 1963, the largest generation ever in U.S. history, is heading into its retirement years. A generational "bubble," moving as a cresting wave along a national population timeline (or as a "pig moving through a python" as demographers have described it), is swelling the relative ranks of the seniors. During the twentieth century, the number of Americans over 65 increased elevenfold, from 3 million to 33 million.[5] As a percentage of the population, the United States has become "grayer" than ever before. Ken Dychtwald calls this aging of America "the most important trend in our time."[6] Moreover, demographers predict that in coming years, these trends toward aging will exacerbate, not abate: by 2035, they tell us, some 70 million Americans will be 65 and older, some 60 million of whom will be elder boomers.[7] The median age in the United States is expected to rise to 39 by 2010 and to 43 by 2050 and could even reach 50 by 2050[8] (which is a far cry from the median age of 16 in 1790). Combine these two demographic variables—greater life expectancy overall and a generation of greater numbers actually joining the ranks of the upper-aged—and the political numbers start skewing heavily in favor of the older folks. In light of these population changes, the original age qualifications in the Constitution start to look like a protracted conspiracy designed to rig the system forever in favor of the middle-aged to elderly, producing a virtual lock, even an entrenched monopoly, on power. In fact, Dychtwald says, after his three decades of deep involvement in the field of aging, that he is utterly convinced that a "gerontocracy" will rule the twenty-first century and that our social-political institutions are woefully unprepared for that prospect.[9]

Indeed, there is overwhelming evidence that our political system is out of generational whack: as I mentioned in the introduction, Congress is getting older and older every session in recent sessions. The 111th Congress is the oldest ever, with an average age of 58.2 for both houses combined.[10] Surely there are a number of factors contributing to this graying of Congress: the graying of the voting public overall, the ever-increasing need for campaign money, and the increased advantages of incumbency owing to more sophisticated polling and computer techniques in the gerrymandering of districts. Yet these numbers and trends also should raise obvious questions about whether such an elderly body can claim to be adequately representing—both procedurally and substantively—the interests of younger American citizens.

Intergenerational Issues

Reading the statistical handwriting on the wall, political analysts have been predicting "generational war" for several years running.[11] It makes sense, at least by the numbers. The pressure between young and old is building. People are living longer, and thus old age pensions and medical care for the retired are absorbing a greater share of the GNP. Social Security cannot stay in the black with fewer and fewer workers supporting more and more retirees. Political scientists, however, have been debating whether age-differentiated self-interest actually translates into predictable patterns of voting behavior[12]—and the voting and polling data, at least those from before the 2008 election, do not reveal well-articulated voting blocs along generational lines—but there is clearly a shift of societal resources upwards: From 1959 to 1990, the poverty rate for the elderly *declined* 56 percent, while the poverty rate among children under the age of 18 *rose* 50 percent from 1969 to 1990.[13] Since 1965, total federal spending on Americans over 65 has increased from 16 percent of the federal budget to 33 percent. Elders, who comprise only 13 percent of the population, receive four times as much federal money as do those under 18, who comprise 26 percent of the population.[14] These numbers would seem to suggest that, politically, the young and the old are barreling toward each other on a collision course: "When our children learn about where Social Security and Medicare are heading, ignorance and apathy will turn to anger," says former U.S. secretary of commerce Peter Peterson.[15] "I believe the young eventually will rebel against tax and other burdens," writes Nobel Prize–winning economist Gary Becker. "They will demand restraints on transfers to the elderly and, possibly, even major modifications in age-discrimination and retirement legislation."[16]

Today, many of our most pressing political, economic, and cultural conflicts do seem to be shaking out along generational lines. Militarism, environmentalism, global warming, education, budget deficits and spending, health care, stem cell research, abortion, stock market investment strategies, and the reliability of other pension plans besides Social Security have all become hot-button issues that, arguably, can look quite different to the young and the old. MIT economist Lester Thurow has voiced his concern that myopic seniors may be wielding too much political power: "All successful societies need to make long-term investments in education, infrastructure, and the basic research that leads to growth industries like biotechnology and new business opportunities on the Internet. How is this going to happen when the largest and most powerful voting bloc is the elderly, who know that they stand no chance of seeing the benefits of these investments?"[17] Thurow's concerns seem to have an empirical basis: During the past twenty years, government investments in infrastructure, education, and research and development have fallen from 24 percent to 15 percent of the federal budget. During the same period, government spending on entitlements for the elderly has grown by 253 percent in real dollars.[18]

Or take war casualties as another hard indicator of intergenerational imbalance: in the Iraq War, over half the casualties were suffered by men and women too young to be in the House of Representatives, over three-quarters by men and women too young to be in the Senate, and at least 90 percent by men and women too young to run for president.[19] From Social Security to combat—it is clear that younger citizens, who have no right to formal representation *as younger citizens*, are shouldering a disproportionate societal burden.[20]

And yet the much-predicted generational war hasn't yet materialized. Studies show that the young more often support higher federal spending for programs that benefit the elderly such as Social Security and health programs than do the old themselves.[21] Younger citizens supported the decision to go to war in Iraq in decisively greater percentages than older ones did.[22] Yet studies also indicate that the young also support higher spending than the old do for the environment, education, space exploration, minority programs, and parks. More and more, according to political scientist Susan MacManus, different age groups *are* giving age-appropriate responses to survey questions about federal policy (notwithstanding the Social Security exception).[23] Still, younger voters haven't staged, or even clamored for, an open revolt against the system, and some commentators are starting to offer explanations why the young haven't yet revolted. Matthew Price suggests two reasons why the young haven't yet revolted: First, he says, the young are politically apathetic, they don't participate, and they lack cohesive clout. Second, the elderly are a "universal interest group" whose current interests may be viewed (by the young) as consistent with the young's *future* interests, which may explain the lack of conflict on an issue such as Social Security.[24]

Note that Price doesn't mention the constitutional age qualifications as a possible root cause for the young's political disengagement

(which isn't to say that an AGE amendment would be a sufficient repair). But imagine the political difficulties facing the young if "they"
attempted to enter the political arena as a voting bloc in order to seek
redress for intergenerational inequities. The AARP has become one of
the nation's most powerful lobbies, thanks to numbers, experience,
organization, and wealth. It has 33 million members and a staff of
twelve hundred.[25] Seniors also belong to other large and powerful mass
membership organizations, such as the National Council of Senior Citizens, the Gray Panthers, and the National Alliance of Senior Citizens.
Even if younger voters could get their act together and form a cohesive
voting bloc and raise sufficient funds to press for their concerns in a
manner comparable to AARP, the system would still be stacked against
them. To parlay their group influence into legislative power, they
would need to channel their energies and direct their monies toward
winning over a critical number of *older* representatives—who then
would need to act against upper-generational interests (and against the
powerful senior lobbies) in order to do right by their younger constituents. In truth, the problem is that the current political system cannot
accommodate a generational revolt. The first step for younger citizens
would seem to be changing the representative structure itself rather
than trying to work in and through it.

Realizing that the current system constitutes a catch-22 for younger
voters who might initially want to repair the country's widening intergenerational imbalances, some commentators have recommended unilateral, top-down, preemptive changes. Paul E. Peterson, a professor
of government at Harvard, has proposed slowing down the increase of
benefits to the elderly.[26] As of 2000, there were almost twice as many
children under the age of eighteen (74 million) as senior citizens (38
million)—and yet federal funds are flowing dramatically to the latter
group while being drained from the former. Although a democratic
government is supposed to respect and reflect the power of majorities,
clearly those under eighteen are not getting adequate representation
under the current system. Peterson suggests solving this problem by
giving children the right to vote. But Peterson presents this far-fetched
idea merely as an exercise, and by the end of his article he admits
that he isn't serious. Unfortunately, he is serious about "the current
imbalance in the structure of the American welfare state and the nation's political incapacity to do anything about it." Peterson's proposal
to enfranchise children came twenty years after a similarly facetious
proposal to disenfranchise the old. In 1970, Douglas Stewart warned
that there were too many older voters and their numbers were growing;

and as a solution, he advocated "that all persons lose the vote at retirement or age 70, whichever is earlier."[27] Both Peterson and Stewart deserve credit for sounding the warning bell, although neither had a solution to the problem.

Philippe Van Parijs, in "The Disenfranchisement of the Elderly, and Other Attempts to Secure Intergenerational Justice," has attempted to give serious and practicable answers to the issue of intergenerationalism.[28] The problem, he points out, is not confined to the United States. The elderly are becoming "too powerful" in a number of countries, especially in Western Europe. Van Parijs asks, "So, how could our democratic institutions be altered in order to reduce the weights of the older generation?" He mentions a family of proposals consisting of various ways to tinker with the age condition for the exercise of political rights. Some examples: one could conceive of statutory parity for young and old; or quotas for the various age groups in representative assemblies; or required proportional representation for the under-twenty-fives;[29] or a general system of age quotas;[30] or a maximum age limit for holding elected office; or simply lowering the age limit for holding elected office. But Van Parijs doesn't find these proposals to be promising, because quotas or lowered age limits would propel young persons into the legislatures "who have had little time to find out what the world is like" and the exclusion of the older would deprive the political system of their services. He believes the main problem isn't the aging of the representatives but the aging of the electorate. Thus Van Parijs wants to concentrate on the age-differentiation of the right to choose, not the right to be chosen (suffrage, rather than eligibility for office).

One possibility, he says, would be to lower the voting age. The minimum voting age for many democracies was still around 25 at the end of World War II. It is down to 18 in most of them, he reports. Some countries have gone further. In Brazil and Nicaragua, voting starts at 16;[31] in Iran, at 15.[32] In Germany, many politicians have advocated lowering the voting age to 16, and some even to 14.[33] But Van Parijs thinks it unreasonable to proceed below certain limits, and any expected impact of lowering the voting age would be offset by low turnout. A proposal more intriguing than setting upper or lower limits to suffrage would be something on the order of Friedrich Hayek's proposal that representatives should be elected every year, for a fixed and nonrenewable term of fifteen years, among the people who reach the age of 40 in that year and only by them.[34] Van Parijs offers this variation on Hayek's proposal: candidates of any age could be elected for renewable terms of four years, but by an electorate consisting exclusively of those who have become 18, 38, 58, or 78 since the last election. But these complicated proposals, while leveling the playing field for different age groups, also reduce the occasions for citizens to express themselves through elections.

Another possibility would be plural voting, weighted with respect to age. For example, the voters under sixty could receive an extra vote each,[35] or an eighteen-year-old could receive a weight of two votes and have that weight reduced by 1 percent every year,[36] or the number of an elector's votes could be proportional to his or her remaining life expectancy.[37] To make this last proposal simpler, Van Parijs suggests that, for instance in the United States, one additional vote could be given for each quarter of a century of remaining life expectancy, so that one would receive three votes at eighteen, two at twenty-seven, and one at fifty-five. But life expectancy rates correlate quite significantly to gender, education, race, and class—so adjusting for age runs up against other inequalities and complications.

Still other possibilities include asymmetrical compulsory voting, such that younger voters would be fined if they do not show up at elections, while older electors would not. Or one could imagine an asymmetrical poll tax to discourage older voters from voting without disfranchising them, or else a poll payment to bribe the young into voting without forcing them to. Or one could devise a system such that each age group elects its own representatives, and therewith, one could require that certain legislation receive a majority among the younger representatives or during important referenda. A final option along these lines would be to target the public funding of election campaigns, using a voucher system that distributes funds to candidates in lower age groups.[38]

For Van Parijs, the best solution probably isn't to disfranchise the old or to devise regulatory mechanisms to check their power. Instead, maybe the best approach would circle back to Peterson's immodest proposal introducing genuine universal suffrage: every member of the population would be given the right to vote from the first day of his or her life. But Van Parijs points out that expanding the franchise in this way doesn't necessarily mean that minors would be required to vote for themselves. A more feasible alternative would be a children's proxy vote, or call it a family vote or a parents' vote. The basic idea is that an adult voter would serve as a legitimate proxy for the number of dependents under his or her legal guardianship. (Van Parijs discusses numerous historical variations on this theme, along with complications, such as whether the mother or the father does the actual voting under a "parents' vote" scenario.) One of the advocates of this plan says that it would reduce "the dictatorship of the present over the future,"[39] but Van Parijs says that this justification for family voting relies on the empirical assumption that adults with minor children in their households will care about a more remote future than other adults. Once again, the viability of a children's proxy vote will depend upon the good graces of their mediating elders.

It is helpful to attend to the full range of possibilities for repairing the growing political problem of intergenerationalism, if only to exhaust many of them as infeasible. In that regard, Van Parijis's comprehensive and comparative approach to the aging issue is certainly instructive, but most of his proposals, in my judgment, are just not politically possible in the United States. Extending the vote to children may have some theoretical purchase in a European context, but not here. Compared with these other "solutions," however, an AGE amendment looks almost like a compromise. It probably wouldn't be very disruptive and surely is more in keeping with American proceduralism. Most of Van Parijs's solutions are "outcome-based" approaches (discounted in the previous chapter). In contrast, lowering the age of eligibility for office doesn't ensure a new distribution of ages in Congress; it doesn't guarantee that younger candidates will in fact run and will in fact get elected, and if elected, will in fact press for legislation in behalf of generation-specific interests. But it would level the playing field, allowing at least the *formal* opportunity for affecting and working toward intergenerational justice—and such equality (and freedom) of opportunity, as opposed to equal outcomes, is surely consistent with American political culture. Expanding the pool of eligible candidates increases market competition, a situation that probably enhances the overall range of proposals put into prominent circulation but also allows heretofore-excluded adult-age candidates to speak in their own behalf. Allowing thus for the possibility of younger candidates and younger elected officials may not be a panacea for all of the impending demographic problems we face, but it is a first step, and a rather obvious one. And until you take that step, you probably cannot agitate credibly for more drastic measures. And yet without altering the representative structure, lesser measures, such as simply imploring the young to vote, start to sound naive.

But back to the question at hand, *why now?*

Technological Change

Every field of endeavor—with the exception of representative politics at the federal level—taps into youth energy and youth culture. The eighteen-to-twenty-nine demographic is considered the prime target audience for advertisers. The age of entry into professional sports gets pushed younger almost every season. Many young minds are at the very forefront of the fast-paced technological world. The old model of democratic politics—a deliberative-discursive model—was based on face-to-face notions of human interaction and negotiation. But that model (or myth) no longer obtains for much of the electronically mediated world that we now occupy. In brief, the world is not only flatter, but also faster.[40] In such a world, many younger persons seem to be cultivating their talents and gaining exposure and experience at ever younger ages[41]—and those new conceptions of talent, energy, and experience probably apply not only to the exceptional candidates for the National Basketball Association but also potentially to exceptional candidates for Congress. Much as the world of commerce lets market forces determine the age of competitive entry, so should competitive democratic forces largely determine the age of political entry. While the founders turned to age limitations as a check on democratic tumult, in today's world of globalized competition we are more apt to question the need for federalized regulation of competitive markets and of such official restraints on speech, persons, and parties, in this case by constitutional fiat.

Military Concerns

We are also living in times of war and terror. Recruiting for the military will be an ongoing national project. For much the same reasons that the age of young draftees became an issue during World War II, the Korean War, and the Vietnam War, we as a republican people should follow through on this continuous if tacit and unfinished obligation to reform the constitutional representative structure with respect to age. If we're going to send young persons off to war, then it is no longer enough that they be permitted merely to vote for older representatives to make those decisions on their behalf yet in their official absence. Besides being a matter of fair representation, it's also an issue of simple stakeholding: Older persons, most beyond the age of military fitness, probably should not have the exclusive right to make the life-or-death decisions about sending largely younger citizens off to fight in the nation's battles. Younger citizens should have at least a chance to sit at the table where those fateful decisions are rendered. The question whether the ages of eighteen to thirty-four are more generally "suited" to militarism than to governance is beside the point. That distinction, often invoked, between young military prowess and eldership rule is false and out-of-date. If certain young persons emerge who, by their talents and wits, deserve a shot as eligible political candidates on the national scene, then it makes little sense that they should be precluded from running simply because they are of an age where they could *also* be fighting on the battlefield.

Worldwide Political Trends

Among the older democracies, only Italy has a more age-encumbered system than the United States (see appendix 1). It is also fair to say that these two countries are clear outliers among the older democracies and that the model isn't being widely emulated among the newer ones. Moreover, Japan, Italy, and the United States are the only countries on the list that do not allow some opportunity for elected representation under the age of 25. For a number of years, 21 seems to have been the common age of eligibility for office, but now that common age has shifted to 18 among the older democracies (a few countries, such as Austria and the United Kingdom, have lowered the age of candidacy from 21 to 18 in just the last few years). Many of the younger democracies are following suit. The trend is quite clear: the world's democracies have been moving in recent decades toward lowering the age not only of suffrage, but of formal opportunities for elected representation as well.[42]

Case Study: Britain

Concerned about lagging rates of participation in its institutions of formal representative democracy, especially among its younger citizens, the British Parliament in November 2000 established the Electoral Commission, an independent public body with statutory authority to review a number of electoral and political matters. The Commission was specifically tasked to investigate a turnout "generation gap" at the polls and at the same time why "fewer than 1% of MPs in the House of Commons elected in 2001 were under 30 years of age."[43] An external lobbying group, the British Youth Council, had publicized such issues as well and pressed vigorously for reducing the age of voting and the age of candidacy. Once established, the Electoral Commission explained its mission thus: "We aim to gain public confidence and encourage people to take part in the democratic process within the UK by modernizing the electoral process." In 2002 the Commission embarked on a yearlong review of the minimum voting and candidacy ages throughout the United Kingdom. The Commission conducted polls, consulted experts, organized public discussions, looked at minimum age requirements at public elections across the country, surveyed international practices, and pursued a case study of the 1995 lowering of age requirements in the German state of Lower Saxony. In 2004 the Commission issued its report, which recommended that Britain lower its age of candidacy from twenty-one to eighteen—but not reduce the age of voting below eighteen, and to keep those two minimum ages, voting and candidacy, coincidental. Even though polls indicated that the public was opposed to lowering the age of candidacy, Parliament accepted the Commission's recommendations, recognizing the age of candidacy to be of "fundamental constitutional importance," and indeed lowered it from twenty-one to eighteen when it passed the Electoral Administration Act of 2006, which went into effect on January 1, 2007.

The Electoral Commission's report focused especially on the following items: international comparators, minimum age limits and maturity, and election turnout and wider participation. The Commission rejected the idea that international practices should be determinative for Britain, but it did think such information was useful and instructive. It found that a "clear majority" (13) of democratic countries worldwide have a minimum voting age of eighteen and that "there is a clear pattern of having the same minimum age for both voting and candidacy" (15). It argued that the widespread acceptance of a minimum voting age of eighteen in the international community should place a special burden of proof on those who wish to lower that age in the United Kingdom, and it added that it was "only fair" to apply the same logic to the candidacy age: "In light of the fact that most of those closely comparable countries also have a minimum candidacy age of 18, it could reasonably be argued that the onus in the UK is on those seeking to make the case for retaining the current minimum age of 21" (17).

The Commission looked at a wide variety of legal minimum ages (marriage, joining the armed forces, liability for taxation, and so on) and the reasons for those various limits. Many of those reasons, it submitted, would "clearly be unacceptable" in relation to electoral matters, since voting and candidacy involve basic rights of adult citizenship. The Commission turned to the general question of "maturity," which is "frequently held to be a fundamental basis on which the question of a legal minimum age should be determined" (23). Many things might be associated with the overall concept of maturity: physical maturity, intellectual development, and social awareness and responsibility or "life experience." The Commission deemed "physical maturity" as having little relevance in the constitutional sphere; intellectual development may be "highly desirable" in voting and campaigning, but that is hardly a criterion to be applied to entitle adults to fundamental rights or not. The notion of "social awareness and responsibility" or "experience" is the only element of "maturity," the Commission argued, worthy of extended consideration with respect to electoral matters. In that regard, "lack of experience," it noted, is the criticism frequently raised by those seeking to maintain or raise minimum ages for holding office. But the Commission noted that one could argue "that it is the capacity to respond to life experiences rather than the quantity of experience that is more important. The number of experiences is of lesser importance than the ability to learn from those experiences that are encountered and the ability to consider and respond to new experiences and information in an appropriate manner" (24).

The Commission considered research evidence that suggests that social awareness develops from the early teens. The question of maturity for politics, then, is one of "sufficiency." The Commission rejected the view that assessing such thresholds could be "framed in exact measurable terms"; such assessments, it reasoned, must rest instead on broad views of society. On that basis, it argued that British society is not yet ready for lowering the voting age to sixteen, nor is that reduction needed or desirable at this time. But the question of lowering the age of candidacy is a separate matter, it held, and the state should be very clear about what maturity means in relation to electoral participation. The main argument to support a minimum candidacy age beyond the voting age is that a greater degree of maturity is required to act as a political representative than as an elector of representatives. They found some merit in the concern that many people might have about the ability of individuals under the age of twenty-one to act effectively in public office. They recognized that those under twenty-one would be less likely to be able to act accordingly, and on the whole might express little desire to run for office. Still, they rejected a blanket preemption of that possibility: "We believe that it is not beyond the realm of possibility that some people of such an age would have both the desire and ability to do so" (26). The Commission insisted on a distinction between eligibility for office and officeholding, such that the two shouldn't be collapsed: "The right to stand as a candidate confers no real powers or obligations in and of itself. Being a candidate merely enables an individual to put themselves before the public for detailed scrutiny to hold political office" (26). In order to screen out unsuitable candidates, the regular electoral process has many advantages, the Commission proffered, over a statutory age ban: "At present, legislation bars all below a certain age from elected office by applying a minimum age to candidacy. Through this means, it is hoped to ensure that a sufficient degree of maturity is evident in all who might become elected representatives. However, the election process itself already provides a far more subtle and flexible mechanism by which the electorate can prevent candidates they consider undesirable or inappropriate from obtaining the power of elected office" (26). Candidates will be screened and nominated by parties, and then they will be vetted and elected by the public. These nonlegislative filters are preferable, the Commission submitted, to crudely disabling legislative age bans. In short, "age should not bar one from electoral office and it should be for the electorate to judge whether a candidate is sufficiently mature to represent their constituency" (27).

But then the question becomes, If age shouldn't be a barrier, why not eliminate *all* age restrictions for candidacy? Why stop at eighteen? The Commission had already determined that broad societal standards, in both the United Kingdom and the international democratic community, recommend holding to a voting age of eighteen. It then held that allowing minors to run for office who would be ineligible to vote would be "anomalous." More to the point, the Commission's "most significant reservations as regards a complete abolition of a statutory minimum candidacy age" are that minors haven't finished school and aren't legally entitled to engage in a broad range of other activities; it thus makes sense to disable the entire group. In consultation, a conservative group explained the rationale for "harmonizing" the age of voting and candidacy thus: "In light of our views that 18 is the age of adulthood and that full citizenship commences at that age, it is a logical step for the minimum candidacy age to be consistent. We thus support a reduction of the age from 21 to 18 for all elections. While there may be questions over whether an 18, 19, or 20 year-old has sufficient experience to be a Parliamentarian, we believe that such subjective considerations are best assessed by political parties during their candidate selection process and ultimately by the electorate"

(27). The Commission endorsed recent initiatives toward enhanced "citizenship education" in the schools, but then worried about the inconsistency of "teaching young people about rights in a democratic society during their compulsory schooling years, and then denying them some of the most fundamental rights for two or more years after the end of that schooling" (32).

Parliament created the Electoral Commission largely because of its concern about declining rates of participation among younger people in the formal processes of politics. The Commission thus paid close attention to the potential effects on turnout that lowering the minimum ages of voting and candidacy might prompt (and used their case study of Lower Saxony to that end). But they contended that any such effects would be, at best, indirect and long-term and extremely hard to measure, let alone to predict. Moreover, they insisted that the question of lowering such age requirements shouldn't be staked on turnout considerations at all but, rather, should be determined "on wider principles" (45). They even went further in moving away from such empirical considerations: "It is important we do not get sucked into debates around voter turnout and apathy. Whether or not young people choose to exercise their vote is not the issue. The issue is that young people have the right to have a say in all decisions that affect them" (45). Ultimately, arguments about how lowering the voting age might affect turnout are "largely based on speculation and hypothesis, with strong views—but little conclusive evidence" (48). Similarly, the Commission found little hard evidence that lowering the age of candidacy would actually increase the numbers of younger candidates who put themselves forward for election. Yet they held that it is important to lower the age of candidacy nonetheless, because "even a small number of younger candidates coming forward and being elected would help bring down the average age of elected representatives and help improve the ability of elected bodies to more closely reflect in demographic terms the communities they serve" (48). It would also promote trust in the government, as elusive as that might be. Hence they issued the main directive of their report: "The Electoral Commission therefore recommend that the minimum age of candidacy be reduced from 21 to 18, the minimum voting age currently in force" (63).

Implications of the British Case for the United States

Several insights and inquiries can be culled from Britain's 2007 lowering of the age of candidacy. Britain's successful and recent lowering the age of candidacy (which was already lower than the U.S. minimum age for candidacy for the House of Representatives) ought to put an onus of explanation upon those who might argue in favor of keeping such constitutional age restrictions in the United States. To be sure, the British political system and society do not align neatly with their American counterparts. But the fact that Britain and so many other advanced democracies have explicitly recognized the importance of extending such a fundamental liberty to their younger adult citizens raises obvious questions about our inability or unwillingness to follow suit: Are our younger citizens somehow less capable or less deserving of such a basic republican privilege? Is our system less able to accommodate a bit of youthful competition in the electoral arena? Why are we so tardy in participating in this conspicuous worldwide trend? What accounts for the growing disparity?

The Electoral Commission's treatment of the question of minimum age limits and maturity is instructive. The elusive standards of "maturity" or "experience" are too often invoked to restrict entire blocs of adult citizens from certain forms of political participation, and thus the burden ought to be on the state to explain clearly and precisely what it means by political maturity and how exactly that quality relates to public office. The possible benefit of a blanket ban in order to ensure some amorphous degree of maturity or experience in all candidates is outweighed by the deprivation of a fundamental liberty to large sections of the citizenry. Besides, candidacy alone confers no power. The regular political processes of nominating, campaigning, and electing candidates are adequate, flexible, and preferable screening devices; and they accord with contemporary democratic sentiments. Let the people ultimately decide the proper virtues for officeholding.

Simply transplanting that argument from Britain to the United States probably isn't enough to convince native skeptics. Holdouts might rightfully respond: Experience *does* matter in politics. Aristotle was right: politics is something you learn how to do and how to perfect largely by way of practice; it isn't something you learn simply by reading a textbook or by exercising a personal proclivity. Therefore, an age qualification, as a general indicator of hands-on experience, is a "reasonable" form of political discrimination.

A possible counter to that response is that experience is, indeed, an empirical proposition, and in fact, a good many young adults these days have acquired a significant track record of politically relevant experience by the time they reach 18 or 20 or 24, and certainly by 27 or 29, and without question by their early 30s. Many political campaigns these days are staffed and even run by college-age kids and younger. Legions of high school students are getting involved in neighborhood, community, church, and service organizations. If, as Benjamin Barber and others remind us,[44] the definition of "political" involvement should be expanded to include all sorts of civil associational activity, then we need to realize that we often may be underestimating the political experience, perspective, savvy, and contributions of many of our citizens of the millennial generation—who volunteer their community services more than any other demographic.[45] As well, as a "wired" generation, the millennials are far more experienced than most of their elders in the communication technologies that will continue to inform and direct our politics.[46] It may also be the case that some young individuals, through dint of sheer will, genius, and hard work, can bypass any normal developmental trajectory—such exceptions in politics may provide the right stuff for extraordinary leadership under certain circumstances.

In other fields of endeavor, many individuals have gained considerable experience by their early to mid-twenties. They found successful businesses, fight wars, write novels, raise children, and so on. Those of us who are fortunate to teach in America's colleges routinely see extraordinary students pass through our doors. Many of these students have been elected or appointed to several positions in their colleges or their communities by the time they are twenty-one; they've served in other responsible capacities; they have work experience; they have travel experience; their resumes already feature a number of internships; they are widely read; they have street smarts; they are well spoken; they are already distinguished in a number of ways; they've served already both as team players and as leaders. They are the potential "LeBron Jameses" or "Bill Gateses" of their political generation, but we tend to recognize and cultivate only athletic, entertainment, and business talents at this age.

Some die-hard opponents of lowering the age of eligibility for office might point to recent neuroscientific studies indicating that persons under twenty-five are more prone to risk-seeking behavior, or that the brain doesn't fully mature until the mid-twenties.[47] The appropriate reply to such appeals to scientific categorization is that generic results—typically the mapping of "normal" distributional curves regarding human physiology or cognition—may or may not be determinate for democratic purposes. In some cases or contexts, a democratic people might want the option, for instance, of choosing candidates who are *less* risk-averse—and a younger candidate might seem to be more appealing on those grounds. Moreover, the significance of these research data would certainly need to be weighed against other physiological and psychological studies that clearly indicate that human beings are at the peak of their physical and mental capabilities in other ways—in terms of strength, psychomotor skills, perception, cognition, short-term memory, problem solving, and creativity—precisely during the ages at which the U.S. Constitution politically disqualifies them.[48]

Since an AGE amendment for the United States would merely lift the formal barriers to eligibility for office rather than mandating youth legislative quotas, any prior concern about youthful inexperience could easily be offset by the accumulated wisdom and experience of the electorate at large. Experience for an entire age-class of citizens would not be at issue, because a good number of experienced voters would be voting for younger candidates, should such candidates prevail. Moreover, the demand for "experience" cuts both ways: We do not make it a formal prerequisite that older candidates necessarily have prior political (or business, administrative, or military) experience. Instead, we leave such important decisions to the electorate, operating on the strong assumption that an open, competitive election is crucial to the workings of a healthy democracy.

Finally, this proposal would not undermine the Madisonian system of so-called checks and balances, according to which one set of interests can be weighed against another, refracting almost all legislation through both houses of Congress as well as the executive branch. The basic differences between the respective purviews of the House and the Senate, for instance, issue from the different terms of office (two years versus six), the different schemes of representation, and the different sizes of those bodies. In *Federalist* 39 and 63, Madison reasons that the structure of the Senate will produce a different form of deliberation, and a different kind of statesmanship, owing to its smaller size and greater stability (compared with the more numerous and more volatile House). Those structural differences, and the benefits that presumably follow from them, have nothing to do with the five-year difference in age qualifications.

As in the British report, shouldn't we worry that a democratizing argument about age, maturity, and experience must necessarily extend to minors? Wouldn't this proposal put us on a slippery slope toward giving children the vote and eligibility for office? Wouldn't the high-minded principle behind eliminating "virtual representation" as opposed to "direct representation" apply to children, too?

Britain's answer bears repeating here: minors haven't reached society's recognized age of adulthood, they haven't finished schooling, and they aren't legally entitled to do a whole range of other activities. For these reasons, all of which distinguish them sharply from adult citizens, it makes practical sense to bar them from voting and holding office. Yet the British Electoral Commission conceded that the boundary between childhood and adulthood is arbitrary in the sense that it is socially constructed and may thus evolve and change. In fact, the Commission recommended that the issue of lowering the voting age from eighteen to sixteen be revisited in five years. Once established and drawn, however, clear distinctions between childhood and adulthood can be widely observed and strictly enforced—though the boundaries and justifications may need to be revisited from time to time. An AGE amendment, as proposed, would lower age qualifications for elected federal office, but it would not eliminate the notion of age qualifications altogether—and certainly not for the age of suffrage. The former need not entail the latter. The amendment would need, therefore, to stipulate, as many other democratic constitutions do, that any person old enough to vote for federal office is old enough to run for federal office. The Twenty-Sixth Amendment sets the minimum voting age in the United States at eighteen. If a few other countries decide to lower this age in the near future, it doesn't mean that we need to follow suit, or abandon any and all age qualifications across the board, even for children. Eighteen seems to be a viable and well-settled cultural threshold for American society, mostly because it tracks with our public education system as well as with most age of consent laws regarding employment, contracts, sexual consent, abortion consent, and military service. The reason that these seemingly arbitrary age standards can be justified (or eliminated, or renegotiated) is that they are based on appeals to cultural norms and practices, rather than on panhuman, or transhistorical, or cross-cultural constants.

All of this is to concede freely that any threshold marking the effective boundary between political childhood and political adulthood is going to seem, and be, rather arbitrary. The case herein for lowering the age qualifications to eighteen isn't, therefore, completely analogous with earlier constitutional amendments that overturned exclusions based on race and gender. Those earlier arguments for extending the franchise were largely based on appeals to natural law: adult-age Native Americans, blacks, and women—as fellow human beings—naturally and inherently deserved equal standing before the law.

While many of the claims used historically to justify the age restrictions on holding office resemble the kind of invidious group stereotyping that kept blacks and women disenfranchised for so long in the
United States, that similarity is not the primary justification for an AGE
amendment today. The main "normative" case (from chapter 2, echo-
ing while amending Rawls) asserts a civic economy between the age
of suffrage and the age of eligibility for office: these twin pillars of
democratic standing (or call it republican liberty) ought to commence
coterminously, as a matter of fair principle in our representative republic,[49] and as a positive right or primary good for the democratic electorate at large, namely to be able to vote, free of unreasonable restrictions,
for candidates of their choosing. The "practical" case asserts that the
potential benefits (electoral competition, generational signaling, and
demographic updating) outweigh the potential liabilities (electoral
risk, constitutional instability, and altering tradition). It would entail
that we continue the nominally antidemocratic practice of granting
virtual representation to Americans from birth to age seventeen and
actual or direct representation to everyone else. Which is to say: the
political distinction between childhood and adulthood would remain
operative in the United States, though perhaps sometime in the future
that division might need to be subjected to thoroughgoing review, on
practical and normative grounds.

Some of my U.S. political science colleagues have suggested to me,
in preliminary terms, various research models by which to provide empirical backing for or against the matter of age qualifications, and most
of these suggestions involve a desire to track turnout and participation
rates among younger voters in local, state, or foreign jurisdictions
where age requirements are lower than the U.S. federal requirements.
But I think it is generally wise to heed the advice of the British Electoral Commission on this score: Do not "get sucked into debates
around voter turnout and apathy" in evaluating minimum age requirements, and resist the concomitant demands for "hard evidence" along
those lines. Whether a group of citizens deserves a formal right should
not depend on how often the members of that group choose to exercise that right, and it certainly should not depend on a prediction of
how often they may choose to do so. Besides, such data would be
extremely hard to collect and even then not very useful. In their national study on Young Elected Leaders (YELS),[50] the Eagleton Institute
of Politics at Rutgers University could not identify any correlation,
positive or negative, between younger candidates and younger voter
turnout. Given the crazy hodgepodge of various age requirements

across local and state districts and for various offices, it was not possible to compare exit poll results to measure, for instance, a city commissioner's election in one state against a district representative's election in another state. The data aren't commensurable, and there are too many other very discrete and very local variables—party, place, personality—to be controlled for. One might be tempted to look at the campaign of an actual younger candidate to see whether that fact alone might increase younger voter turnout; or one might try to evaluate against some kind of stipulated standards the success of younger office occupants. But such evidence would need to be overwhelmingly and unassailably conclusive in order to gain enough confidence to preempt and to restrict the choice of a democratic electorate. Yes, in Lower Saxony, the British Electoral Commission discovered when it tried to undertake just such a study, turnout among younger voters seemed to increase a few percentage points in the election immediately following a reduction in the voting age (similar to the U.S. experience in 1972, after the passage of the Twenty-Sixth Amendment). From that datum, however, not much at all follows, concluded the Electoral Commission—not for Lower Saxony, and not for Britain, and, we might add, not for the United States.

Still, one might wish to entertain the plausible conjecture that lowering minimum age requirements would jolt the youth out of their formal political apathy and inspire them, as a class, into greater formal involvement. But it can't be proved, and it doesn't help us decide whether or not younger citizens should be allowed to run for office. About all we can reasonably assert regarding that alleged nexus between formal citizenship rights and the actual and robust exercise thereof is that without the former, one can hardly insist upon the latter. The fact that so many other advanced democracies have lowered the age of candidacy and haven't collapsed should be enough to commence some democratic soul-searching in the United States.

Truth be told, I for one wouldn't expect the results of an AGE amendment to be very dramatic anytime in the near term. It isn't a revolutionary proposal. It isn't a push toward radical democracy. Rather, it is a proposal that works squarely within the framework of the representative system and keeps that checks-and-balances system very much intact. Having said that, I wouldn't expect that many previously age-ineligible citizens would in fact get elected into federal office anytime soon. In fact, very few would—the numbers will continue to favor a veritable gerontocracy in the United States. It would be a rare candidate who could leapfrog from holding no federal office to becoming a serious candidate for the highest positions. It is simply the case that few if any eighteen-year-olds will ever emerge as viable contenders for the presidency. Their candidacies will have a hard time getting off the ground, a hard time getting national exposure and credibility, and a hard time surviving the harsh scrutiny of a national campaign over the long haul. The democratic electorate will still value hard-won and demonstrated experience gained through traditional stepping-stone positions.

The foreseeable short-term effects of this amendment, if passed and approved, would probably be modest. We would probably see some movement toward earlier entry into politics. It probably would have a slight ripple effect downward; a few more younger citizens might run for various local political offices—as candidates for local board elections, municipal commissions, and mayoral positions—which eventually would create upward ripples through the local, county, and state systems. Perhaps a few extraordinary individuals will eventually break the former age barriers for the House and Senate—and someday, maybe, a thirty-three-year-old will be elected president. We would also probably see some symbolic movement toward greater scrutiny and perhaps appreciation of younger citizens both as politically engaged individuals and as members of a potential voting bloc. At the same time, we would probably see growing suspicion of older representatives who presume to be able to speak on behalf of their younger constituents. We might see some younger candidates who emerge as viable candidates for the "wrong" reasons, who gain national exposure not primarily on the basis of their political ideas, talent, or accomplishments but largely through their family pedigrees, personal wealth, or celebrity.[51] The amendment could have this effect in particular cases or overall, thus exacerbating those tendencies in American politics today rather than truly opening the doors for increased democratic competition. But it also makes sense to suppose that if younger candidates were to gain some heavy traction in national races, they would have to prove their political mettle on their own at some point (more so, we would hypothesize, than need older candidates who attempt a late, lateral entry into politics) rather than relying mainly on extrapolitical laurels, connections, and credentials. The early American fear of reestablishing aristocratic family lineages in the New World, as documented by Gordon Wood[52] and Akhil Reed Amar,[53] really should not be reprised as a rationale for denying contemporary eligibility for office to a large group of adult citizens. Indeed, a credible argument can be made that following one's parents in the family business is a common way (not just in politics) of gaining valuable early experience in a particular field.[54] Such familial connections slant what is supposed to be a completely level playing field, but they hardly place us on a slippery slope to restoring noble privileges and certainly don't justify disqualifying *all* younger candidates in order to disqualify a chosen few.

Some doubters might fret that the whole political system, in opening the doors to a few younger candidates, is liable to become more reckless and volatile, slouching toward *neocracy*, government by untested upstarts. The 1968 cult film *Wild in the Streets* portrays a horror scenario in which drug-crazed youth take over Congress and the presidency after the voting age is lowered (surely a cautionary/satirical tale to be put in the context of the debates leading up to the passage of the Twenty-Sixth Amendment in 1971). Similarly, *Prez: First Teen President*, a four-issue DC Comics series published in the early 1970s, chronicles the odd adventures of Prez Rickard, the first teenage president, whose election had been made possible by a constitutional amendment to lower the age of eligibility.[55] Prez fought legless vampires and named a shamanistic Native American to head the FBI. Such pop culture satires surely reflected the fears that the boomer generation youth culture would gain too much political traction. But the worst-case scenarios didn't happen then, and they wouldn't happen now. The Madisonian system would stubbornly retain its checks and restraints, even against occasional electoral excitations.

While disclaiming any hard connection between lowering the age of candidacy and increasing youthful participation in politics, the British Electoral Commission concluded nonetheless "that lowering the minimum age would go some way towards persuading younger people that politicians were treating their views more seriously than they might otherwise do."[56] We, too, might indulge in a few ruminations about the imaginable derivative benefits of an AGE amendment. Opening up the competition for national offices could, quite conceivably, invigorate the system at all levels. Perhaps a few younger candidates could bypass the entrenched party hierarchies that all too frequently reward lifelong insiders for little more than persistence. Yet the payoff, symbolic and otherwise, need not be limited to how many actual younger candidates seriously compete for or successfully gain office. Merely opening the door to youthful participation, to the sheer prospect thereof, would surely put into circulation, and lend greater credence to, a variety of intergenerational or generation-aligned policy issues, ideas, and concerns that otherwise might not receive the same kind of attention. Instead of an older politician purporting to speak on behalf of the putative Social Security concerns of a hypothetical twenty-year-old, you might find actual twenty-year-olds speaking *officially* in their own behalf on that issue, or a public expectation thereof. (As J. S. Mill[57] and Thomas Paine[58] both argued, even if benevolent trustee-minded statespersons act out of noble intentions, it is far preferable to have implicated parties speaking for themselves and representing their own interests.) Imagine a race for a seat in the House or the Senate, or even for the presidency, in which one of the candidates is under twenty-five. It would take only one such candidate to alter the tenor and direction of the entire race—and the unlikelihood of that ever occurring does not mean it should be forbidden.

What Is the Right (Age) to Run, According to U.S. Courts?

The issue of a minimum age requirement for elected eligibility for (mostly) state and local office has been tested and adjudicated in various U.S. courts.[59] The Supreme Court has ruled on the issue of age discrimination in several landmark cases as well, although not with respect to the issue of a minimum age of federal candidacy. It might be helpful to review some of this case history, as a way of clarifying the case for an AGE amendment. Some of the legal reasoning in those cases may apply—and we thus need to read those cases selectively. The very turn to a constitutional amendment presumes, or follows from the acquired determination, that current law is insufficient and that the politics of structural repair or reorientation needs to intervene.

Mancuso v. Taft (1973) established a "First Amendment" basis for the right of candidacy to public office and also asserted "that both candidates and voters may challenge on its face on equal protection grounds a candidacy restriction because of its impact on voting rights."[60] The case involved the right of a local city police chief to run for city office, and the Circuit Court of Appeals for the First Circuit viewed the right to run for public office to be a fundamental right, concluding that it implicates two basic freedoms, the freedoms of individual expression and of association:

> Whether the right to run for office is looked at from the view of individual expression or association effectiveness, wide opportunities exist for the individual who seeks public office. The fact

of candidacy alone may open previously closed doors of the media. . . . In short, the fact of candidacy opens up a variety of communicative possibilities that are not available to even the most diligent of picketers or the most loyal of party followers. A view today, that running for public office is not an interest protected by the First Amendment, seems to us an outlook stemming from an earlier era when public office was a preserve of the professional and the wealthy. Consequently we hold that candidacy is both a protected First Amendment right and a fundamental interest. Hence the legislative classification that significantly burdens that interest must be subjected to strict equal protection review.[61]

Thus the court declared that the basic right to be a candidate for public office is protected by the First Amendment and that proscriptive state restrictions on candidacy would need to meet strict standards of scrutiny. Legal scholar Alexander Bott points out that the court in *Mancuso* cited the U.S. Supreme Court decision in *Williams v. Rhodes* (1968), which also drew a close connection between the right of eligibility for office and the First Amendment freedoms of expression and association: "In the present situation the state laws place burdens on two different, though overlapping, kinds of rights—the right of individuals to associate for the advancement of political beliefs, and the right of qualified voters, regardless of their political persuasion, to cast their votes effectively. Both of these rights, of course, rank among our most precious freedoms." The court in *Williams* had determined furthermore that while a citizen "has no right" to any particular public office, all persons "do have a federal constitutional right to be considered for public service without the burden of invidiously discriminatory disqualification. The State may not deny to some the privilege of holding public office that it extends to others on the basis of distinctions that violate federal constitutional guarantees."[62] Bott mentions the *Mancuso* decision, however, as an *aberration*, since subsequent courts, including the Supreme Court, have not viewed the political right to be a candidate as a fundamental right under the First Amendment and therefore entitled to the strict scrutiny standard of review.[63] Other courts have considered whether state and local eligibility for office restrictions violate the Fourteenth Amendment's equal protection clause. In those cases, a strict standard of scrutiny applies if a "suspect" basis of classification can be shown to exist that distinguishes unfairly between persons in the exercise of their fundamental rights. To meet the substantial burden of proof under a strict scrutiny test, the government has to show a tight fit between the restrictive means and the state's desired end or interest in the restriction. In an age-eligibility case in particular, the government would need to demonstrate, under strict scrutiny review, that, for instance, only persons twenty-five years old and older could perform the tasks of a given office. A lesser standard of review under the equal protection clause is the rational relationship test. The rational relationship test is invoked if a court finds that no fundamental right or suspect classification is involved. This test places a very low burden of demonstration on the government, requiring only that a restriction bear a "rational relationship" to a state interest not prohibited by the Constitution.

As for the history of minimum age restriction cases at the state level, Bott points out that the Supreme Court has not addressed the constitutionality of these clauses.[64] Lower courts have generally applied, he says, the rational basis standard of review rather than the strict scrutiny standard and thereby have upheld age requirements as constitutional.[65] Bott's summary of the courts' rationale accords almost precisely with, for instance, John Rawls's rationale for allowing age qualifications: "These courts conclude that the states have an interest in insuring that the candidates possess a certain maturity so as to enhance the probability that competent and experienced individuals will fill the positions. The assumption is that older people will act more responsibly, effectively, and prudently in public office than people below a minimum age. Such age requirements have been considered as not permanently excluding any candidate since a person who reaches the required age may then qualify to run for public office" (58). The courts have not accepted the argument that eighteen-year-olds who vote should be able to run for office. In those cases, courts disentangle the right to suffrage from the prospect of eligibility for office, contending that the former implies nothing about the latter. Voting for an office is not the same as administering an office, the argument goes—and under a rational relationship test, courts commonly invoke and accept the blanket "maturity" assumption about older persons and their comparative fitness for office (along with the corollary "immaturity" assumption about the prohibited younger persons).

Bott argues, however, that if the courts would apply a strict scrutiny standard to these age requirements, it would be very difficult for a state to meet that high burden of demonstration. He mentions that when a federal district court in *Manson v. Edwards* (1973) required the state to show a compelling reason why a councilperson had to be twenty-five years old, "the state could make no showing that the knowledge or wisdom arguably necessary to fulfill the duties of councilman was absent in all or most persons between the ages of eighteen and twenty-four" (58). An appeals court, however, reversed the decision on the grounds that there was no "suspect classification" that required the strict scrutiny test instead of the rational relationship test. The cumulative effect of these decisions is that states can pretty easily impose reasonable minimum age requirements for candidates. Bott submits that in order to trigger a higher standard of review, plaintiffs would probably have to show that "an identifiable group has been denied its right to a representative candidate by the restriction on candidacy" (59). Proving that a group has been in fact denied a benefit because of the absence of a hypothetical candidate is nearly impossible. The problem is further compounded, says Bott, because "there is no history of discrimination against young people as a class" triggering a suspect class categorization (59).

This last statement is rather curious—"there is no history of discrimination against young people as a class"—especially since Bott cites numerous court cases that have deployed a starkly invidious distinction between the young and the old as the linchpin of the rational relationship test. Yet it seems to be something of an unexplored truism that several courts have repeated. In these cases state litigants invoke a disqualifying generalization against the "immature" or "inexperienced" young adults, and somehow that commonplace designation passes muster as a "reasonable" exception to equal protection (even when all parties know fully well that such "reasonableness" would surely fail stricter scrutiny tests). True enough, it is unclear how one could define "young persons" as an enduring and thus suspect class, a "discrete and insular" entity, that would grant them legal standing on those class-based grounds (as opposed to pressing for individual rights). Yet circumscribing youth as a class becomes an even more vexing proposition if almost any discriminatory practice against young persons can be effectively excused through the "normal life expectancy" or "mutability" loopholes, such that no age-based discrimination would ever constitute a permanent exclusion. But the legal assumption that "young persons" don't face structural inequities, simply as a function of their age, shouldn't go uncontested. If older legislators engage in deficit spending that defers and shifts tax burdens onto younger voters whose interests have not been directly represented at the legislative table, one wonders why that structural exclusion could not be viewed as an example of a discriminatory practice that redounds to the detriment of age-ineligible citizens as a bounded class, a deprivation that cannot be redressed through the regular political process.[66]

Other Supreme Court cases have reinforced the prevailing view that invidious, age-based practices do not deserve suspect class designations and thus are not generally entitled to strict scrutiny tests. *Massachusetts Board of Retirement v. Murgia* (1976) sanctioned a form of age discrimination (of older workers), with the court finding that age discrimination generally deserves less judicial scrutiny than discrimination based on race or gender. Agedness, the state could now argue, involves an objective decline in physical and cognitive abilities, and thus the physiological and psychological demands of a job can be rationally related to age requirements. (*Murgia* also held that the Massachusetts statutory scheme in question did not violate any fundamental right of the plaintiffs.) *Kimel v. Florida Board of Regents* (2000) effectively sealed this view, with the majority declaring emphatically that under equal protection jurisprudence, "age is not a suspect classification." Age discrimination (unlike discrimination based on race or gender)[67] therefore needs to meet only a rational basis review: an age classification in question can be justified by a rational relation to a legitimate state interest and thereby won't violate the Fourteenth Amendment.

Still, the above analytic (if somewhat convoluted) exercise—attempting to evaluate the constitutional age requirements via First and Fourteenth Amendment case precedents—probably leads us into a blind alley and isn't, after all, very relevant or revealing, except perhaps as a cautionary saga. What lessons we can extract from those cases for constitutional purposes is a mixed bag at best: if strict scrutiny tests are applied (and a few courts have in fact done so),[68] state litigants lose, but strict scrutiny tests are seldom recognized either because most courts don't regard eligibility for office to be a fundamental right or because they refuse to recognize a suspect classification for discrimination against youth. Maybe all that can be generally concluded, therefore, is that one can find little in the First and Fourteenth Amendments that can be used as leverage against federal age qualifications in preceding parts of the Constitution. We would need instead to assert the case, *pace* the Constitution, that eligibility for office *ought* to be implicitly recognized as a fundamental right of democratic citizens, on par with the republican right to vote—an acknowledgment that would form the basis and indicate the need for a constitutional amendment as latter-day repair.

What Would the State and Local Implications Be?

If an AGE amendment were to be ratified, would such an amendment affect or influence the minimum age requirements at the state and local levels of government, even if the wording of the amendment didn't refer explicitly to a "fundamental right" to candidacy?

There is no uniform or default age standard for eligibility for local and state office across these United States. Instead, our various state and local governments feature a hodgepodge of age requirements. Forty-four states feature some form of minimum age requirement for the state legislature and the governorship. A few have upper age restrictions. Over the years, some individuals have challenged these restrictions in court, but for the most part, minimum age qualifications, as I have noted, have been widely upheld. One group, Youthelect,[69] has organized an interstate network to challenge this patchwork of state and local age requirements, trying to persuade legislators in the various municipalities and states to rewrite their laws and to amend their respective constitutions.[70]

The U.S. Supreme Court, in *Oregon v. Mitchell*, said clearly that the federal government cannot set election qualifications for the states—so Congress could not, if it wished, simply pass a law to lower age qualifications for eligibility for office at the state and local levels. Nor could Congress pass a law to lower age qualifications for federal elections, since the age qualifications are inscribed in the Constitution. It would take a constitutional amendment to change the federal requirements. But how exactly would such an amendment affect the state and local requirements? Conceivably (following the 2007 British example), an AGE amendment could, in one fell swoop, lower and coordinate age qualifications at local, state, and federal levels—but there'd be little reason to do so (and justifying such an omnibus approach is beyond the scope and intent of this book). My arguments have been tailored to issues of federal representation, and the federal circumstances may not obtain at the local levels (e.g., current issues about municipal sewage disposal may not be breaking in fact into intergenerational cleavages). In my view, the proper venues for challenging and possibly lowering state and local age qualifications are state and local ones, respecting a federalist separation of powers. Hence an AGE amendment (and campaign) would need to stipulate that it would lower only those age qualifications specified in the U.S. Constitution, and thus would be applicable only to federal elections. The agglomeration of state and local requirements would remain intact.

But that proviso raises a host of questions that deserve exploration. If an AGE amendment is an attempt to respond to an antiquated and occluded form of discrimination—akin to earlier campaigns to eliminate original constitutional exclusions—then why not have the courage of one's convictions and propose an amendment eliminating *all* adult-age qualifications for elected office, including the state and local levels? If slavery is wrong at the federal level, it is wrong at the state and local levels. If denying women the right to vote is wrong at the federal level, it is wrong at the state and local levels. If the age restriction is to be eliminated at the federal level, shouldn't it be eliminated at the state and local levels as well?

The answer is that we can indeed distinguish among federal, state, and local levels on this issue precisely because rectifying age discrimination can be distinguished from rectifying discrimination by race or gender. They involve different normative claims. The campaigns against exclusion by race and gender were based on so-called civil rights platforms that were really *human rights* platforms. Granting political standing for women and African Americans was part of a larger, more extensive effort to remedy their historic denigration as something less than full human beings in America. Again (as discussed in chapter 2), the argument for their political exclusion went back to Aristotle: women and slaves could be denied citizenship because they were not full human beings at all. But no one claims that young adults as such are not full human beings. Those who have been denied eligibility for office under the Constitution have still been granted the franchise and all other rights of citizenship. The normative basis for their full inclusion into representative government is not a *human rights* claim, but merely and strictly a *civic rights* claim. In much the same way that John Rawls argued that his notion of fairness was "political, not metaphysical," from which he nonetheless deduced "fundamental liberties" such as the right to vote and the right to eligibility for office, so too are we saying that an AGE amendment would not be grounded in a normative metaphysics about human personhood or human dignity or human equality. Rather, the normative arguments have to do with delimited claims about political fairness, political equality, issues of political representation, and so forth. Thus one can properly relegate those decisions to the state and local jurisdictions without compromising one's commitments at the federal level. For the same reason—that the normative claim is based on political rights as such,[71] not metaphysical or human rights across the board—one could coherently support an AGE amendment without being obliged to support a transnational human rights campaign that seeks to eliminate age qualifications in every democracy the world over.

But could a "federalist" solution be sustained, that is, with an amendment lowering age restrictions for federal elections while leaving the states to determine their own policies regarding political age limits? First, we should note that such an amendment would not trigger a federal-state electoral crisis along the lines created by the *Oregon v. Mitchell* decision. Having different age qualifications for federal versus state and local office would not require separate ballots, separate voting machines, or separate elections, as would have been the case if the states had not also lowered their voting ages to eighteen when the Twenty-Sixth Amendment was ratified. The real question is whether an AGE amendment would inspire a rush of state and local challenges to state and local age qualifications by claimants now encouraged and emboldened by the federal example. Could they now stand a better chance of pressing for recognition of eligibility for office as a fundamental First Amendment right or as a Fourteenth Amendment equal protection case? It's possible. My guess is that some individuals might be more inclined to make this case if an AGE amendment were to pass, but such arguments wouldn't necessarily go very far in state courts. True, judges might be marginally more inclined to recognize an implicit "fundamental right" to candidacy at the state and local levels, now discerning the background logic of the federal amendment. Yet lowering the constitutional age requirements would not bestow a new class of positive rights on eighteen- to thirty-four-year-olds across the board; it would merely lower an explicit and specified bar. It thus wouldn't set any *explicit* principle or precedent for state and local cases—the amendment wouldn't *say* that all adult citizens enjoy a fundamental right to candidacy—so that any influence would be through judicial osmosis and interpretive transference rather than by constitutional decree and mechanism. Moreover, we have ample precedent that such differentiated federal versus state standards do not necessarily establish an implicit or spillover precedent. The Constitution's stipulation that the highest federal executive must be "natural born" has not prompted any states to follow suit for their constitutional requirements for governorships, and several states have in fact elected foreign-born governors. As well, after its passage several state and federal courts held that the Twenty-Sixth Amendment did not impact various local, state, or tribal voting ages.[72] In sum: the founders' federalist idea of "unmixed and extensive republics"[73] isn't so difficult to grasp and maintain (on some issues).

Is a Temporary Exclusion from Office a Form of Discrimination?

The "not-a-permanent exclusion" argument is a standard refrain: the young will eventually get their chance. A minimum age qualification isn't, according to this view, analogous to forms of permanently exclusionary discrimination, such as those based on race or gender. In the language of the courts, an age group doesn't constitute "a discrete and insular" entity but, instead, is a "fluid group of which everyone will become a member."[74]

But imagine if one tried to apply the "not-a-permanent exclusion" rationale symmetrically, namely, to *maximum* age qualifications: because old people have already had their chance earlier in life (even if they chose to pass it up at the time), it is acceptable to exclude them from eligibility for office past a certain age. Most of us would probably reject this reasoning as a transparent rationalization of age discrimination. Why we don't see this logic as faulty and insidious when applied to age discrimination against younger adults is a good question. As I suggested in chapter 2, the "not-a-permanent exclusion" rationale (or rationalization) of minimum age requirements naturalizes discrimination through the legerdemain of a "normal life course" trajectory that allegedly applies to all persons. Such is, after all, a specious way of trying to explain and justify the official exclusion of entire blocs of adult citizens, namely by excusing the present discriminatory act through the promise of future compensation. The "not-a-permanent exclusion" argument should be challenged and probably discredited as a ploy to keep the young in their place. Discrimination on the basis of race or gender is not ameliorated one iota by the deconstruction of stable racial identity based on genetics or the possibility of gender-reassignment surgery. Discrimination on the basis of religious creed is not ameliorated one iota by the argument that a believer *could* convert, if he or she really wished to, thereby avoiding the discriminatory exclusion and rendering it as something other than permanent. Group discrimination is group discrimination, wherever it occurs. We should be mightily suspicious about any attempt to justify it, and the burden of doing so should fall fully and heavily on those who advocate it.

The "not-a-permanent exclusion" or "you'll get your day" argument also dovetails with the epistemic claim that favors the accumulated wisdom of elders. Elders benefit, the argument goes, from a kind of Hegelian or DuBoisian "double-consciousness": since they've lived through their younger years, they now have the advantage of seeing things from the perspectives of both the young and the old. Of course that basic point can be affirmed as a truism, generally according with common developmental accounts of the stages of a "normal life course" for adulthood.[75] Yet the claim oddly inverts the Hegelian or DuBoisian master-serf relationship, asserting that those in charge, the masters, not the serfs, are the ones who uniquely see the world from expanded sensibilities. Eliding such power dynamics, the claim also glosses over the particularly open-ended, unresolved views of the future now held by the youthful underclass: an elderly memory of experiencing such unwritten futures is necessarily skewed or tainted as teleological, as leading eventually to the future that actually became the present at hand. With similar license, one could plausibly posit that the old, with a foreshortened purview of their own futures, are liable to dispense with an other-regarding viewpoint that genuinely cares about the young; they might well presume or conclude that there's little reason to attempt to inform their political judgments by taking into account younger views and interests. All of this is to say that the seniors can't necessarily claim, from a "been there, done that" experiential vantage, to understand fully the plight and purview of a younger generation. Besides, they will never be young again, whereas many younger citizens, looking toward their evolving futures, putting themselves imaginatively and prospectively (if prematurely) in the place of their elders, are perhaps in a better position to develop a vicariously expanded outlook that is more likely to empathize across generations. In sum, such abstractions about epistemic advantage can be construed either way, as favoring age over youth, or for that matter youth over age.

Is This a Liberal or a Conservative Proposal?

Those who see the world of American politics as bifurcated irremediably into a "liberal" versus "conservative" dichotomy might naturally suspect that an AGE amendment constitutes a backdoor plan for installing a liberal youth brigade into the halls of Congress, thus shifting the balance of power in America toward progressive forces. Youth politics are mainly liberal politics, it would be argued, and therefore this proposal will necessarily work to the advantage of liberal interests. Those predictions could come true. The young historically seem to be the bastion of antiestablishment sentiments, and maybe admitting those outsiders into the club would translate effectively into a liberal power grab. Yet the amendment also has the potential to defy the liberal-conservative dichotomy and could, conceivably, generate an appeal that crosses traditional partisan lines—and maybe it would produce new, unexpected alignments. Conservatives of various stripes might find good reasons, both principled and partisan, to support it. The amendment naturally accords with the views of libertarian, independent, and limited-government conservatives, who believe, above all, in increased competition and who also might wish to break up entrenched forms of government power. Libertarian conservatives often advocate applying market principles to governmental practices, and in that light, the original age qualifications would appear to be a form of unnecessary regulation that impedes competition in the political sphere. Limited-government conservatives increasingly lament the growth of entitlements flowing to the retiring boomer generation. It may take a younger cohort of representatives (were they somehow to break through the demographic barriers to win elections) to stem the tide of irresponsible deficit spending and impose fiscal restraint on their elders. Younger representatives, reflecting the on-the-ground interests of the rank-and-file majority of the armed services, might become more sparing in their use of military force—using it only for truly defensive or clearly defined national security purposes rather than as a tool of an aggressionist foreign policy. (Or, depending on the issues, they might become more daring and aggressive.) In other matters—the environment, energy policy, health care, education, infrastructure investment—it may turn out that a significant number of young voters today represent the true Burkean brand of conservative. Instead of being the hedonists or anarchists or subversives of the 1960s, today's youth may prove to be the genuine custodians of the long-range interests of the nation, the true conservatives who fight against the destructive, short-sighted practices of their short-sighted boomer-generation elders.

Despite Obama's 2008 success among young voters, the battle for their hearts and minds is far from over. Conservative organizations have spent far more on outreach to college students—through groups such as the Young America's Foundation and the Leadership Institute—than their liberal counterparts have. "Conservatives are trying harder to hook students," says David Halperin, executive director of Campus Progress, a start-up liberal group that provides seminars and crash courses to strengthen "progressive student leadership." Halperin says that Republican organizations are "taking a group of students and giving them the tools to succeed. With the resources, the training and the skills they have been taught, they can win. They win with smaller numbers."[76] Patrick Henry College is actively grooming young Christian conservatives for political office.[77] In a given election, in a given district, the most attractive candidate for conservatives may happen to be a young conservative (likewise for liberals), so it is hard to say at this point that simply expanding the candidacy options for all voters will necessarily tilt the country one way or another.

There are other signs that an AGE amendment could attract support beyond liberal strongholds: Republican presidents were the ones who took the lead in promoting and eventually passing the Twenty-Sixth Amendment, and it was a Republican—Philip English of Pennsylvania—who in 2004 introduced a resolution (H.J.Res. 105) for a constitutional amendment to lower the age of eligibility for the Senate and the House to twenty-one. If an AGE amendment gets off the ground, it's probably safe to say that neither party will want to risk alienating the eighteen-to-thirty-four-year-old age group—so it's not clear that a politics of derogatory labeling would commence.

Shouldn't Vested Stakeholders Be Given a Special Privilege?

The argument lurking behind this question is a serious one. The age qualifications these days serve as the functional equivalent (in a good sense, it would be contended) of bygone property qualifications. Age qualifications are, in other words, a property qualification by other means. A property qualification ensures that government is conducted, literally, by stakeholders. Before the ratification of the Constitution many of the states had property qualifications for suffrage and for holding office, and those state provisions survived in various forms, one of them being the appointment of senators by the state legislatures. It was over the objections of George Mason and others that explicit property qualifications—for suffrage or eligibility for office—were kept out of the Constitution; and any official vestige of them for purposes of national suffrage was supposed to be expunged by the Twenty-Fourth Amendment, which eliminated all poll taxes. While latter-day democratic sentiment widely eschews such politically incorrect signs of class-based privilege, an abiding and countervailing view of democracy regards property as a proper grounding for responsible participation. In his essay, "Politics," Emerson examines this age-old tension between (unequal) property and (democratic) personhood:

It was not . . . found easy to embody the readily admitted principle that property should make law for property, and persons for persons; since persons and property mixed themselves in every transaction. At last it seemed settled that the rightful distinction was that the proprietors should have more elective franchise than non-proprietors, on the Spartan principle of "calling that which is just, equal; not that which is equal, just."

That principle no longer looks so self-evident as it appeared in former times, partly because doubts have arisen whether too much weight had not been allowed in the laws to property and such a structure given to our usages as allowed the rich to encroach on the poor, and to keep them poor; but mainly because there is an instinctive sense, however obscure and yet inarticulate, that the whole constitution of property, on its present tenures, is injurious, and its influence on persons deteriorating and degrading; that truly the only interest for the consideration of the State is persons; that property will always follow persons; that the highest end of government is the culture of men; and that if men can be educated, the institutions will share their improvement and the moral sentiment will write the law of the land.[78]

But Emerson dismisses such wildly romantic democratic views as issuing from "young and foolish persons." Even if magistrates and governors accede to an "ignorant and deceivable majority," they will not, after all, eclipse the influence of property holding in government, nor should they: "Things have their laws, as well as men; and things refuse to be trifled with. Property will be protected. Corn will not grow unless it is planted and manured; but the farmer will not plant or hoe it unless the chances are a hundred to one that he will cut and harvest it. Under any forms, persons and property must and will have their just sway."[79]

The contemporary version of the argument would go thus: Property qualifications are culturally and legally proscribed today. But we still need some kind of check on democratic passions, plus we need real-world incentives to attract serious and productive citizens into public service. An age qualification, it might be said, becomes a virtual property qualification for politics (and, for example, *Kimel v. Florida Board of Regents* explicitly recognizes age as a legitimate proxy for advancing other state interests). As Americans get older, they go through natural life stages that correspond pretty closely with natural economic stages: they get jobs, they marry, they get raises and start accumulating some wealth, they have children, they buy houses and assume debt and gain equity, they start businesses, they invest in stocks and pensions, their savings and net worth grow, and so on.[80] The bottom line is that it is better and wiser to have someone in office who has successfully managed his or her own money than to entrust the finances of the U.S. government to penniless upstarts.

The response to this line of thinking is that lowering the age qualifications will hardly inaugurate into federal office a postadolescent gang of pinko redistributionists. Until we find a new way to reform the expensive nature of financing campaigns or else find a way to reform the entire representative system—neither is likely soon—Congress will remain largely an enclave of the well-to-do. Along those lines it ought to be said that a good number of American citizens these days have indeed accumulated significant wealth by the age of 20, or 25, or 30—the modern economy can and does reward many young persons quite richly. But a more compelling answer may be that the "youth" constitute a different kind of stakeholding that deserves a fair opportunity for official self-representation. For instance, abortion policy is a hotly contested issue in American politics. The age of fertility for most women ends about age 43, with chance of pregnancy declining steadily after age 35. Combine this fertility-age range-limit with the eligibility for office qualification, and the result is a government populated almost exclusively by women who are past the age of bearing children. It could be argued that fertile women are the primary stakeholders in the dispute (the unborn may or may not count as persons, but no one argues that they should qualify as voters)—or at least, however one wants to order the ranking of stakeholding, the interests of *financial* stakeholders is not the first priority in abortion policy by any means. One could make a similar case for the military: the primary or first-line stakeholders in any military dispute are the members of the armed forces themselves. Since the great majority of these fighting forces are under the age of 30, the age qualification for holding office effectively divests this constituency of its fair share of power. The overall point is, focusing on the constitutional age qualifications as a form of legitimate stakeholding narrows the concept of stakeholding to only one kind of stakeholding, namely financial. But once you admit the general argument about stakeholding, then you discover other, equally valid stakeholding grounds on which to reduce the age qualifications as well.

Do the Age Restrictions Warrant Constitutional Repair?

The U.S. Constitution is far from perfect. It contains many inherent design flaws and many definitional ambiguities, and many of these defects appear downright "stupid," especially in hindsight.[81] Constitutional stupidities, however, are to be distinguished from constitutional "evils," such as the original acceptance of slavery.[82] Stupidities are more than harmless but less than tragic, and one must ask oneself whether attempting to correct them will do more harm than good.[83]

Matthew Michael considers the presidential age qualification one of the Constitution's stupidities.[84] He contends that it has certainly prevented any Generation X presidential candidates from emerging, which is, in his opinion, one of the main reasons why there has been little or no public debate on intergeneration issues. Michael focuses exclusively on the presidential age qualification because he sees access to the presidency as key to all policymaking. He doesn't examine or even mention the other constitutional age provisions, let alone their effect on the representative system.

As I mentioned in chapter 1, the only other contemporary author besides Michael (and Levinson) to examine the constitutional age qualifications is William E. Cooper.[85] Cooper contends that all sorts of constitutional stupidities have their origin in the age qualifications— and unlike Michael, he cites all three of them as pieces of a collective problem. He points out that the Constitution is not clear about how to apply any of the restrictions on eligibility for office—native birth (for the presidency), residency, or age. The confusion surrounding the term "natural-born" is well known. The residency requirements have never been strictly enforced—many would-be senators, for instance, have suddenly claimed to be "inhabitants" of a state for purposes of candidacy, even though their established living routines were situated elsewhere. The age qualifications have been strictly enforced, except in the case of Henry Clay, who served in the Senate before he turned thirty. Today, says Cooper, Clay's underage status would not have gone unchallenged.[86] But what if a slightly underage candidate were to be elected—how long could we wait for that person to reach the proper age? The Constitution doesn't specify, even though the age qualifications sound very cut and dried. They have been *interpreted* to apply at the time of swearing in, but there is no explicit provision to prohibit underage *candidates* from running, and winning, and then waiting until they come of age before taking office.[87] How long could they be permitted to wait? The Constitution does not say. Cooper notes that the Twentieth Amendment tacitly acknowledges the possibility that a president-elect may, at the beginning of the term, still fail to meet all of the constitutional qualifications for the presidency, in which case, the vice president-elect "shall act as President until a President shall have qualified." This qualification cannot apply to the birth requirement, of course, but it could apply to residency and age requirements. Cooper reasons that the Twentieth Amendment provides a means by which a slightly underage president-elect could assume the office after some delay, but there are no corresponding provisions for new members of the House and Senate.

Suppose a major political party in a particular state wanted to nominate a slightly underage but otherwise dynamic candidate for an office that he or she is one year too young to hold. An open Senate seat, for example, represents an opportunity that might not come around again for six years. An extremely attractive and ambitious candidate may not wish to wait that long. So like Joe Biden or Henry Clay, such an individual might be tempted to push the constitutional envelope to avoid waiting two, four, or six years for the next election.

Yet the age qualifications present other, more serious inconsistencies and questions, says Cooper. If the main rationale for age qualifications is to ensure maturity of judgment, then why does the Constitution restrict the age of elected officials but not appointed ones? Why not ensure maturity of judgment for, for instance, justices of the Supreme Court or ambassadors and cabinet members? The arguments for age requirements lose credibility by their selective application throughout the Constitution.

Cooper considers the inconsistency of the age qualifications a design flaw that in the event a president is incapacitated could produce confusion and havoc, even provoke a constitutional crisis, at a most inopportune time. The Twelfth Amendment clearly states that the vice president must also meet the minimum age for holding the presidency. But others in the line of presidential succession, from the Speaker of the House to the president pro tempore of the Senate and on down the line, might not meet the presidential age qualifications and thus could not serve as president—a potential crisis not handled by the Constitution or by existing succession law.[88] Would we pass over a capable but age-ineligible Speaker of the House in order to elevate a thirty-six-year-old president pro tempore of the Senate to the presidency, or would the entire order of succession be rendered illegitimate thereafter? This flaw of the Constitution, owing directly to the inconsistent age requirements, could result in just such a constitutional impasse. While some might think this scenario overly hypothetical, Cooper points out that the Twenty-Fifth Amendment involving presidential succession was passed in 1967 to rectify a problem in the Constitution before a foreseeable but improbable crisis emerged,[89] and is credited with providing for Gerald Ford's smooth transition to the presidency after Nixon resigned in 1974, only seven years later.[90]

Cooper goes so far as to suggest actual language for an amendment to eliminate all age qualifications in the Constitution:[91]

Amendment
Section 1. The age qualifications contained in Article I, Sections 2.2 and 3.3 in Article II, Section 1.5 are hereby repealed.

5Section 2. No person shall be eligible to the office of President or to membership in Congress who shall not have attained to the age of eighteen years.

Nevertheless, Cooper concludes his article by saying that he doesn't think it likely "at present" (writing in 1988) that eliminating age qualifications will gain widespread support, and thus he offers his analysis merely in the spirit of contributing to "informed dialogue." We take exception to that pessimistic appraisal and propose an alternative.

The eminent Yale political scientist Robert Dahl, in his important recent book, *How Democratic Is the American Constitution?* laments the many profoundly antidemocratic aspects of the American system of government. He regards the Senate, for instance, as a quirky enclave that unduly favors small-state representation, the Electoral College as an unwieldy and illogical anachronism, and the idea of judicial review by an unelected and largely unaccountable Supreme Court as based on dubious democratic theory. But he concedes that not much can be done about them. He is especially certain that no constitutional amendment could ever get ratified that would make the Senate more democratic. The small states would never ratify a proposal that would cost them so much political power. "The likelihood of reducing the extreme *inequality of representation in the Senate* is virtually zero."[92] And because the inequality in representation in the Senate will persist for the foreseeable future, the possibility for a constitutional amendment to change the Electoral College is also "virtually impossible."[93] So, according to Dahl, we have reached an impasse. What, then, is the point of his admittedly pessimistic book? On the one hand he believes that significant constitutional change is impossible, but he also wants "to invigorate and greatly widen the critical examination of the Constitution and its shortcomings," so that the public learns not to revere the Constitution as sacred. Even constitutional scholars and political scientists rarely subject the Constitution, Dahl complains, to sufficient scrutiny and skepticism. At the end of his book, he issues a measured, if somewhat wistful, hope for changing the course of American democracy somewhere, somehow, sometime in the distant future: "I can envision the possibility . . . of a gradually expanding discussion that begins in scholarly circles, moves outward to the media and intellectuals more generally, and after some years begins to engage a wider public. I cannot say what the outcome might be. But surely it would heighten understanding of the relevance of democratic ideas to the constitution of a democratic country, and specifically of the existing constitution viewed from that perspective and of the possibilities of change."[94]

Dahl makes absolutely no mention of the constitutional age qualifications that explicitly restrict access to elected office.[95] He analyzes the Senate as an enclave granting woefully unequal privileges on the basis of geography, but he does not assess that body in terms of generational privilege. Dahl's oversights notwithstanding, we should apply his general common sense to the present issue: Is it reasonable to think that such an amendment could ever come about? Even if the issue of age discrimination in the Constitution were to reach some level of public currency, how likely would it be for an amendment to pass through Congress and be ratified by the states into law?

With the uphill nature of passing *any* constitutional amendment in mind,[96] I want to outline how such a constitutional amendment could still come about. At the moment, the issue of age discrimination is not even on the national radar screen, but that could change very quickly. In the last several election cycles, a great deal of attention was paid to the youth vote. More than a hundred organizations came forward to research and mobilize the eighteen-to-twenty-four-year-old demographic.[97] In my opinion, these efforts indicate a massive misunderstanding about the nature of the American political system. Our representative democracy is a game rigged against young voters. They probably already know this at some level. They are being treated like second-class citizens in their own country. Why should they (or we) overlook that systemic inequality any longer and pretend that it doesn't exist?

Once you point out the obvious to all of those dedicated people affiliated with those organizations, you might start to initiate some serious discussion about redirecting and refocusing their efforts. Some will find it hard to carry on "business-as-usual"—simply asking youth for their votes yet again—once the argument gets broached that when the young vote, they are helping to perpetuate a flawed scheme of representation that works to their detriment. Yes, opponents to an AGE amendment will undoubtedly voice the predictably dismissive refrains: "The youth don't vote." "The youth are immature." "The youth shouldn't govern." These comments, perceived as self-evident and perhaps put forward without malice, should nevertheless be identified and confronted for what they are, namely, prejudicial slurs. (What else should one call such sweepingly derogatory comments about the political capacities of 70 million adult citizens?)

In a national campaign, I can easily imagine (grant me some speculative license here) a major-party candidate seizing the opportunity to support an AGE amendment, sincerely or not, to attract younger voters to his or her platform and party. That would pressure his or her opponent to respond in kind, for what candidate would dare make a robustly public and transparently self-serving argument *in favor* of the current age qualifications? For either side, supporting such an amendment would be an easy, feel-good, relatively cost-free campaign promise. It would also help preempt and deflect attention away from competing, wedge-issue amendment proposals. In other words, the proposal would be a good attention-getter, a "high concept" with good talking points, and it wouldn't take much for the topic to be introduced into a national campaign. Momentum could build, and a vast organizational advocacy structure is already effectively in place.

Still, individual or even party campaign promises have to translate somehow into actual votes in Congress and in state legislatures—no small task. It's true that the passage of the Twenty-Sixth Amendment was largely an elite-driven movement, introduced and passed by politicians and *not* supported by the public at large or by the youth in particular. Yet it *was* a calculated response to the antiwar movement, and not simply a benevolent gift bestowed unilaterally upon an unassuming public. In contrast, today we do not have a comparable student protest movement that might put similar pressure on elites, even though we as a nation are again at war—and such widespread protest probably won't be forthcoming precisely because of the passage of the Twenty-Sixth Amendment along with the elimination of the military draft in favor of the all-volunteer army. Were such an amendment to be passed by Congress nonetheless, it's not clear why the states would ratify it: there'd be no *Oregon v. Mitchell* conflict with the states to make it in the states' interests to go along with the federal initiative. Normative arguments aplenty can be marshaled on behalf of this proposal, but that's not enough.

In a more perfect world, the members of the boomer generation now in office would somehow find it in their hearts to enact an AGE amendment as their unique political legacy to future generations. That magnanimous gesture could add a nice touch to the normative arguments for passage. But it is hard to imagine them taking proactive, unilateral action on such a measure. It is hard to imagine them acting on such a measure at all until a youth movement—or something comparable to the former Voting Rights Coalition or the more recent British Youth Council—rises to press aggressively for such rights. If several of the youth-voter-outreach groups close ranks and find common cause in calling for a constitutional amendment along these lines, the issue could well draw national attention—and itself could become a rallying cry for youthful engagement and mobilization in politics. Chances are, such explanations of the lacunae in our representative system will find a receptive audience among the young. It could become seen as *the* political linchpin for addressing issues of environmentalism, social security, militarism, and so forth.

But my own view is that this won't be enough. I would *like* to be able to recommend that younger American voters continue to work diligently and in good faith within the system in order to change it—and to consider extraordinary measures only as a very last resort. But sadly, I must agree with Dahl: the chances of successfully working within the system on some key constitutional features to change that very system are virtually nil (at least in the political climate as I read it at this time). Younger voters are not likely to change the representative structure by voting in representatives who would have little vested interest in changing the very system that brings their ilk into power.[98] It's just not likely to happen in the normal course of events.

Yet I can think of another way—admittedly, an extreme, desperate, last-gasp measure—of applying pressure in order to change the political landscape: a boycott of voting (or, call it *civil forbearance*), or the threat thereof. The young, along with the young at heart, could threaten to refuse (and maybe *should* refuse) to participate in a representative system that officially excludes any one of them from becoming an elected representative of, by, and for themselves. At the same time, if they were to organize and threaten such a boycott, they should use every unofficial means at their discursive disposal to explain why they were refusing to vote. It would thus be a *principled* boycott. It would be proclaiming that the system isn't just, change isn't at all likely through conventional methods, and thus we deliberately withhold and withdraw our consent (as latter-day Lockeans). Suppressing the vote through speech and boycott might stand a chance of prompting a legitimacy crisis of sorts, such that elected representatives would feel some pressure to demonstrate their own integrity and the integrity of the system by passing a constitutional amendment that would alter the structure of representation itself. A youth boycott of the U.S. electoral system—with possible reprieves and selective turnouts for particular candidates who vigorously support an amendment lowering the constitutional age barriers[99]—would draw attention to the very problem that needs correction. The threat alone might get people to take the issue seriously. Right-minded (and opportunistic) elites, responding to growing pressure, might just eventually take action and change the rules of the game. Getting such an amendment through the states might take redoubled efforts, and I can't see much of anything happening without sustained pressure, outcry, and righteous indignation from below (below thirty-five years old, that is). A youth movement, coalescing around the prospect of a constitutional amendment and galvanized by way of boycotting speech and action, is probably necessary at both the federal and state levels—to demonstrate with some dramatic force that the normative and historical claims of justice are backed by resolve, commitment, even resentment and anger. In a time again of war, it is not inconceivable that another youth movement, demanding greater representative fairness in the political process, could get off the ground and make a difference.

Part of me, I will freely admit, is skittish about urging the young to boycott the ballot box. Who am I to make such a recommendation? Well past any constitutional age prohibition myself, I cannot and do not presume to speak on behalf of voters in the affected eighteen-to-thirty-four-year-old bloc.[100] In my own defense, I will say that this book grows out of twenty-five years of close association with many inspirational, eminently capable, and highly qualified young citizens who have populated my classrooms over that span. Privileged to witness firsthand their tremendous abilities and energies while observing their coming-of-age frustrations and looming estrangement from the U.S. political system, I have long pondered this disconnect—and this book is the result of those face-to-face encounters in the classroom rather than the result of any esoteric epiphany. While I believe that a constitutional amendment lowering the age qualifications is necessary and justified and that an election boycott, while extreme, could be a means toward that end, I heartily welcome countervailing concerns as well as alternate suggestions for credible reform. I might point out that a call for a boycott falls short of a declaration of independence—yet an obvious slogan for such a boycott would echo the revolutionary slogan "No taxation without representation." The youthful protesters holding up placards before the Iraq War that read "No War Without Representation" were attesting to the sham, the hoax, the hypocrisy, the insidious nature of the commonplace claim that our government is properly representative. Today, the jig ought to be up, and the days of codified "virtual representation" of adult citizens ought to be over: the franchise alone is not sufficient for generational representation and equal political standing. However you spin it, all adult American citizens should be eligible to participate as potential candidates in well-contested national elections.

Postscript: An Appeal to U.S. Civics Educators

Youth cannot have a very great faith in democracy if we insist that they have to be denied some of the privileges of democracy in order to protect it.

—Homer P. Rainey, President, University of Texas, "Education for Citizenship" (1943)

Democratic action operates in the transitory realm that Hannah Arendt called the gap between the past and future, the spatial-temporal lag between that which is "no more" and that which is "not yet"—or, to put it yet another way, between that which is known and settled in the faculty of understanding and that which can be only projected in the imagination.[1] The inherent problem with organizing "the youth" as a political force is not simply, as Aristotle would have it, that "they" are inexperienced, shortsighted, and hormonally distracted. "They" as a group also stand squarely in the "gap" of the moving present as described by Arendt; in fact, young adults could be called the epitome or the quintessential embodiment of Arendtian political possibility (she commonly used birthing metaphors and the term *natality* to convey the ongoing sense of the ever-newness of politics, but youthful adults better convey and occupy that political trope than do pregnant mothers as such or their newborns). From the perspective of a young voter in America, by the time you realize that the political system has been shafting you by keeping you and your peers out of office—worse, not even eligible for consideration—you've probably already outgrown or nearly outgrown your official exclusion (and you'll look like an even greater chump for caring after the fact). "The youth," in other words, is a shifting and continuously changing political constituency. This transitory character presents inherent difficulties for taking action as a group. For Thomas Paine, the ongoing problem of political generationalism is *the* problem of democracy itself: "A nation, though continually existing, is continually in a state of renewal and succession. It is never stationary. Every day produces new births, carries minors forward to maturity, and old persons from the stage. In this ever running flood of generations there is no part superior in authority to another."[2]

Concerted collective action takes time to organize, but before it can be organized, its organizers must first understand the system. They must understand where the system may need to change and where the system can be changed in a way that has no exact precedent. Coordinating the understanding, the imagination, and the capacity for action naturally takes some time and thoughtfulness. The youth of the young puts them at a political disadvantage. This shortcoming does not justify barring the young from holding office, but it does help explain why they have not proactively sought to reform the system on their own behalf (as opposed to reactively protesting against its policies). Taking the time to reflect and plan and organize is a place and role that the educators of the young might properly occupy.

Could "civics" educators—American political scientists, constitutional law professors, political theorists, and social studies teachers[3]—actually play a leadership role in American political life today? Could we take an issue that few are talking about and, because of our seasoned insight into political affairs, manage somehow to parlay our classroom and academic ruminations into significant change and lasting effect?

I propose that those of us who study and teach the mechanics and dynamics and aspirations of American government ought to consider advocating (cautiously, not wildly) for the constitutional amendment I have proposed, which might moderately improve our representative system. Turning our expertise in this one instance toward public service, we might become collective catalysts for thoughtful reform. The spirit of these remarks is not to incite partisan activism but, rather, to recall Hamilton's foremost "important question" about our Union, namely "whether societies of men are really capable or not of establishing good government from reflection and choice, or whether they are forever destined to depend for their political constitutions on accident and force."[4] We political scientists, theorists, and educators are certainly well positioned for such constitutional deliberations, and in this case we may recognize a special obligation and opportunity to assert ourselves since the issue affects our most immediate constituency: our students. Those persons sitting in front of our lecterns and seated around our seminar tables belong to a group of citizens that has been constitutionally branded as *second-class*. We can, do, and should help them understand the system, a system we share with them, but at the same time help them understand the possibilities and the difficulties of changing the system—and that much of the burden will fall on them. But we must do our part, too. I am convinced that American

political scientists can and should assume—in Hamiltonian fashion—
the lead role in eliminating this uniquely political form of age discrimination. Once alerted to the problem, it becomes difficult to teach
American government without raising the issue prominently. What's
more, if we don't assume a lead role in the effort, we run the risk of
being seen as part of the problem. I frankly question how long American college-age students will tolerate a double silencing and suppres-
sion of their interests, in both the political arena and in their education
about politics. Outspoken individuals will eventually demand an account from those recalcitrant instructors who, from their position of
authority and power, remain indifferent or dismissive of an issue that
so directly affects their students, eclipsing their status as fully enfranchised citizens. But make no mistake: I think an election boycott may
someday be in order, but not a classroom boycott. I remain convinced
that in the latter sphere, young adults are still encouraged, formally
and informally, to speak their minds and that in academia there exist
not just ample, but abundant opportunities to do so. American higher
education, unlike American politics, features no official age barriers for
full participation by all otherwise qualified adults.

There is no need to trust my judgment, however, on whether our
elected officials adequately represent those citizens barred by age from
holding office. Ask your students.

Appendix 1: Federal Age Requirements in Other Democracies

Advanced Democracies

Country	Voting age	Lower house	Upper house	Executive office
			Age requirement for holding office	
Australia	18	21	21	None (appointed by British monarch)
Austria	16	18	Not specified (appointed)	35
Belgium	18	21	21	18 (monarch attains majority)
Canada	18	18	30 (appointed)	None (appointed by British monarch)
Costa Rica	18	21		30
Denmark	18	18		18 (monarch attains majority)
Finland	18	18		18
France	18	23	30 (appointed)	23
Germany	18	18	Not specified (appointed)	40
Iceland	18	18		35
Ireland	18	21	21	35
Israel	18	21		30
Italy	18 (25 for senatorial elections)	25	40	50
Japan	20	25	30	Titular head of state not part of government
Luxembourg	18	21		18 (grand duke attains majority)
Netherlands	18	18	18	18 (monarch attains majority)
New Zealand	18	18		None (appointed by British monarch)
Norway	18	18		18 (monarch attains majority)

Country	Voting age	Age requirement for holding office		
		Lower house	Upper house	Executive office
Sweden	18	18		18 (monarch attains majority)
Switzerland	18	18		18
United Kingdom	18	18		18 (monarch attains majority)
United States	18	25	30	35

Note: The abbreviation N/A means "not applicable." If there is no entry for the upper house, the country in question has a unicameral legislature.

Sources: Robert Dahl, *How Democratic Is the American Constitution?* (New Haven: Yale University Press, 2002), table 1, p. 164; Zachary Elkins, Tom Ginsburg, and James Melton, *Characteristics of National Constitutions, Version 1.0*, Comparative Constitutions Project, http://www.comparative constitutionsproject.org/index/htm/ (accessed May 14, 2010).

Other Countries

Country	Voting age	Age requirement for holding office		
		Lower house	Upper house	Executive office
Antigua and Barbuda	18	21	21	None (appointed by British monarch)
Argentina	18	25	30	30
Armenia	18	25		35
Azerbaijan	18	25		35
Bahamas	18	21	30	None (appointed by British monarch)
Bangladesh	18	25		35
Barbados	18	21	21	None (appointed by British monarch)
Belarus	18	21	30	35
Belize	18	18	18	None (appointed by British monarch)
Bolivia	18	25	35	35
Brazil	16	21	35	35
Chile	18	21	35	35
Colombia	18	25	30	30
Czech Republic	18	21	40	40
Dominica	18	21		40
Dominican Republic	18	25	25	30
Ecuador	18	25		35
El Salvador	18	25		30
Estonia	18	21		40
Finland	18	18		N/S

Country	Voting age	Lower house	Upper house	Executive office
			Age requirement for holding office	
Georgia	18	25		35
Greece	18	25		40
Grenada	18	18	None (appointed by British monarch)	
Guatemala	18	Not specified		40
Guyana	18	18		18
Haiti	21	25	30	35
Honduras	18	21		30
India	18	25	30	35
Jamaica	18	21	21	None (appointed by British monarch)
Kazakhstan	18	25	30	40
Latvia	18	21		40
Lithuania	18	25		40
Malta	18	18		None (appointed by lower house)
Mauritius	18	18		40
Mexico	18	21	25	35
Moldova	18	18		40
Nicaragua	16	21		25
Pakistan	18	25	30	45
Panama	18	21		35
Paraguay	18	25	35	35
Peru	18	25		35
Poland	18	21	30	35
Portugal	18	18		35
Russia	18	21	Not specified	35
South Africa	18	18	18	18
Spain	18	18	Not specified	18 (monarch attains majority)
Suriname	18	21		30
St. Kitts and Nevis	18	21		None (appointed by British monarch)
St. Vincent	18	21		None (appointed by British monarch)
Ukraine	18	21		35
Uzbekistan	18	25		35
Uruguay	18	25	30	35
Venezuela	18	21		30
Vietnam	18	21		21

Note: If there is no entry for the upper house, the country in question has a unicameral legislature.

Source: Zachary Elkins, Tom Ginsburg, and James Melton, *Characteristics of National Constitutions, Version 1.0*, Comparative Constitutions Project, http://www.comparative constitutionsproject.org/index/htm/ (accessed May 14, 2010).

Appendix 2: Average Age of Congress Since 1949

Average Age of House and Senate

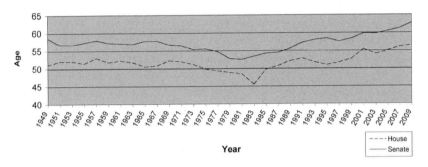

Average Age of Congress

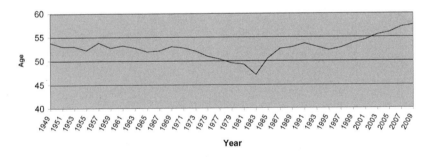

Sources: *Guide to Congress*, 5th ed., vol. 2 (Washington, D.C.: CQ Press, 2000), 840; *Guide to Congress*, 6th ed., vol. 2 (Washington, D.C.: CQ Press, 2008), 840; author's calculations.

Notes

Introduction

1. Michael Connery, *Youth to Power: How Today's Young Voters Are Building Tomorrow's Progressive Majority* (Brooklyn, N.Y.: IG Publishing, 2008); Eric H. Greenberg and Karl Weber, *Generation We: How Millennial Youth Are Taking Over America and Changing Our World Forever* (Emeryville, Calif.: Pachatusan, 2008); Michelle Conlin, "Youthquake Shakes Up Electoral Politics," *Businessweek.com*, January 11, 2008; Damien Cave, "Generation O Gets Its Hopes Up," *New York Times*, November 7, 2008, "Fashion and Style," 1.

2. "New Census Data Confirm Increase in Youth Voter Turnout in 2008 Election," CIRCLE (The Center for Information and Research on Civic Learning and Engagement), April 28, 2009, http://www.civicyouth.org/?p=339.

3. Ibid.

4. Thomas L. Friedman, "Generation Q," *New York Times*, October 10, 2007, http://www.nytimes.com/2007/10/10/opinion/10friedman.html.

5. See Connery, *Youth to Power*, 191–93, and Greenberg and Weber, *Generation We*, 32–35.

6. Neil Howe and William Strauss, *Millennials Rising: The Next Great Generation* (New York: Vintage Books, 2000).

7. Harvard University Institute of Politics, "The 12th Biannual Youth Survey on Politics and Public Service, March 8–26, 2007," http://www.iop.harvard.edu/var/ezp_site/storage/fckeditor/file/pdfs/Research-Publications/springoll0060pline.pdf.

8. Becky O'Malley, "Obama Leads the Way for Young Candidates," *Berkeley Daily Planet*, July 24, 2008, http://www.berkeleydailyplanet.com/issue/2008-07-24/article/30669?headline=Obama-Leads-the-Way-for-Young-Candidates; Carl Hulse, "An Age Shift Brings a Youthful Feel to the Senate," *New York Times*, January 31, 2009, http://www.nytimes.com/2009/02/01/us/politics/01web-hulse.html?_er=1.

9. See appendix 2.

10. At age forty-five, Senator Michael F. Bennett from Colorado assumed office January 21, 2009, as an interim replacement, appointed by Governor Bill Ritter, to fill the seat vacated by U.S. Secretary of the Interior Ken Salazar.

11. Obama was the fourth-youngest U.S. president elected but the fifth-youngest at the time of inauguration.

12. The Socialist Workers Party (USA) ran Linda Jenness in 1972 as its presidential candidate, though she was only thirty-one at the time. In 2004, the SWP nominated Arrin Hawkins as its vice-presidential candidate even though she was twenty-eight.

13. See appendix 1.

14. Sheldon S. Wolin, "Political Theory as a Vocation," *American Political Science Review* 63 (December 1969): 1062–82.

15. Here and throughout the book, I am using the term "normative" advisedly, as a synonym for "prescriptive," thus following a conventional usage in American political science. But I am also aware of the limitations of this commonplace and of the problems of characterizing the writing of political theory mainly as a normative enterprise in this sense. See Hanna Pitkin, *Wittgenstein and Justice: On the Significance of Ludwig Wittgenstein*

for Social and Political Thought (Berkeley and Los Angeles: University of California Press, 1972), esp. 219–21, 228–31.

16. John Rawls, *A Theory of Justice* (Cambridge: Harvard University Press, 1971), 61.

17. Ibid., 223–24.

18. See Peter Levine, *The Future of Democracy: Developing the Next Generation of American Citizens* (Medford: Tufts University Press, 2007), 60–61.

19. See Daniel M. Shea and John C. Green, "Young Voter Mobilization Projects in 2004," in *Fountain of Youth: Strategies and Tactics for Mobilizing America's Young Voters,* ed. Shea and Green (Lanham, Md.: Rowman and Littlefield, 2007), 181–207.

20. Hannah Arendt, *On Revolution* (New York: Penguin, 1963), 199–205. Also see Sanford Levinson, "Introduction: Imperfection and Amendability," in *Responding to Imperfection: The Theory and Practice of Constitutional Amendment,* ed. Levinson (Princeton: Princeton University Press, 1995), 3–11.

21. Article 5 of the Constitution outlines two processes by which the Constitution can be amended. Amendments may be proposed by a two-thirds vote of each house of Congress or by a national convention called by Congress at the request of two-thirds of the states. Amendments must then be ratified by legislatures of three-quarters of the states or by conventions in three-quarters of the states. For some of the hidden complexities of these processes, see William F. Harris II, *The Interpretable Constitution* (Baltimore: Johns Hopkins University Press, 1993), 164–208.

22. Richard M. Valelly makes the point emphatically and eloquently that black officeholding did not follow automatically from black suffrage; in fact, the Fifteenth Amendment included no explicit provision for officeholding because, he contends, Congress chose to drop any such stipulation so as to ensure ratification. Valelly, *The Two Reconstructions: The Struggle for Black Enfranchisement* (Chicago: University of Chicago Press, 2004), 5.

23. Some state courts did deny the link between suffrage and eligibility for office after the passage of the Nineteenth Amendment. See Gretchen Ritter, *The Constitution as Social Design: Gender and Civic Membership in the American Constitutional Order* (Stanford: Stanford University Press, 2006), 48–52. It should also be noted that Jeannette Rankin, the first female member of the U.S. Congress, was elected in 1916, namely, four years before suffrage was extended to women.

24. Americans for a Society Free from Age Restrictions (or ASFAR Youth Liberation) has been advocating for the youth rights since its founding in 1996, though the constitutional age requirements aren't foremost among its concerns. The National Youth Rights Association (NYRA) was founded in 1998 as an offshoot of ASFAR, and it has pressed for lowering the voting age in several states but not at the national level.

25. Judith N. Shklar, *American Citizenship: The Quest for Inclusion* (Cambridge: Harvard University Press, 1991); Robert A. Dahl, *On Political Equality* (New Haven: Yale University Press, 2006).

26. "First, by their very presence, young elected leaders serve as role models and inspirations to other young people evaluating their own prospects. If we believe that youth civic engagement at any level—from simply voting to running for office—matters, then there is value in offering young people examples of leaders from their peer group." Ruth B. Mandel and Katherine E. Kleeman, *Political Generation Next: America's Young Elected Leaders,* Spring 2004, 24–25, http://www.eagleton.rutgers.edu/research/documents/YELPFullReport.pdf.

27. The Czech Republic, Montenegro, Norway, and Dominica have all had prime ministers in their early thirties and younger. Switzerland in particular has elected young parliamentarians.

28. Joseph Smith, for example, founded the Church of Jesus Christ of Latter Day Saints at age twenty-four; and in 1835, the youngest member of the first Quorum of the Twelve Apostles was twenty-three and the oldest was thirty-five.

29. Harry T. Burn was twenty-four and the youngest member of the Tennessee House of Representatives, when, on August 18, 1920, he cast the deciding vote for Tennessee to become the final state needed to ratify the Nineteenth Amendment.

30. In 2003 LeBron James entered the NBA at age eighteen and became a star player almost immediately.

31. Joseph A. Schlesinger, *Ambition and Politics: Political Careers in the United States* (Chicago: Rand McNally, 1966), 176–93.

32. For an up-to-date state-by-state guide to age restrictions on political office, see http://runforoffice.org/.

33. Young Elected Officials Network, "About the Young Electeds," 1, http://www .yeonetwork.org/content/about-young-electeds.

34. Mandel and Kleeman, *Political Generation Next*, http://www.eagleton.rutgers.edu/ YELP/YELPFullReport.pdf.

35. Anna Greenberg, "OMG! How Generation Y Is Redefining Faith in the iPod Era," April 1, 2005, http://www.greenbergresearch.com/index.php?ID=1218; cited in Greenberg and Weber, *Generation We*, 32.

36. Harvard University Institute of Politics, "The 11th Biannual Youth Survey on Politics and Public Service, October 4–October 16, 2006," 12, http://www.iop.harvard.edu/Research-Publications/Polling/Fall-2006-Youth-Survey; cited in Connery, *Youth to Power*, 12.

37. Harvard University Institute of Politics, "The 12th Biannual Youth Survey on Politics and Public Service, March 8–26, 2007," http://www.iop.harvard.edu/Research-Publications/Polling/Spring-2007-Survey; cited in Connery, *Youth to Power*, 13–14.

38. Pew Research Center for People and the Press, "A Portrait of 'Generation Next,'" January 9, 2007, http://people-press.org/report/300/a-portrait-of-generation-next.

39. UCLA Higher Education Research Institute, "Political Engagement Among College Freshmen Hits 40-year High," Fall 2008, http://www.gseis.ucla.edu/heri/pr-display.php?prQry=28.

40. The Electoral Commission, "Age of Electoral Majority: Report and Recommendations," April 2004, http://www.electoralcommission.org.uk/document-summary?asset id=63749.

41. As of the summer of 2009, 54 percent of the U.S. troop casualties in Iraq have been incurred by young American soldiers aged 18 to 24; 78 percent by those 18 to 29; and 90 percent by those 18 to 34. http://www.icasualties.org/oif/Stats.aspx; Phil Ochs, *I Ain't Marchin' Anymore*," Elektra Records, 1965.

42. See Patrick J. Deneen, *Democratic Faith* (Princeton: Princeton University Press, 2005).

43. I've been influenced on this point of a post- (or pre-) political fantasy by Jodi Dean's *Democracy and Other Neoliberal Fantasies: Communicative Capitalism and Left Politics* (Durham: Duke University Press, 2009).

44. See, for instance, Kathleen B. Jones, *Compassionate Authority: Democracy and the Representation of Women* (New York: Routledge, 1993), and Carole Pateman, *The Sexual Contract* (Stanford: Stanford University Press, 1988).

45. See Ralph Ellison, *Invisible Man* (New York: Random House, 1952); Charles W. Mills, *The Racial Contract* (Ithaca: Cornell University Press, 1997); Joel Olson, *The Abolition of White Democracy* (Minneapolis: University of Minnesota Press, 2004); Judith Butler, *Gender Trouble: Feminism and the Subversion of Identity* (New York: Routledge, 1990); Edward Said, *Orientalism* (New York: Pantheon Books, 1978); Martha C. Nussbaum, *Frontiers of Justice: Disability, Nationality, Species Membership* (Cambridge: Harvard University Press, 2006); Dianne Pothier and Richard Devlin, eds., *Critical Disability Theory: Essays in Philosophy, Politics, Policy, and Law* (Vancouver: UCB Press, 2006); and Barbara Arneil, "Disability, Self Image, and Modern Political Theory," *Political Theory* 37, no. 2 (April 2009): 218–42.

46. Kantorowicz notes the erasure of aging in the metaphors of the medieval "body politic." See Ernst H. Kantorowicz, *The King's Two Bodies: A Study in Medieval Political Theology* (Princeton: Princeton University Press, 1957), 7–14.

47. See Margaret Morganroth Gullette, *Aged by Culture* (Chicago: University of Chicago Press, 2004); Kathleen Woodward, *Aging and Its Discontents: Freud and Other Fictions* (Bloomington: Indiana University Press, 1991); and Stephen Katz, *Cultural Aging: Life Course, Lifestyle, and Senior Worlds* (Buffalo, N.Y.: Broadview Press, 2005).

48. Gill Jones's excellent book, *Youth* (Cambridge: Polity Press, 2009) is an exception. Jones challenges various constructions of "youth" and often reveals the underlying power relations sustaining such conceptions: "Intergenerational power relations may therefore be the key to understanding youth. To talk about young people as though they were a social unit, with common interests, strengths and weaknesses at a biologically defined age, is itself an obvious manipulation" (3–4).

49. Randolph Bourne, "Youth," in *Youth and Life* (Boston: Houghton Mifflin, 1913), 12–13. Judith Baer has suggested to me that I should point out that Bourne published this essay when he was twenty-seven, and that he died when he was thirty-two.

Chapter 1

1. Bernard Bailyn, ed., *The Debate on the Constitution*, 2 vols. (New York: Library of America, 1993), 2:1091.

2. Michael Barone speculates that the framers were harking back to British parliamentary history in the seventeenth century, during which time members of the House of Commons could be elected before reaching the age of twenty-one. For instance, Christopher Monck, heir to George Monck, first duke of Albemarle, was elected to Parliament in 1667 at the age of thirteen! He was appointed to several committees and made a speech when he was only fourteen. Barone suspects that the framers wanted to ensure that rich and powerful American families would not be able to concentrate their power as British lords had been able to. But there's no evidence that this seventeenth-century practice was their main concern, and it would explain only the need for setting the age of office eligibility at the age of majority and not for the staggered minimum age requirements beyond twenty-one upon which the framers eventually agreed. Barone seems to be drawing heavily upon Holly Brewer's excellent book, *By Birth or Consent: Children, Law, and the Anglo-American Revolution in Authority* (Chapel Hill: University of North Carolina Press, 2005), 26–27. Michael Barone, "Must Be of Age," *U.S. News and World Report: Politics and Policy*, April 2, 2005, http://politics.usnews.com/opinion/blogs/barone/.

3. Holly Brewer points out some seventeenth-century debates and practices regarding minimum age requirements. Puritans in Massachusetts, she notes, passed the first such minimum age legislation in 1641, setting twenty-one as the age of suffrage and of eligibility for office. Virginia passed a similar law in 1655. In a 1652 pamphlet English activist Gerrard Winstanley claimed that a person is a child until age forty. James Harrington suggested thirty in *Oceana* (1656) as the appropriate minimum age for office. The Royalist Arise Evans urged in 1659 that both the king and members of Parliament be over fifty. After Parliament passed a law in 1696 establishing twenty-one as the age of eligibility, a flood of pamphlets argued for even higher age limitations. In 1699 Virginia passed a law that nullified the elections of all those under age twenty-one and established twenty-one as the age of office eligibility. Brewer, *By Birth or Consent*, 17, 18, 32.

4. William G. Carr, *The Oldest Delegate: Franklin in the Constitutional Convention* (Newark: University of Delaware Press, 1990), 169–71.

5. I use the term "legislative" advisedly here, since in 1787 the framers decided that the executive branch should not be excluded from the legislative process, as had been the model for several colonial state constitutions.

6. Hannah Arendt, *On Revolution* (New York: Penguin, 1963), esp. 215–81.

7. Jeff Broadwater affirms that Mason has a "legitimate claim" to being called the "Father of the Bill of Rights." Broadwater, *George Mason: Forgotten Founder* (Chapel Hill: University of North Carolina Press, 2006), viii.

8. Mark David Hall, *The Political and Legal Philosophy of James Wilson, 1742–1798* (Columbia: University of Missouri Press, 1997), 1. Farrand claims that Wilson in some ways was "Madison's intellectual superior." Max Farrand, *The Framing of the Constitution of the United States* (New Haven: Yale University Press, 1913), 197.

9. Kate Rowland, *The Life of George Mason, 1725–1793*, 2 vols. (New York: G. Putnam's Sons, 1892), 2:184.

10. Charles Page Smith, *James Wilson, Founding Father, 1742–1798* (Chapel Hill: University of North Carolina Press, 1956), 282.

11. *New Hampshire Spy*, November 30, 1787; cited in Rowland, *Life of George Mason*, 2:184.

12. Hall, *Political and Legal Philosophy of James Wilson*, 196.

13. Max Farrand, ed., *The Records of the Federal Convention of 1787*, 4 vols. (New Haven: Yale University Press, 1911), 1:48. Note that these quotations are from notes taken by delegates to the Convention and thus only paraphrase the actual debate.

14. Virginia's colonial political system, Adam Bellow submits, was a "gerontocracy dominated by the twelve-man Royal Council, composed of the wealthiest planters." Adam Bellow, *In Praise of Nepotism: A Natural History* (New York: Doubleday, 2003), 261.

15. Robert Allen Rutland, *George Mason: Reluctant Statesman* (New York: Holt, Rinehart, and Winston, 1961), 86.

16. In a June 1 letter to his son, Mason expresses well his middle-ground point of view: "When I first came here, judging from casual conversations with gentlemen from the different States, I was very apprehensive that soured and disgusted with the unexpected evils we had experienced from the democratic principles of our governments, we should be apt to run into the opposite extreme and in endeavoring to steer too far from Scylla, we might be drawn into the vortex of Charybdis, of which I still think there is some danger, though I have the pleasure to find in the convention, many men of fine republican principles." George Mason to George Mason Jr., Philadelphia, June 1, 1787, in Farrand, *Records of the Federal Convention*, 3:32.

17. Robert McCloskey, "Introduction," in James Wilson, *The Works of James Wilson*, ed. Robert G. McCloskey (Cambridge: Harvard University Press, 1967), 1:1; cited in Hall, *Political and Legal Philosophy of James Wilson*, 197.

18. On Wilson's commitment to natural law, see Hall, *Political and Legal Philosophy of James Wilson*.

19. James Wilson, *Considerations on the Nature and the Extent of the Legislative Authority of the British Parliament*, JHL Pamphlet 44 (Philadelphia, 1774), 9; cited in Bernard Bailyn, *The Ideological Origins of the American Revolution* (Cambridge: Harvard University Press, 1967), 171.

20. Wilson on Blackstone, in Andrew C. McLaughlin, *The Foundations of American Constitutionalism* (New York: New York University Press, 1932), 83–84; cited in Bailyn, *The Ideological Origins of the American Revolution*, 173–74.

21. Farrand, *Records of the Federal Convention*, 1:20.

22. Ibid., 210, 215.

23. Ibid., 211.

24. David Hutchison, *The Foundations of the Constitution* (Secaucus, N.J.: University Books, 1975), 32.

25. Farrand, *Records of the Federal Convention*, 1:375.

26. Holly Brewer argues convincingly that Mason's language of "bargains" reflected a concern about the deficiencies of minors in making personal contracts. She speculates that Mason had read Whig pamphleteer Henry Care's *English Liberties*, a piece published in 1680 which argued that maturity is necessary for elected members of Parliament.

Henry Care, *English Liberties; or, The Free-born Subject's Inheritance* (London, 1680); cited in Brewer, *By Birth or Consent*, 32–35.

27. Farrand, *Records of the Federal Convention*, 1:375. William the Pitt the Younger (1759–1806) was the British prime minister at the time and, at twenty-four, the youngest ever; and he remained prime minister through the French Revolutionary and Napoleonic wars. Henry St. John, 1st Viscount Bolingbroke (1678–1751), was a statesman and writer who was returned to Parliament in 1701, at age twenty-three, as a Tory, and soon gained extraordinary ascendancy over the House of Commons.

28. Ibid., 367, 498; 2:536.

29. Rowland, *Life of George Mason*, 2:124.

30. Farrand, *Records of the Federal Convention*, 2:940; "Yates Minutes," in *The Debates in the Several State Conventions on the Adoption of the Federal Constitution*, ed. Jonathan Elliot (Washington, D.C.; Printed for the Editor, 1836), 1:440; cited in Rowland, *Life of George Mason*, 2:125–26.

31. Rowland, *Life of George Mason*, 2:126–27.

32. Farrand, *Records of the Federal Convention*, 1:69.

33. Ibid., 2:31.

34. Ibid., 99.

35. Ibid., 119.

36. See Robert A. Dahl, *How Democratic Is the American Constitution?* (New Haven: Yale University Press, 2001).

37. *Wesberry v. Sanders*, 376 U.S. 1 (1964), followed upon the decision in *Reynolds v. Simms*, 377 U.S. 533 (1964), which first affirmed the one-person, one-vote principle, albeit for state legislatures. *Wesberry v. Sanders* extended the decision to the U.S. House of Representatives, but not to the Senate.

38. Hall, *Political and Legal Philosophy of James Wilson*, 197.

39. "James McHenry Before the Maryland House of Delegates," November 29, 1787, in Farrand, *Records of the Federal Convention*, 3:147.

40. David Robertson, comp., *Debates and other proceedings of the Convention of Virginia: convened at Richmond, on Monday the 2d day of June, 1788, for the purpose of deliberating on the Constitution recommended by the Grand Federal Convention . . . ; To which is prefixed, the Federal Constitution*, 2nd ed. (Richmond, Va.: Printed at the Enquirer-Press for Ritchie & Worsley and Augustine Davis, 1805), 18; cited in Brewer, *By Birth or Consent*, 35–36.

41. Joseph Story, *Commentaries on the Constitution of the United States; With a Preliminary Review of the Constitutional History of the Colonies and States, Before the Adoption of the Constitution*, 3 vols. (Boston: Little, Brown, 1851), 2:428.

42. An American Citizen [Tench Coxe], "On the Federal Government, and first on the safety of the people, from the restraints imposed on the President," *Independent Gazetteer* (Philadelphia), September 26, 1787, in Bailyn, *Debate on the Constitution*, 1:22. This article may also be found in *Pamphlets on the Constitution of the United States*, ed. Paul Ford (New York: Burt Franklin, 1971), 137–38.

43. An American Citizen [Coxe], "On the Federal Government," in Bailyn, *Debate on the Constitution*, 1:23, also in Ford, *Pamphlets on the Constitution*, 138–39.

44. An American Citizen [Tench Coxe], "On the safety of the people, from the restraints imposed upon the Senate," *Independent Gazetteer* (Philadelphia), September 28, 1787, in Bailyn, *Debate on the Constitution*, 1:26. This article may also be found in Ford, *Pamphlets on the Constitution*, 141.

45. Bailyn, *Debate on the Constitution*, 1:25.

46. A Citizen of America [Noah Webster], "An Examination into the Leading Principles of the Federal Constitution," Philadelphia, October 17, 1787, in Bailyn, *Debate on the Constitution*, 1:132; also in Ford, *Pamphlets on the Constitution*, 31–32 (in Ford, the date for the article is given as October 10, 1787).

47. [Webster], "Examination," in Bailyn, *Debate on the Constitution*, 1:133; also in Ford, *Pamphlets on the Constitution*, 33.

48. Webster, "Examination," in Bailyn, *Debate on the Constitution*, 1:142; also in Ford, *Pamphlets on the Constitution*, 42.

49. Webster, "Examination," in Bailyn, *Debate on the Constitution*, 1:136; also in Ford, *Pamphlets on the Constitution*, 36.

50. Elaine K. Swift sees the U.S. Senate as an American House of Lords. But Swift doesn't account for the differences in those bodies, especially with respect to the American animus against birthright, and she doesn't examine age as a proxy for republican virtue. Elaine K. Swift, *The Making of an American Senate: Reconstitutive Change in Congress, 1787–1841* (Ann Arbor: University of Michigan Press, 1996).

51. Daniel Wirls and Stephen Wirls, in their otherwise excellent book, *The Invention of the United States Senate* (Baltimore: Johns Hopkins University Press, 2004), do not investigate the age issue in the formation of the U.S. Senate, except to speculate that the founders thought a minimum age "prudent" (112).

52. William Smith, ed., *A Dictionary of Greek and Roman Antiquities* (New York: American Book Company, 1843), 864.

53. Ibid., 866.

54. Ibid., 867.

55. Oskar Seyffert, *Dictionary of Classical Antiquities* (New York: Meridian Books, 1957), 573.

56. [Webster], "Examination," in Bailyn, *Debate on the Constitution*, 1:136; also in Ford, *Pamphlets on the Constitution*, 36.

57. Smith, *Dictionary of Greek and Roman Antiquities*, 866.

58. The scholarship on such minimum age requirements in Rome remains contestable. Thomas Broughton, for instance, contended that the first law to regulate the legal age of candidacy and entrance upon office was the Lex Villius Annalis (180 B.C.). T. R. S. Broughton, *The Magistrates of the Roman Republic*, 2 vols. (New York: American Philological Association, 1951), 1:388. Earlier, Theodor Mommsen had claimed that the Lex Villius Annalis didn't directly fix minimum ages; instead, various requirements for extended military service and a two-year cooling-off period between offices were responsible for setting the effective minimum ages thresholds for magistrates in Rome. Mommsen, through indirect evidence, speculated that the minimum age for quaestor was 27, for curule aedile 30, for praetor either 30 or 33, and consul either 33 or 36. Theodor Mommsen, *Römisches Staatsrecht* (Leipzip: S. Hirzel, 1876). A. E. Astin refutes Mommsen's claim the Lex Villius Annalis didn't specify any set age requirements, and Astin also contends that there is a high probability that the minimum ages for aedileship, praetorship, and consulship were, respectively, 36, 39, and 42 (Cicero clearly designates 42 as the minimum age for consulship, he points out). A. E. Astin, *The Lex Annalis Before Sulla* (Bruxelles: Latomus, 1958). G. Walsh submits that the minimum ages for those offices were 31, 34, and 37; cited in John Briscoe, *A Commentary on Livy: Books 38–40* (Oxford: Oxford University Press, 2008), 522.

59. Although Webster wrote this essay almost two decades before his conversion to Calvinism, the general concern expressed in his essay with the need to staff the upper body of a bicameral system with elders could reflect an ambient Calvinism, not to mention the prevalence of Presbyterians in colonial state houses and the army (the Greek *presbuteros* means "elder"). Yet I'm not inclined to push the religious casting to this debate too far, if only because no one during this period seems to have been advocating fifty as the proper age of ruling eldership (drawing on the Levitical age of senior office, based on Numbers 4:3, 8:25–26). David Hume quite explicitly refers to a senatorial system as "Presbyterian government." David Hume, "Idea of a Perfect Commonwealth," in *Essays: Moral, Political and Literary* (Indianapolis: Liberty Fund, 1985), 520.

60. Hume, "Idea of a Perfect Commonwealth," 522–23.

61. H. F. Russell-Smith, *Harrington and His Oceana: A Study of a 17th Century Utopia and Its Influence in America* (Cambridge: Cambridge University Press, 1914); Gordon S.

Wood, *The Creation of the American Republic, 1776–1787* (Chapel Hill: University of North Carolina Press, 1969), 8, 206–14; J. G. A. Pocock, *The Machiavellian Moment: Florentine Political Thought and the Atlantic Republican Tradition* (Princeton: Princeton University Press, 1975), 395.

62. Michael Walzer contends that eldership is underspecified in the Hebrew Bible and that the political function of biblical elders is "enigmatic." Walzer, "Biblical Politics: Where Were the Elders?" *Hebraic Political Studies* 3, no. 3 (Summer 2008): 225–38.

63. James Harrington, *The Commonwealth of Oceana* (London: D. Pakeman, 1656), 231.

64. James Madison, "*Federalist 62*," in Alexander Hamilton, James Madison, and John Jay, *The Federalist Papers*, ed. Clinton Rossiter (New York: Penguin, 1961), 376. William Rawle simply repeats this line from *Federalist* 62 in his 1829 constitutional commentary: "The senatorial trust requiring great extent of information and stability of character, a mature age is requisite." Rawle, *A View of the Constitution of the United States* (Philadelphia: Philip H. Nicklin, 1829), 37.

65. Holly Brewer also cites *Federalist* 63 as possible evidence of Madison's views of the benefits of an age qualification for the Senate—yet *Federalist* 63 doesn't mention the age qualifications at all and instead is preoccupied with the structure of the Senate as a smaller and more permanent body than the House. Brewer, *By Birth or Consent*, 35.

66. Alexander Hamilton, "*Federalist 68*," in Alexander Hamilton, James Madison, and John Jay, *The Federalist Papers*, ed. Clinton Rossiter (New York: Penguin, 1961), 414; Matthew D. Michael makes this point about *Federalist* 68 in "The Presidential Age Requirement and Public Policy Agenda Setting," in *Constitutional Stupidities, Constitutional Tragedies*, ed. William N. Eskridge Jr. and Sanford Levinson (New York: New York University Press, 1998), 67–68.

67. Alexander Hamilton, "*Federalist 35*," in Alexander Hamilton, James Madison, and John Jay, *The Federalist Papers*, ed. Clinton Rossiter (New York: Penguin, 1961), 214.

68. Ibid.

69. Ibid., 215.

70. Akhil Reed Amar, *America's Constitution: A Biography* (New York: Random House, 2005), 159.

71. An American Citizen [Coxe], "On the safety of the people," in Ford, *Pamphlets on the Constitution*, 141.

72. Amar, *America's Constitution*, 71.

73. Gordon S. Wood, *The Radicalism of the American Revolution* (New York: Alfred A. Knopf, 1992), 181; cited in Amar, *America's Constitution*, 163, 554n86.

74. Amar, *America's Constitution*, 71.

75. Wood, *The Radicalism of the American Revolution*, 48; Amar, *America's Constitution*, 162.

76. "Native of Virginia: Observations upon the Proposed Plan of Federal Government, 2 April," in *The Documentary History of the Ratification of the Constitution*, vol. 9, *Ratification by the States: Virginia, No. 2*, ed. Merrill Jensen, John Kaminski, and Gaspare J. Saladino (Madison: Wisconsin Historical Society Press, 1990), 679; cited in Amar, *America's Constitution*, 161.

77. Amar, *America's Constitution*, 163.

78. Ibid., 160.

79. St. George Tucker, *Blackstone's Commentaries: With Notes of Reference, to the Constitution and the Laws of the Federal Government of the United States; and of the Commonwealth of Virginia, in Five Volumes* (1803; rpt.; New York: Augustus M. Kelley, 1969), 1:214.

80. Ibid., 223.

81. James Kent, *Commentaries on American Law* (New York: O. Halsted, 1826), vol. 1, pl. 214.

82. Story, *Commentaries on the Constitution*, 1:427–28.

83. Ibid., 512

84. Ibid., 2:298.

85. Wilson, *Works*, 1:411–12.

86. Actually, there are two others: Sanford Levinson, drawing upon an early version of my manuscript for this book, explores the age restrictions at some length in his *Our Undemocratic Constitution* (New York: Oxford University Press, 2006), 143–45. The other treatment is a humorous one, to be found in Jon Stewart's *America: The Book* (New York: Warner Books, 2004), 40–41: "The Founders did see fit to place three small requirements on who could be president . . . technicalities, really. . . . 3. *You must be at least 35 years old.* Though one would think this was to ensure people seeking the office had the requisite experience and wisdom, in reality the clause again safeguarded against tyranny. The average life span in colonial times was 41.3, so with 35 as the minimum, even a brutal tyrant would have only five, seven years tops, before gout, cholera, and/or syphilis re-democratized the nation."

87. William E. Cooper, "A Reappraisal of Constitutional Age Requirements for Congress and the President," *Congress and the Presidency* 15, no. 1 (Spring 1988): 93.

88. Michael, "Presidential Age Requirement," 67.

89. Ibid.

90. For a fine analysis of the various arguments and perspectives surrounding the Twenty-Sixth Amendment, see Jenny Diamond Cheng, "Uncovering the Twenty-Sixth Amendment" (Ph.D. diss., University of Michigan, 2008), http://deepblue.lib.umich.edu/handle/2027.42/58431.

91. Judith N. Shklar, *American Citizenship: The Quest for Inclusion* (Cambridge: Harvard University Press, 1991), 18.

92. See, for instance, Alexander Keyssar, *The Right to Vote: The Contested History of Democracy in the United States* (New York: Basic Books, 2000), 280–81; Edward S. Corwin, *The Constitution and What It Means Today*, 14th ed. (Princeton: Princeton University Press, 1978), 556; and Wendell W. Cultice, *Youth's Battle for the Ballot: A History of Voting Age in America* (New York: Greenwood Press, 1992), 177–81.

93. David E. Kyvig, *Explicit and Authentic Acts: Amending the U.S. Constitution, 1776–1995* (Lawrence: University Press of Kansas, 1996), 364–68; Benjamin Ginsberg, *The Consequences of Consent: Elections, Citizen Control and Popular Acquiescence* (Reading, Mass.: Addison-Wesley, 1982), 13–14.

94. See Cultice, *Youth's Battle for the Ballot*, 221–25.

95. Ginsberg, *Consequences of Consent*, 11–13.

96. See ibid., 13, and Kenneth Janda, Jeffery M. Berry, and Jerry Goldman, *The Challenge of Democracy: Government in America* (Boston: Houghton Mifflin, 2005), 231–32.

97. Kris E. Palmer, ed., *The Constitutional Amendments: 1789 to the Present* (Detroit: Thomson Gale, 1999), 568; Julia E. Johnsen, *Lowering the Voting Age* (New York: H. W. Wilson, 1944), 110.

98. Johnsen, *Lowering the Voting Age*, 132.

99. Wynell Schamel, "The 26th Amendment and Youth Voting Rights," *Social Education* 60, no. 6 (1996): 374–76.

100. Carl M. Cannon, "Generation 'We'—The Awakened Giant," *National Journal Group*, March 9, 2007.

101. Jane Eisner, "Jennings Randolph's Obsession: Why One Man Worked for Nearly Thirty Years to Secure the Right to Vote for Eighteen-year Olds," in *Taking Back the Vote: Getting American Youth Involved in Our Democracy* (Boston: Beacon Press, 2004), 9–32.

102. Ibid., 377.

103. Senate Committee on the Judiciary, Subcommittee on Constitutional Amendments, *Hearings Before the Subcommittee on Constitutional Amendments on S.J. Res. 8, S.J. Res. 14, and S.J. Res. 78 Relating to Lowering the Voting Age to 18*, 90th Cong., 2nd sess., May 14, 15, and 16, 1968 (Washington, D.C.: U.S. Government Printing Office, 1968), 3; cited in Ginsberg, *Consequences of Consent*, 13–14.

104. Ibid., 11–12.

105. Schamel, "26th Amendment," 377.

106. Louis M. Seagull, *Youth and Change in American Politics* (New York: Franklin Watts, 1977), 31.

107. Keyssar does note that popular groups did form in the 1960s to lobby and exert pressure toward lowering the voting age, including Let Us Vote (LUV) and the Youth Franchise Coalition, the latter an umbrella group backed by a coalition of youth groups, Democratic activists, the NAACP, church organizations, the National Student Association, the United Auto Workers, and some Republicans. Keyssar, *Right to Vote*, 279–80.

108. See ibid., xx–xxiv.

109. Ibid., xxi.

110. Wood, *The Radicalism of the American Revolution*, 145–65; Bellow, *In Praise of Nepotism*, 272–76.

111. One interesting way to flesh out the anxieties animating a nervous patriarchy that is trying to legitimize, reform, and stabilize itself through contract theory would be via Don Herzog's analysis of "masterless men" in sixteenth- and seventeenth-century England, those largely young, single, unattached men who appear as potentially threatening to the received social order. Don Herzog, *Happy Slaves: A Critique of Consent Theory* (Chicago: University of Chicago Press, 1989).

112. Celler wasn't the only one proffering such views. In 1967 the *New York Times* editorialized, "The requirements for a good soldier and for a good voter are not the same. For the soldier, youthful enthusiasm and physical endurance are of primary importance; for the voter, maturity of judgment outweighs other qualifications." Cannon, "Generation 'We,'" 3.

Chapter 2

1. One can find a few passing references in the political theory canon and near-canon to the proper age for holding office. Plato in the *Laws* writes that 40 is the limiting age for holding office for women, 30 for men (*Laws* 785b). James Harrington suggests 30 in *Oceana* (1656). Gerrard Winstanley considered one to be a child until age 40 (1652). Robert Owen, always concerned about pressing youth into work prematurely, also thought that holding office should be deferred to the age of 40 (1813).

2. Robert Dahl, *On Democracy* (New Haven: Yale University Press, 1998), 38.

3. As Marcus Bickford, a delegate to the Constitutional Convention of the State of New York of 1867, argued (in favor of lowering the voting age to eighteen), "Before the flood, when man lived to the age of nearly a thousand years, a child of a hundred was still a child. Afterward we find Isaac emancipating his sons Esau and Jacob at the age of forty. Under the Jewish economy the age of majority was fixed at twenty-five. Now, sir, the age in which we live, in this fast age, men arrive to maturity both in body and mind at a great deal earlier period than formerly." Jane Eisner, *Taking Back the Vote: Getting American Youth Involved in Our Democracy* (Boston: Beacon Press, 2004), 11.

4. See Anthony M. Orum, *The Seeds of Politics: Youth and Politics in America* (Englewood Cliffs, N.J.: Prentice-Hall, 1972). 1. Earlier American youth movements raised very general issues on behalf of the young but weren't pressing for formal political inclusion as such. In the 1930s Eleanor Roosevelt's prominent support of youth rights culminated in the formation of the American Youth Congress (1935), which pressed for the introduction of an American Youth Bill of Rights to the U.S. Congress and issued a "Declaration of the Rights of American Youth" on July 4, 1936 (see http://newdeal.feri.org/students/ayc.htm).

5. John Rawls, *A Theory of Justice* (Cambridge: Harvard University Press, 1971), 61.

6. Dahl, *On Democracy*, 85–86.

7. There are a few countervailing moments in the classical canon. For instance, in Sophocles's *Antigone*, Creon curtly questions whether he should listen to the views of a younger generation, Haemon's in particular: "Men of my age—are we indeed to be schooled, then, by men of his?" Haemon responds, "In nothing that is not right; but if I am young, thou shouldest look to my merits, not to my years." Sophocles, *Plays: Antigone*, trans. R. C. Jebb (London: Bristol Classical Press, 2004), 137 (lines 726–29).

8. See, for example, Gregory Vlastos, *Socrates: Ironist and Moral Philosopher* (Ithaca: Cornell University Press, 1991); Jacques Derrida, "Plato's Pharmacy," in *Disseminations*, trans. Barbara Johnson (Chicago: University of Chicago Press, 1981); Leo Strauss, *The City and Man* (Chicago: University of Chicago Press, 1964); and John Seery, *Political Returns: Irony in Politics and Theory from Plato to the Antinuclear Movement* (Boulder, Colo.: Westview Press, 1990).

9. Aristotle, *Nicomachean Ethics*, trans. Martin Ostwald (Indianapolis: Bobbs-Merrill, 1962), 5–6.

10. Aristotle, *Politics* (New York: Penguin, 1981), 52.

11. Ibid.

12. For Aristotle's influence on Juan Ginés de Sepúlveda and Sepúlveda's influence on the earliest American wars against Native Americans, see Lewis Hanke, *Aristotle and the American Indians* (Chicago: Henry Regnery, 1956); for Aristotle's influence on slavery in the early colonies, see C. Duncan Rice, *The Rise and Fall of Black Slavery* (New York: Harper and Row, 1975), 40–41; for Aristotle's influence on proslavery writers in the periods before and after the Constitutional Convention, see William Sumner Jenkins, *Pro-Slavery Thought in the Old South* (Chapel Hill: University of North Carolina Press, 1935), 40–41, 110–11, 120, 123–24, 137, 290; for Aristotle's influence on mid-nineteenth-century proslavery writers, see James Oakes, *Slavery and Freedom: An Interpretation of the Old South* (New York: Alfred A. Knopf, 1990), 30–31, and Page DuBois, *Slaves and Other Objects* (Chicago: University of Chicago Press, 2003), 19. Jenkins makes the strongest summary of the connection between Aristotle's thought and American slavery: "The Aristotelian influence upon Southern thought was strong and may be traced through much of the proslavery literature. Probably to no other thinker in the history of the world did the slaveholder owe the great debt that he owed Aristotle." Jenkins, *Pro-Slavery Thought in the Old South*, 137.

13. Aristotle, *Politics*, 286.

14. Marcus Tullius Cicero, *On the Commonwealth*, trans. George Holland Sabine and Stanley Barney Smith (Indianapolis: Bobbs-Merrill, 1976), 184–86.

15. Marcus Tullius Cicero, *On the Commonwealth; and, On the Laws*, trans. and ed. James E. G. Zetzel (Cambridge: Cambridge University Press, 1999), 159–60. Regarding Cicero's acceptance of the prevailing age requirements of his day, determined by the Lex Villia Annalis (180 B.C.), A. H. J. Greenidge speculates in a footnote, "It probably accepted the age of twenty-eight for the quaestorship; the minimum age for the consulship in the time of Cicero was forty-three (*Phil.* v. 17, 48); that for the praetorship is quite unknown; thirty-five and forty have been conjectured." Greenidge, *Roman Public Life* (London: Macmillan, 1911), 186n3.

16. Marcus Tullius Cicero, "On Old Age," in *On Old Age and On Friendship*, trans. Frank O. Copley (Ann Arbor: University of Michigan Press, 1967), 11–12.

17. Ibid., 12.

18. J. G. A. Pocock, *The Machiavellian Moment: Florentine Political Thought and the Atlantic Republic Tradition* (Princeton: Princeton University Press, 1975).

19. Niccolò Machiavelli, *The Prince* (New York: Hendricks House, 1964), 176.

20. Niccolò Machiavelli, *Discourses on Livy*, trans. Julia Conaway Bondanella and Peter Bondanella (Oxford: Oxford University Press, 1997), 147–48.

21. James Harrington, *Oceana*, in *Ideal Commonwealths*, introduction by Henry Morley (London: Colonial Press, 1901), 239.

22. Ibid., 360.

23. John Locke, *Two Treatises of Government* (Cambridge: Cambridge University Press, 1960), bk. 2, chap. 6, sec. 75.

24. Ibid., sec. 62.

25. Edmund Burke, *Reflections on the Revolution in France*, ed. V. C. O. Clark (Stanford: Stanford University Press, 2001), 261.

26. Thomas Paine, *Rights of Man* (New York: Penguin, 1984), 41–42.

27. Thomas Paine, *Dissertation on First-Principles of Government* (London: Daniel Isaac Eaton, 1795), 9.

28. John Stuart Mill, "On Liberty," in *Three Essays* (Oxford: Oxford University Press, 1975), 15.

29. Ibid., 16.

30. Mill, "Considerations on Representative Government," in *Three Essays*, 341.

31. Walt Whitman, "Democratic Vistas," in *Prose Works, 1892*, vol. 2, *Collect and Other Prose*, ed. Floyd Stovall (New York: New York University Press, 1964), 393.

32. Walt Whitman, "The Eighteenth Presidency! Voice of Walt Whitman to each Young Man in the Nation, North, South, East, and West," in *Complete Poetry and Collected Prose* (New York: Library of America, 1982), 1308.

33. Ralph Waldo Emerson, "Politics," in *The Essays of Ralph Waldo Emerson* (Cambridge: The Belknap Press of Harvard University Press, 1979), 335.

34. Henry David Thoreau, *Walden*, in *Henry David Thoreau: Essays, Journals, and Poems*, ed. Dean Flower (Greenwich, Conn.: Fawcett Crest, 1975), 172–73.

35. Hannah Arendt, "Reflections on Little Rock," in *Responsibility and Judgment*, ed. Jerome Kohn (New York: Schocken Books, 2003), 204–5.

36. Michel Foucault, *The Use of Pleasure*, vol. 2 of *The History of Sexuality*, trans. Robert Hurley (New York: Vintage Books, 1990), 213.

37. Ibid., 217.

38. Oribasius, *Collection des médecins*, 3.181; cited in Foucault, *Use of Pleasure*, 207.

39. Foucault, *Use of Pleasure*, 210.

40. Ibid., 211.

41. John Rawls, *A Theory of Justice* (Cambridge: Harvard University Press, 1971), 60; italics added.

42. Ibid., 61.

43. Ibid., 62.

44. Rawls's original position, first outlined in *A Theory of Justice*, is a hypothetical situation, analogous to a fictive "state of nature" in social contract theorizing, in which rational actors agree to principles of justice prior to (as it were) their knowing what role and identity and social position they will actually occupy in life (operating under a "veil of ignorance" about those subsequent social roles is integral to the workings of the original position). The original position is thus an abstracting device that introduces that frames the rudiments of social justice with a certain kind of impartiality.

45. Constant distinguished between ancient liberty (participatory and republican) and modern (representative and rights based). See Benjamin Constant, "The Liberty of the Ancients Compared with That of the Moderns," in *Political Writings*, trans. Biancamaria Fontana (Cambridge: Cambridge University Press, 1988), 309–28.

46. Rawls, *Theory of Justice*, 223.

47. Since Rawls asserts that office eligibility is a basic liberty, a fundamental right, he cannot justify denying it on the grounds that doing so is a reasonable means to an end. The reduced judicial scrutiny that permits such judgments is appropriate only when the right in question is not a "fundamental" one or when denying it does not constitute a "constitutional wrong."

48. Margaret Morganroth Gullette, *Aged By Culture* (Chicago: University of Chicago Press, 2004), 192. Or, as Bonnie Honig asks, "What is linear time's normativity?" Honig,

Emergency Politics: Paradox, Law, Democracy (Princeton: Princeton University Press, 2009), 15.

49. For similar criticisms of Rawls, albeit from varying disabilities studies perspectives, see Martha C. Nussbaum, *Frontiers of Justice: Disability, Nationality, Species Membership* (Cambridge: Harvard University Press, 2006), and Barbara Arneil, "Disability, Self Image, and Modern Political Theory," *Political Theory* 37, no. 2 (April 2009): 218–42.

50. Another way of putting this is as an objection to Justice O'Connor's reasoning in *Kimel v. Florida Board of Regents* (528 U.S. 62 [2000]) that age generalizations can be construed in usefully tendentious ways, whereas generalizations about race and sex cannot.

51. Bernard Bailyn, ed., *The Debate on the Constitution*, 2 vols. (New York: Library of American, 1993), 2:1087–92.

52. Dahl, *On Democracy*, 10.

53. Ibid., 12.

54. Ibid., 75.

55. Ibid., 86.

56. Robert A. Dahl, *Democracy and Its Critics* (New Haven: Yale University Press, 1989), 127.

57. Ibid.

58. Ibid., 129–30.

59. Dahl, *On Democracy*, 12.

60. Charles R. Beitz, *Political Equality: An Essay in Democratic Theory* (Princeton: Princeton University Press, 1989), 4.

61. Judith N. Shklar, *American Citizenship: The Quest for Inclusion* (Cambridge: Harvard University Press, 1991), 15.

62. James H. Kettner, *The Development of American Citizenship, 1608–1870* (Chapel Hill: University of North Carolina Press, 1978), 288; quoted in Shklar, *American Citizenship*, 14–15.

63. Shklar, *American Citizenship*, 15.

64. Judith N. Shklar, "The Boundaries of Democracy," in *Redeeming American Political Thought* (Chicago: University of Chicago Press, 1998), 127–45.

65. Shklar cites Steven F. Lawson, *Black Ballots: Voting Rights in the South, 1944–1969* (New York: Columbia University Press, 1976), 286.

66. Shklar, *American Citizenship*, 43.

67. Ibid., 51.

68. Richard M. Valelly takes explicit exception with Judith Shklar's elision of the issue of black officeholding: "Black office-holding has always been in part a matter of 'civic status.' Social standing in America, Judith Shklar cogently argued, has two great emblems: the right to vote and the 'opportunity to earn.' She might well have added that free access to public office, regardless of class, gender, ethnicity, or race, also entitles a group defined by such divisions to general respect." Valelly, *The Two Reconstructions: The Struggle for Black Enfranchisement* (Chicago: University of Chicago Press, 2004), 6.

69. Ibid., 55

70. Ibid.

71. Ibid., 60–61.

72. Hanna Fenichel Pitkin, *The Concept of Representation* (Berkeley and Los Angeles: University of California Press, 1967), 3.

73. Ibid., 60.

74. John Adams, "Letter to John Penn," in *Works* (Boston: Little, Brown, 1852–65), 4:205; cited in Pitkin, *Concept of Representation*, 60.

75. "Proceedings of Committee of the Whole House, May 30–June 19," in *The Records of the Federal Convention of 1787*, ed. Max Farrand, 4 vols. (New Haven: Yale University Press, 1927), 1:141–42; cited in Pitkin, *Concept of Representation*, 61.

76. Carl Friedrich, *Constitutional Government and Democracy* (Boston: Ginn, 1950), 304–5; cited in Pitkin, *Concept of Representation*, 61.

77. Pitkin, *Concept of Representation*, 128.

78. Ibid., 130.

79. Ibid., 210.

80. Ibid., 190.

81. For contested histories of African American and female struggles for office-eligibility after suffrage, see Valelly, *The Two Reconstructions*, and Gretchen Ritter, *The Constitution as Social Design: Gender and Civic Membership in the American Constitutional Order* (Stanford: Stanford University Press, 2006).

82. One might be tempted to mention here Bernard Manin's general thesis that political representation, from the founding of the United States on, has inherently involved a difference between the representatives and the electorate, a functional difference between the rulers and ruled, and that principles of proximity do not necessarily apply. Manin mentions the constitutional age qualifications briefly and contends that the age qualifications contain "no trace of the principle of distinction" of representative government that constitutes the rest of his book. Thus he denies that the age qualifications pertain to his main point about representative government. Manin, *The Principles of Representative Government* (New York: Cambridge University Press, 1997).

83. Rawls, *Theory of Justice*, 284–93; Brian Barry, "Justice Between Generations," in *Liberty and Justice: Essays in Political Theory 2* (Oxford: Clarendon Press, 1991), 242–58.

84. Barry, "Justice Between Generations," 254.

85. Arendt, "Reflections on Little Rock," 205.

86. William E. Connolly, *The Ethos of Pluralization* (Minneapolis: University of Minnesota Press, 1995); Connolly, *Identity/Difference: Democratic Negotiations of Political Paradox*, expanded edition (Minneapolis: University of Minnesota Press, 2002).

87. Honig, *Emergency Politics*, 54.

88. Ibid.

89. Ibid., 15.

Chapter 3

1. Hannah Arendt, "Introduction *into* Politics," in *The Promise of Politics* (New York: Schocken Books, 2005), 93–200.

2. Elizabeth Arias, "Life Expectancy by Age, Race, and Sex: Death-registration States, 1900–1902 to 1919–21, and United States, 1929–31 to 2002," *National Vital Statistics Reports* 53, no. 6, November 10, 2004.

3. Susan A. MacManus, *Young v. Old: Generational Combat in the 21st Century* (Boulder, Colo.: Westview Press, 1996), 4.

4. Ken Dychtwald, *Age Wave: The Challenges and Opportunities of an Aging North America* (New York: St. Martins Press, 1989), 4.

5. Ken Dychtwald, *Age Power: How the 21st Century Will Be Ruled by the New Old* (New York: Putnam, 1999), 2.

6. Dychtwald, *Age Wave*, 21–23; Dychtwald, *Age Power*, xix.

7. U.S. Census Bureau; cited in Dychtwald, *Age Power*, 2.

8. MacManus, *Young v. Old*, 5.

9. Dychtwald, *Age Power*, xix, 1.

10. See appendix 2.

11. S. W. Sterling and S. White, *Boomernomics: The Future of Your Money in the Upcoming Generational Warfare* (New York: Ballantine Books, 1998); Dychtwald, *Age Wave*, 63–66; Dychtwald, *Age Power*, 203–322; MacManus, *Young v. Old*, esp. 37; Matthew C. Price, *Justice Between Generations: The Growing Power of the Elderly in America* (Westport, Conn.: Praeger Publishers, 1997), 106–9.

12. See MacManus, *Young v. Old*, 190–91, and Christine L. Day, *What Older Americans Think* (Princeton: Princeton University Press, 1990), 41–52.

13. Paul E. Peterson, "An Immodest Proposal," *Daedalus* 121, no. 4 (Fall 1992): 151–74.

14. Dychtwald, *Age Power*, 212.

15. Peter Peterson, speech at the "United We Stand" Conference, Dallas, Texas, August 8, 1995; cited in Price, *Justice Between Generations*, 106.

16. Gary Becker, "Cut the Greybeards a Smaller Slice of the Pie," *Business Week*, March 28, 1994, 20; cited in Price, *Justice Between Generations*, 106.

17. Richard B. du Boff, "Thurow on Social Security: The 'Left' Strikes Again," *Monthly Review*, October 1996, 1–9; cited in Dychtwald, *Age Power*, 213.

18. Dychtwald, *Age Power*, 213.

19. See www.icasualties.org/.

20. For an inkling of things to come, see Anya Kamenetz, *Generation Debt: How Our Future Was Sold Out for Student Loans, Bad Jobs, No Benefits, and Tax Cuts for Rich Geezers—And How to Fight Back* (New York: Riverhead Trade, 2006).

21. MacManus, *Young v. Old*, 161.

22. Pew Research Center for People and the Press, "Generations Divide over Military Action in Iraq: A Pew Research Center Note," October 17, 2002, http://people-press.org/commentary/?analysisid=57.

23. MacManus, *Young v. Old*, 161–62.

24. Price, *Justice Between Generations*, 107.

25. MacManus, *Young v. Old*, 124.

26. Peterson, "An Immodest Proposal."

27. Douglas J. Stewart, "Disfranchise the Old," *New Republic*, August 29, 1970, 20–22.

28. Philippe Van Parijs, "The Disenfranchisement of the Elderly, and Other Attempts to Secure Intergenerational Justice," *Philosophy and Public Affairs* 27, no. 4 (Fall 1998): 292–333.

29. Anne Phillips, *The Politics of Presence* (Oxford: Oxford University Press, 1995), 63; cited in Van Parijs, "Disenfranchisement of the Elderly," 302.

30. Claus Offe, "Zusatzstimmen für Eltern. Ein Beitrag zur Reform von Demokratie und Wahlrecht?" in *Zukunft wählen—Zusatzstimmen für Eltern?* ed. G. Grözinger and H. Geiger (Bad Boll: Evangelische Akademie, 1993), 1–26; cited in Van Parijs, "Disenfranchisement of the Elderly," 302.

31. Josep M. Vallès and Agustí Bosch, *Sistemas electorales y gobierno representativo* (Barcelona: Ariel, 1997), 44; cited in Van Parijs, "Disenfranchisement of the Elderly," 302.

32. Jean-Pierre Perrin, "Un mollah outsider à la présidence de l'Iran," *Libération;* cited in Van Parijs, "Disenfranchisement of the Elderly," 303.

33. Klaus Hurrelmann and Christian Palentien, "Jugendliche an die Wahlurnen! Argumente zur Verbesserung der politischen Partizipation der jungen Generation," *Diskurs* 2 (1997): 44; cited in Van Parijs, "Disenfranchisement of the Elderly," 303.

34. Friedrich A. Hayek, *Economic Freedom and Representative Government*, 4th Wincott Memorial Lecture, Occasional Paper no. 39 (London: Institute of Economic Affairs, 1973), 19–21; cited in Van Parijs, "Disenfranchisement of the Elderly," 304.

35. Jacques Lefèvre claims that this proposal was unsuccessfully put to a referendum in a Swiss canton. See "Le troisième âge: riche mais inexploité," *Le Soir*, August 5, 1997, 15; cited in Van Parijs, "Disenfranchisement of the Elderly," 305.

36. Silvano Möckli, "Demokratische Struktur und Volksabstimmmungen" (Hochschule St-Gallen, Institut für Politikwissenschaft, 1993), 13; cited in Van Parijs, "Disenfranchisement of the Elderly," 10.

37. Gerd Grözinger, "Achtung, Kind wählt mit! Ein Beitrag zur allmählichen Aufhebung der Diktatur der Gegenwart über die Zukunft," *Blätter für deutsche und internationale Politik* 10 (1993): 1265; cited in Van Parijs, "Disenfranchisement of the Elderly," 305.

38. Bruce Ackerman, "Crediting the Voters: A New Beginning for Campaign Finance," *American Prospect* 13 (1993): 71–80; cited in Van Parijs, "Disenfranchisement of the Elderly," 308.

39. Grözinger, "Achtung, Kind wählt mit!" 1261; cited in Van Parijs, "Disenfranchisement of the Elderly," 314.

40. Thomas L. Friedman, *The World Is Flat: A Brief History of the Twenty-first Century* (New York: Farrar, Straus and Giroux, 2005); Paul Virilio, *Speed and Politics: An Essay on Dromology*, trans. Mark Polizzotti (New York: Columbia University Press, 1986).

41. See Cliff Zukin, Scott Keeter, Molly Andolina, Krista Jenkins, and Michael X. Delli Carpini, *A New Engagement? Political Participation, Civic Life, and the Changing American Citizen* (New York: Oxford University Press, 2006); Neil Howe and William Strauss, *Millennials Rising: The Next Great Generation* (New York: Vintage Books, 2000).

42. See Robert A. Dahl, *How Democratic Is the American Constitution?* (New Haven: Yale University Press, 2001), 164.

43. Compiling comprehensive comparative data on the ages of actual elected officials in these various countries is a project beyond the scope of the present study. It would be extremely useful to have such a vast survey, but since my main argument in favor of a constitutional amendment rests on normative rather than consequentialist grounds, I thankfully leave such an ambitious project to my political science colleagues. But a few quick anecdotes may be in order. In 2003, Iceland elected to the Althing a twenty-three-year-old, Birkir J. Jónsson. In the 2003 elections to the Swiss National Council, two parliamentarians elected were twenty-five years old, and seven out of the remaining two hundred were thirty years old or younger. Asa Elvik was elected to the Norwegian parliament, the Storting, at age twenty-two in 2001, and several other current Norwegian MPs were twenty-five or under at the time of election.

44. The Electoral Commission, "Age of Electoral Majority: Report and Recommendations," April 2004, 8, http://www.electoralcommission.org.uk/document-summary?asset id=63749.

45. Benjamin Barber, *Strong Democracy: Participatory Politics for a New Age* (Berkeley and Los Angeles: University of California Press, 1984); Benjamin Barber, *A Place for Us: How to Make Society Civil and Democracy Strong* (New York: Hill and Wang, 1998).

46. Robert Putnam, *Citizenship and the Six Spheres of Influence: An Agenda for Social Capitals*, National Conference on Citizenship 2005 Report, 13, http://www.ncoc.net/conferences/2005conference_report.pdf.

47. See Eric H. Greenberg with Karl Weber, *Generation We: How Millennial Youth Are Taking Over America and Changing Our World Forever* (Emeryville, Calif.: Pachatusan, 2008), 24–26; Brian D. Loader, ed., *Young Citizens in the Digital Age: Political Engagement, Young People and New Media* (New York: Routledge, 2007); Scott Keeter, Cliff Zukin, Molly Andolina, and Krista Jenkin, *The Civic and Political Health of the Nation: A Generational Portrait*, CIRCLE (The Center for Information and Research on Civic Learning and Engagement), September 19, 2002, http://www.civicyouth.org/research/products/Civic_Political_Health.pdf; and Peter Levine, *The Future of Democracy: Developing the Next Generation of American Citizens* (Medford: Tufts University Press, 2007), 77–91.

48. Elizabeth Williamson, "Brain Immaturity Can Be Deadly," *Washingtonpost.com*, February 1, 2005. A study presented at the 2006 British Association's Science Festival show that "the adolescent brain undergoes massive changes and does not reach maturity until 20 or 30 years old." See, Elli Leadbeater, "Seeing the Teenager in the Brain," September 8, 2006, http://news.bbc.co.uk/go/pr/fr/-/2/hi/science/nature/5327550.stm. Neuropsychologist Ruben Gur of the University of Pennsylvania speculates that the biological age of brain maturity is generally around age 21 or 22. Abigail Baird of Dartmouth College estimates the age of brain maturity to be more like 25 or 26. MRI research shows that myelin formation in the brain does not peak until age 45. See Bruce Bower, "Teen Brains on Trial," *Science News*, May 8, 2004, http://www.sciencenews.org/view/feature/id/

4995/title/Teen_Brains_on_Trial, and Craig M. Bennett and Abigail A. Baird, "Anatomical Changes in the Emerging Adult Brain: A Voxel-Based Morphometry Study," *Human Brain Mapping* 27 (2006): 766–77.

49. See Judith Stevens-Long, *Adult Life* (Palo Alto: Mayfield Publishing, 1984), esp. 96, 106–9, 111.

50. I do not mean to assert this normative principle too axiomatically; rather, I'm assuming here the contemporary U.S. context, which generally associates the age of majority with the age of adulthood. If Germany, for instance, eliminates age requirements for suffrage and allows some mechanism to tally the votes of minors, I'm not at all convinced that "coterminality" between suffrage and office-eligibility has to follow. The point, rather, is that full enfranchisement in the United States, covering both voting and office-eligibility, ought now to include all citizens that the polity deems to have reached the age of adulthood.

51. Ruth B. Mandel and Katherine E. Kleeman, *Political Generation Next: America's Young Elected Leaders*, http://www.eagleton.rutgers.edu/YELP/YELPFullReport.pdf.

52. See Joseph A. Schlesinger, *Ambition and Politics: Political Careers in the United States* (Chicago: Rand McNally, 1966), 181–84.

53. Gordon S. Wood, *The Radicalism of the American Revolution* (New York: Alfred A. Knopf, 1992); Akhil Reed Amar, *America's Constitution: A Biography* (New York: Random House, 2005).

54. See Adam Bellow, *In Praise of Nepotism: A Natural History* (New York: Doubleday, 2003).

55. See http://en.wikipedia.org/wiki/Prez_(DC_Comics).

56. The Electoral Commission, "Age of Electoral Majority," 61.

57. J. S. Mill, "Considerations on Representative Government," in *Three Essays* (Oxford: Oxford University Press, 1975), 188; Thomas Paine, *Rights of Man* (New York: Penguin, 1984), 41–42.

58. Schlesinger, *Ambition and Politics*, 176.

59. This section draws on the excellent work of Alexander J. Bott, *Handbook of United States Election Laws: Political Rights* (Westport, Conn.: Greenwood Press, 1990).

60. *Mancuso v. Taft* (1973), http://openjurist.org/476/f2d/187/mancuso-v-l-taft.

61. *Mancuso v. Taft*, 476 F.2d 187, 196 (1st Cir. 1973); cited in Bott, *Handbook*, 55.

62. *Williams v. Rhodes* (1968), http://www.oscn.net/applications/oscn/deliverdocument.asp?citeid=428479.

63. See, for instance, *CSC v. Letter Carriers*, 413 U.S. 548, 555 (1973) and *Magill v. Lynch*, 560 F.2d 22 (1st Cir. 1977).

64. One might suspect that an unsympathetic court would invoke the language of *Kimel v. Florida Board of Regents* (528 U.S. 62 [2000]), which struck down part of the Age Discrimination in Employment Act, in part on the grounds that senior citizens are not a "discrete and insular minority" worthy of special protection because all Americans, if they live out the natural course of life, will reach old age. One could probably surmise that a court would extend such reasoning in reverse to "youth." Or else a likely move would be to extend to office candidacy the decision of *Kramer v. Union School District* (395 U.S. 621 [1969]) regarding the right of a state to set age requirements for voting.

65. Annotation: "Validity of Age Requirements for State Public Office," 90 *American Law Reports* 3d 900 (1979); cited in Bott, *Handbook*.

66. *United States v. Carolene Products Company*, 304 U.S. 144 (1938).

67. The Supreme Court in *United States v. Virginia et al.* (518 U.S. 515 [1996]) asserted that courts must take a "hard look" at generalizations or "tendencies" based on "fixed notions concerning the roles and abilities of males and females." For our purposes, perhaps a similar "hard look" could be taken with respect to "fixed notions concerning the roles and abilities" of different age groups. But the courts have not extended such sharp skepticism about race or gender categories to age discrimination along with the

purported "tendencies" of younger or older citizens to behave in particular ways. Justice Ginsburg's exalted language about women simply has not translated into similar views about age classifications: "Neither federal nor state government acts compatibly with equal protection when a law or official policy denies to women, simply because they are women, full citizenship stature—equal opportunity to aspire, achieve, participate in and contribute to society based on their individual talents and capacities." Cornell University Law School, Legal Information Institute, "Supreme Court of the United States: Syllabus, *United States v. Virginia et al.*, http://www.law.cornell.edu/supct/html/94-1941.ZS.html.

68. *Korematsu v. United States*, 323 U.S. 214 (1944).

69. See http://www.youthelect.com/.

70. In 2002 Oregon voters considered (and rejected) a proposal to amend the state constitution to lower the age qualifications for membership in the Oregon legislature from twenty-one to eighteen (http://www.sos.state.or.us/elections/nov52002/guide/measures/m170pp.htm). In 2008 Colorado voters rejected a state ballot measure to lower the age of office eligibility for the state legislature from twenty-five to twenty-one (http://www.boulderweekly.com/20081009/statewidereferenda.html).

71. I am following here Hannah Arendt's sharp distinction between political rights and human (or metaphysical, or natural) rights. See Arendt, *On Revolution* (New York: Penguin, 1963).

72. See Edward S. Corwin, *The Constitution and What It Means Today*, 14th ed. (Princeton: Princeton University Press, 1978), 557.

73. James Madison, "*Federalist* 14," in Alexander Hamilton, James Madison, and John Jay, *The Federalist Papers*, ed. Clinton Rossiter (New York: Penguin, 1961), 101.

74. *Massachusetts Board of Retirement v. Murgia* (1976), http://altlaw.org/v1/cases/398018.

75. John Scanlon, *Young Adulthood* (New York: Academy for Educational Development, 1979); Allen J. Moore, *The Young Adult Generation: A Perspective on the Future* (Nashville: Abingdon Press, 1969); Gene Bocknek, *The Young Adult: Development After Adolescence* (New York: Gardner Press, 1986); Frances Goldscheider and Calvin Goldscheider, *The Changing Transition to Adulthood: Leaving and Returning Home* (Thousand Oaks, Calif.: Sage Publications, 1999).

76. Cynthia H. Cho, "Left Follows the Right on Campus Outreach Path," *Los Angeles Times*, July 24, 2005, A20.

77. Hanna Rosin, "God and Country: A College That Trains Young Christians to Be Politicians," *New Yorker*, June 27, 2005, 44–49.

78. Ralph Waldo Emerson, "Politics," in *The Essays of Ralph Waldo Emerson* (Cambridge: The Belknap Press of Harvard University Press, 1979), 337–38.

79. Ibid., 338.

80. Schlesinger, *Ambition and Politics*, 177–79; MacManus, *Young v. Old*, 135–36.

81. William N. Eskridge Jr. and Sanford Levinson, eds., *Constitutional Stupidities, Constitutional Tragedies* (New York: New York University Press, 1998).

82. See Mark A. Graber, *Dred Scott and the Problem of Constitutional Evil* (Cambridge: Cambridge University Press, 2006).

83. Philip Bobbit makes the case that the Constitution should be viewed as an organic whole, and latter-day reformers should resist second-guessing and overcorrecting it. "Parlor Games," in Eskridge and Levinson, *Constitutional Stupidities, Constitutional Tragedies*, 18–21.

84. Michael, "Presidential Age Requirement," in Eskridge and Levinson, *Constitutional Stupidities, Constitutional Tragedies*, 67–70.

85. William E. Cooper, "A Reappraisal of Constitutional Age Requirements for Congress and the President," *Congress and the Presidency* 15, no. 1 (Spring 1988): 91–96.

86. Congressional Research Service, *The Constitution of the United States of America, Analysis and Interpretation*, 82nd Cong., 2d sess., 1973, S. Doc. 92–82; *Congressional Record* 79 (June 21, 1935): 9824–42; as cited in Cooper, "A Reappraisal," 94.

87. Cooper, "A Reappraisal," 94.

88. Ibid., 95.

89. J. D. Ferrick, ed. *The Twenty-Fifth Amendment: Its Complete History and Earliest Applications* (New York: Fordham University Press, 1976), 213–14; cited in Cooper, "A Reappraisal," 95.

90. Cooper, "A Reappraisal," 95.

91. Dahl, *How Democratic Is the American Constitution?* 154.

92. Ibid., 155.

93. Ibid., 156.

94. In his subsequent book, Dahl mentions an age requirement in passing: "Citizens are entitled to run for and serve in elective offices, though requirements as to age and place of residence may be imposed." Robert A. Dahl, *On Political Equality* (New Haven: Yale University Press, 2006), 12.

95. Nearly eleven thousand constitutional amendments have been proposed over the past two hundred-plus years of U.S. history. Of those eleven thousand proposals, only twenty-seven have been successful. Kris E. Palmer, ed., *The Constitutional Amendments: 1789 to the Present* (Detroit: Thomson Gale, 1999), 391.

96. "More than 100 organizations in the Youth Vote coalition devoted their efforts to raising youth participation in the election. Partners in the Coalition included MTV's 'Choose or Lose,' Project Vote Smart, Speak Out, and World Wrestling Entertainment's 'Smackdown Your Vote!' The organizations had a goal of bringing 20 million youths out to the polls." Amy Kwolek, "Youth Voter Turnout Highest Since 1972," *Michigan Daily*, November 4, 2004, http://www.michigandaily.com/content/youth-voter-turnout-highest-1972.

97. See David R. Mayhew, *Congress: The Electoral Connection* (New Haven: Yale University Press, 2004), for arguments about legislators taking action only when it serves their interests narrowly construed.

98. Selective use of a boycott or the threat of boycott, along with the possibility of throwing full support to favored candidates, must be retained as an option to avoid partisan manipulation or gaming of a boycott by a particular candidate or party.

99. Dick Pels, *The Intellectual as Stranger: Studies in Spokespersonship* (New York: Routledge, 2000).

100. William Chaloupka, *Everybody Knows: Cynicism in America* (Minneapolis: University of Minnesota Press, 1999).

Postscript

1. Hannah Arendt, "Preface: The Gap Between Past and Future," *Between Past and Future: Eight Exercises in Political Thought* (New York: Viking, 1954), 3–15; Arendt, "Understanding and Politics," *Partisan Review* 20, no. 4 (1953): 377–92; Arendt, *The Life of the Mind, Part 2, Willing* (San Diego: Harcourt Brace Jovanovich, 1977), 217; Arendt, "No Longer and Not Yet," *Nation*, September 2, 1946, 300–302.

2. Thomas Paine, *Dissertation on First-Principles of Government* (London, 1795), 11.

3. These educational efforts need not be confined to those eighteen and older. The "Constitution Day" activities in the high schools could be a good time to draw attention to the age requirements. Perhaps it would be appropriate at an even younger age: the popularity of Dan Gutman's books, which portray a twelve-year-old running for president, suggests that the issue could have some nonfictional currency among a younger constituency. Dan Gutman, *The Kid Who Ran for President* (New York: Scholastic, 1996); Gutman, *The Kid Who Became President* (New York: Scholastic, 1999).

4. Alexander Hamilton, "*Federalist 1*," in Alexander Hamilton, James Madison, and John Jay, *The Federalist Papers*, ed. Clinton Rossiter (New York: Penguin, 1961), 33.

Index